PUBLIC POLICY
A COMPREHENSIVE INTRODUCTION

MARTIN POTŮČEK
ET AL.

KAROLINUM PRESS
PRAGUE 2017

KAROLINUM PRESS
Karolinum Press is a publishing department of Charles University
Ovocný trh 560/5, 116 36 Prague 1, Czech Republic
www.karolinum.cz

Layout by Jan Šerých
Set and printed in the Czech Republic by Karolinum Press
First English edition

A catalogue record for this book is available from the National Library
of the Czech Republic

ISBN 978-80-246-3556-9
ISBN 978-80-246-3570-5 (pdf)

The original manuscript was reviewed by Prof. PhDr. Ľudmila Malíková, PhD.
(Faculty of Social Sciences, University of St. Cyril and Methodius in Trnava);
Prof. Douglas J. Besharov (School of Public Policy, University of Maryland)

CONTENTS

Introduction

The book of public policy in front of you follows in the footsteps of an earlier publication, *Public Policy in Central and Eastern Europe: Theories, Methods, Practices*.[1] Since it came out, the field went through a relatively rapid development. Today, students of public administration, economics, political science, sociology, social policy, demography, international relations, regional development and other social sciences can avail themselves of a range of other educational texts offering novel insights to public policy. Having more than two decades of experience teaching at Charles University in Prague as well as at other universities in the Czech Republic and abroad, I considered it necessary to provide a new, comprehensive and synoptic account of the state of the art. I placed emphasis on the field's conceptual foundation, description of the most frequently used theories, and an illustrative account of how these can be applied in policy analysis and policy making – here, in the form of selected case studies.[2]

Should you choose to pursue your interest in public policy by studying this publication, then several avenues towards that end are opening in front of you.

The easiest way forward is to follow the sequence of chapters in Part A. It starts with the most general topics (definition of key terms, value fundamentals, issues of governance) and continues to more specific texts characterizing actors, institutions and instruments of public policy. This is followed by chapters on four stages of the policy process – problem delimitation and recognition, policy formulation and decision-making, implementation, and

---

1 Potůček, M., L. LeLoup, G. Jenei, L. Váradi. 2003. *Public Policy in Central and Eastern Europe: Theories, Methods, Practices*. Bratislava: NISPAcee.

2 Readers with a command of the language may prefer to consult a Czech version of this textbook: Potůček, M. a kol. 2016. *Veřejná politika*. Prague: C. H. Beck.

evaluation. The final chapter of this part brings attention to obstacles in the process of examining public policies and possible methods to overcome them.

At the same time, you may choose a cross-sectional way of studying the most influential public policy theories. They are referred to throughout the textbook in accordance with the focus of the respective chapters. The table "Overview of the public policy theories presented" that immediately follows can help you find where the different theories are presented in Part A and where they are applied in Part B.

Another method will be found useful by those with a preference for narratives and vivid accounts of events. Part B demonstrates the ways selected public policy theories can be applied in telling the story of pension reform in the Czech Republic: repeated attempts to utilize expertise in policy decision-making, executive and legislative responses to a ruling of the Constitutional Court on the unconstitutionality of applicable law, or an attempt to structurally reform the pension system as a whole by establishing a new element, a fully funded, private, so-called "second pillar", relying in part on mandatory social insurance premiums transferred from the pay-as-you-go first pillar.

The book bears the imprint of the country of its origin, the Czech Republic, and the specific historical legacy of Central Europe. Students of public policy should consider complementing their study with other textbooks of the subject, influenced by other cultural and socio-political traditions, such as Cairney (2011), Howlett, Ramesh (2009) or Peters (2015).[3]

I am much obliged to the co-author of Part B, Veronika Rudolfová, for an inspiring collaboration. I am also thankful to a number of colleagues at the Department of Public and Social Policy, Institute of Sociological Studies, Faculty of Social Sciences, Charles University in Prague, who proved to be important sources of critique and advice in the process of preparing this book: Arnošt Veselý, above all, and also to Martin Nekola and Vilém Novotný – even though we kept different perspectives on some particular topics. Jan Morávek participated in the final draft not only by conducting an excellent translation but also through inspiring comments on the text as such. I am grateful to him as well as to the book's editor, Hana Märzová. Responsibility for the concept of the textbook and for my chapters is, of course, mine alone.

Prague, November 2017
Prof. Dr. Martin Potůček, PhD.

3   Cairney, P. 2011. *Understanding public policy: Theories and issues.* Palgrave Macmillan; Howlett, M., A. Perl and M. Ramesh, *Studying Public Policy.* 2009. Toronto: Oxford University Press; Peters, B. G. 2015. *Advanced introduction to public policy.* Cheltenham, UK and Northampton, MA, USA: Edward Elgar Publishing.

Overview of the public policy theories presented[4]

Theory	Part A, chapter	Part B, chapter
Historical institutionalism	A2	–
Corporatism	A3	–
Policy networks	A3	–
Actor-centered Institutionalism	A4	B3
Actors generating agendas in arenas	A4	–
Advocacy Coalition Framework (ACF)	A5	B4
Discursive institutionalism	A5	B2
A Stage model of the policy cycle	A6	B3
Agenda setting	A6	–
Veto payers	A7	–
Multiple streams	A7	–
Bureaucracy	A8	–
Principal–agent (politico-administrative relations)	A8	–
Rational choice	A9	B3
Framework analysis	–	B2

---

4   This is the author's selection of theories which proved to be instrumental in various research contexts. There are of course many other public policy theories applied in specific application fields at different levels of generality. Refer to John (2013) for their overview.

List of Abbreviations

AC	Advocacy Coalition
ACF	Advocacy Coalition Framework
ANO	Ano bude líp (political movement)
ASEAN	Association of Southeast Asian Nations
BBC	British Broadcasting Corporation
CESTA	Center for Social Market Economy and Open Democracy
ČMKOS	Czech-Moravian Confederation of Trade Unions (abbreviation in Czech)
ČNB	Czech National Bank (abbreviation in Czech)
ČR	Czech Republic
ČSSD	Czech Social Democratic Party (political party)
ČSSZ	Czech Social Security Administration (CSSA, abbreviation in Czech)
CZK	Czech Crown (national currency)
DB	Defined Benefit (pension scheme)
DC	Defined Contribution pension scheme
EG	Expert Group (government and opposition party, ČSSD)
EU	European Union
EUR	Euro
FF	Fully Funded pension system
G20	Group of Twenty
G8	Group of Eight
GDP	Gross Domestic Product
GNH	Gross National Happiness
GNI	Gross National Income
HDI	Human Development Index
IADF	Institutional Analysis and Development Framework

ICT	Information and Communication Technologies
ID	Identity Document
ILO	International Labor Organization
KDU-ČSL	Christian and Democratic Union – Czechoslovak People's Party
KSČM	Communist Party of Bohemia and Moravia (political party)
MLG	Multi-level Governance
MP	Member of Parliament
MPSV	Ministry of Labor and Social Affairs of the Czech Republic (abbreviation in Czech)
NDC	Notional Defined Contribution (pension scheme)
NERV	The National Economic Council of the Government, Czech Republic (abbreviation in Czech)
NGO	Non-Governmental Organization
NHS	National Health Service, United Kingdom
ODA	Civic Democratic Alliance (political party)
ODS	Civic Democratic Party (political party)
OECD	Organisation for Economic Co-operation and Development
OK	Expert Committee on Pension Reform, Czech Republic (abbreviation in Czech)
PAYG	Pay-as-you-go (pension system)
PČR	Parliament of the Czech Republic
PES	Expert Advisory Board/Bezděk Commission II (abbreviation in Czech)
PS PČR	Chamber of Deputies of the Parliament of the Czech Republic
RCT	Rational Choice Theory
RHSD	Council of Economic and Social Agreement (abbreviation in Czech)
RIA	Regulatory Impact Assessment
SP ČR	Confederation of Industry of the Czech Republic (abbreviation in Czech)
SZ	Green Party
TOP 09	Tradition. Responsibility. Prosperity (political party)
UK	United Kingdom of Great Britain and Northern Ireland
UN	United Nations
ÚS	Constitutional Court of the Czech Republic (abbreviation in Czech)
USA	United States of America
VÚPSV	Research Institute of Labor and Social Affairs (abbreviation in Czech)
VV	Public Affairs (political party)
WB	World Bank
WWII	Second World War (1939–1945)

PART A

/A1/
Public Interest and Public Policy

Some time ago, William Dunn (1981: 8–19) argued that "the study of public policy is as old as Plato's concern for The Republic" (as paraphrased by McCool 1995: 1). But even long before ancient philosophers, people had been trying to solve conflicts between interests and ways of satisfying them intuitively, on the fly. Albeit many armed conflicts arose, other struggles were, fortunately, solved peacefully.

Public policy in practice serves to prevent and solve conflicts, a natural trait of social life which is here to stay. Our lives and deeds depend on the lives and deeds of other people – and not only those. We are confined to societal frameworks that mediate and enable coexistence between people: money, law, organizations, language, culture... it is in these complex relations that our individual interests mix and intersect with those of other people, social groups, corporations, and/or states. Such interests are often conflicting, and there are many actors who will lose a lot if their interests fail to be reconciled. Economic and social crises, wars, coups and revolutions are, among other things, manifestations of a conflict of particular interests gone out of control.

Building on the basis of philosophy and other existing social sciences, **public policy** became established as a new scientific discipline in the second half of the 20ᵗʰ century. Academics did not invent it as their new toy or source of income. The main reason public policy emerged was that the more responsible part of politicians and public officials felt the need to study the nature of these conflicts of particular interests systematically in order to derive recommendations on how to prevent such conflicts, avoid violent escalation, get them under control – and possibly even solve them, at least for the time being. **The discipline serves to analyze and formulate policies** – such policies that affect people's lives in specific ways, whether by increasing their quality or by making them more difficult. Examples include transportation, health care, education, sports, housing, monument preservation, protection of nature, and a myriad other concerns.

Every day, politicians and public officials deal with problems that are not easy to solve. Is it reasonable to introduce mandatory vaccination of children against communicable diseases? While children themselves are often unable to express their opinion, many parents oppose such a policy. Should we abolish regulations that prohibit surface mining in defined areas? Such a measure would ensure new jobs and cheaper coal, but also annihilate communities where people have been living for centuries. Is it a good idea to build nuclear power stations? We are not sure how to deposit nuclear waste in a safe and permanent way. Are we better off building more kindergartens, or supporting industrial innovations? Should we devote our limited public resources to providing better pensions to seniors, or better salaries to civil servants? Or should we rather increase welfare benefits for children?

Before attempting to answer questions like these, we need to clarify how public interest can be defined.

WHAT IS MEANT BY PUBLIC INTEREST?

Leading American policy scientist Walter Lippman defines public interest as follows: "Living adults share, we must believe, the same public interest. For them, however, the public interest is mixed with, and is often at odds with, their private and special interests. Put this way, we can say, I suggest, that the public interest may be presumed to be what men would choose if they saw clearly, thought rationally, acted disinterestedly and benevolently" (Lippman 1955: 42). The concept of public interest is undoubtedly of descriptive power but also of a high value loading.

As Lane (1993) notes, there is a constant tension between the term "public" with its relation to the whole and the term "interest" with its individualist connotation. For that reason, some theorists who rely on methodological individualism and philosophical objectivism reject the term "public interests" as misleading (Kinkor 1996).

In defining public interests, one can proceed procedurally or analytically. The procedural approach is typically applied in policy practice and the analytical one in the scientific discipline of public policy.

The procedural approach to formulating public interests in a democratic society conforms to certain rules regarding debating about what the public interest is and what it is not, of reaching a consensus on such a definition, and of pursuing public interests in practice. Community, civil society institutions, law and government provide procedural mechanisms for articulating, aggregating, coordinating and, if possible, also satisfying particular interests in a form in which it starts to be useful to speak of public interests. However, an important complication is caused by competition between the particular interests of the actors who necessarily take part in this process: politicians, officials, and interest group representatives. Formulation and realization of public interest becomes the subject of negotiation and, sometimes, social or political struggle. It is an intense historical, social and political process. Of course, conflicts emerge between competing "public interests" associated with the interests of different communities or social groups.

The analytical approach to formulating public interests relies on their shared characteristics:
- they pertain to the quality of life of a given society's members, or other values they find important;
- they can be related to the quality or the effects of the function of society as a whole;
- they are embedded historically, in a given stage of civilization development, and may change;
- they enter an arena where they clash with differentiated individual, group and institutional interests and come to be identified, articulated, acknowledged, and satisfied. The decisions adopted affect the ways public goods are produced, distributed and used; the quality of life of large social groups; and the satisfaction of the functional needs of society as a whole;
- they are related to current social problems or possible futures;
- their realization often goes beyond the competencies of a single institution or an entire department of government, or even a nation.

The benefit of the social whole is shaped by the context of competing value orientations or visions of the world. Therefore, people's place in it comes to be defined in divergent ways. This in turn gives rise to competing values underlying different public policies.

In debates about public finance, parliaments often see a clash between "penny pinchers," who associate public interest with balanced budgeting, and "investors for the future," who believe it is in public interest to support education, science and the like, even at the price of a budget deficit, because they will bring a return in future.

Efforts to promote public interests are embraced by certain types of political orientation (as well as individual orientation, as long as such individuals are well-informed) – namely on advancing the community and solving its problems. In this sense, public interests aggregate the interests of individual members of the community – they arise from the individual level. Yet the same public interests may run against conflicting interests of other individuals or groups. Thus, public interests become the subject of frequent negotiation and occasional struggles as well. There are conflicts between competing "public interests" associated with the interests of different communities or social groups. This is the point where they become the domain of public policy, which studies the processes of identifying, formulating, presenting, recognizing and satisfying the public interest.

The lessons humanity took from the rise of totalitarian regimes after World War I provide a good example of how a new global-level public interest emerged, was formulated, and prevailed. These regimes were established in spite of existing norms of international law or traditional political mechanisms of representative democracy at the national level. All this led to the largest humanitarian disaster in the history of mankind, World War II. When WWII ended, nations quickly agreed on introducing a newly defined public interest – the general **criterion of human rights protection** – into policy documents at the international (Universal Declaration of Human Rights adopted by the United Nations (1948)) and European levels (Convention for the Protection of Human Rights and Fundamental Freedoms adopted by the Council of Europe (1950)).

However, public interests can also be generated on the basis of autonomous requirements of the function and development of larger social entities that arise from the evolution of the social division of labor and technology. Furthermore, they spread more and more across the frontiers of individual states.

As another example, the rise of automobile transportation requires the construction of a public road network. That, however, may be in conflict with the interests of some groups, individuals or environmental protection. Should we authorize the construction of an expressway through a nature preserve? If the owners of the land within the expressway's corridor disagree, is the state entitled to confiscate their property?

The concept of public interest is associated with an array of similar terms that are used in different contexts. The social teaching of the Catholic Church operates with the term **common good.** Martenas (1991) uses the term **public good** as a moral umbrella term which also covers public interests. The term **general interest** is used by the European Union's Lisbon Treaty and is reflected in specific regulations covering various forms of services at the European level (The Publications Office of the European Union 2012a, 2012b). The rhetorical figure of "sacrifice for the country" is also used to denote a deed which benefits a given national community at the cost of a particular interest.

In a way, the concept of public interest plays a central role in public policy. However, one rarely comes across the term in practical use. This is because an overwhelming majority of public policies are formulated and implemented at lower levels of generalization. There, the benefit of the social whole is translated into specific objectives such as to reduce school failure or the burden of bureaucracy, to build a bicycle path or a new theatre, to expand the capacity of a shelter or of an electricity transmission network, etc.

WHAT IS MEANT BY PUBLIC POLICY?

The term "public policy" is used in two basic meanings: to refer to a scientific discipline, and to denote a social practice. When using the term, it is necessary to make a clear distinction between both meanings.

THE EMERGENCE AND DEVELOPMENT OF PUBLIC POLICY AS A SCIENTIFIC DISCIPLINE: A HISTORY

Public policy as a scientific discipline was developed in the United States after World War II. In Europe, it started to obtain significant influence around the turn of the 1960s and the 1970s, building, in some countries, on the older **disciplinary tradition of social policy**. Both disciplines indeed share a multitude of research topics and some methodological instruments. In the context of the Czech Republic, public policy has been developing since 1989,[5] inspired by both the American and the European schools of thought.

RELATION OF PUBLIC POLICY TO OTHER DISCIPLINES

Among the disciplines that have contributed the most to public policy are philosophy, sociology, economics, political science, public administration, law, and management theory.[6] This list can be further expanded to include the broader frameworks of history and the art of taking policy lessons from the past, anthropology and the meaning of culture, demographics with its population forecasts, or various disciplines of science and engineering that

Table A1.1 Disciplines and topics related to public policy

Discipline	Example topics
Philosophy	Logics, values and ethics, theory of justice
Sociology	Understanding society as a whole, social structure in terms of classes and other groups, social status, social problems, social interests, social exclusion
Economics	Instrumental rationality, institutional economics, cost-benefit analysis, political economy, special economic policies
Political science	Political processes, institutions and actors
Public administration	The role of bureaucracy in shaping policies and implementing decisions
Legal sciences	Law as a normative and regulatory framework
Management theory	Processes of decision making, implementation and evaluation

Source: Potůček et al. (2010: 11; adapted and expanded).

---

5 The history of policy studies in the Czech Republic is elaborated in more detail by Potůček (2007), Novotný (2012), Veselý, Nekola, Hejzlarová (2016).
6 For a more in-depth discussion of the disciplinary context of public policy, see Potůček, M., L. LeLoup, G. Jenei, L. Váradi (2003: 11–19).

help us better understand health, energy or environmental issues. Public policy makes specific uses of these disciplinary inspirations on the basis of its own theoretical foundations and methodological instruments in order to directly help analyze and propose solutions to such social problems that none of these disciplines alone would be able to grasp and address alone. See Table A.1.

Thus, public policy is a cross-cutting scientific discipline of its own kind. Through the structure of its topics as well as through the explanatory frameworks and research methods applied, it transcends the boundaries of traditional social sciences.[7]

DEFINING PUBLIC POLICY AS A SCIENTIFIC DISCIPLINE

To define the characteristics of a scientific discipline is not a popular endeavor among academics. This is understandable as the boundaries between disciplines are becoming increasingly blurred in the context of an immense accumulation of innovative knowledge, paradigms and methods, and a growing emphasis on problem- and issue-oriented science. And many, albeit not all, would add that those boundaries are also becoming more and more permeable. In spite of that, I believe a definition of public policy is due, even if it continues to be contested, even in the USA (see above) where the discipline has its deepest roots.

> **Public policy** (sometimes also policy studies or policy science) is **defined** as a discipline which elaborates and applies the interpretative frameworks of sociology, economics, political sciences, law, management theory, and other disciplines in analyzing and foresighting the processes of formation and assertion of public interests with respect to solving differentiated social problems. It primarily deals with the institutional mediation of those processes by the public sector, the civic sector and, to some extent, also the commercial sector, in a form that is useful for political practice.

This is, of course, not the only definition. According to Peters (1993), the discipline of public policy studies "the sum of government activities, whether pursued directly or through agents, as those activities have an influence on the lives of citizens" – which operate at three levels: policy choice, policy outputs, and policy impacts. From another perspective, public policy examines

---

7   Unfortunately, many authors use these concepts without defining them, and one can only
     guess by the context in which meaning their terms are to be understood.

what Dewey called "the public and its problems" as early as in 1927. According to Lasswell (1936), policy studies are understood as a discipline that integrates available cognitive approaches in a comprehensive analysis of the overall context of the policy process, policy decisions, and their consequences. As such, they are problem-oriented, multidisciplinary, and pluralistic in terms of methods. In an introduction to his encyclopedia of policy studies, Nagel (1994: xi) defines them as "the study of the nature, causes, and effects of alternative public policies."

According to Dunn, **policy analysis** is "an applied social science discipline which uses multiple methods of inquiry and argument to produce and transform policy-relevant information..." (Dunn 1981: 35) "..., because policy-relevant information has the potential to improve policy making" (Dunn 2012: 53).

POLITY, POLICY, POLITICS

English is the most popular language of science. Unlike some other languages, it provides scholars with a number of terms to grasp essential analytical distinctions. For public policy as a scientific discipline, different meanings of terms *polity, policy,* and *politics* represent its conceptual cornerstones.

The term **polity** refers to the general foundation or orientation of a society, or what is referred to by some authors as the "choice of society" – the direction and nature of its basic aims (Roebroek 1992).

The term **policy** refers to public policy as conceptualized in this chapter.

The term **politics** denotes processes in which actors cooperate, clash, negotiate and reconcile their conflicting interests through political institutions.[8]

At the price of considerable simplification, Fiala and Schubert (2000: 19) succeeded to define all three terms in a single sentence: "The political order constitutes a framework (polity) in which the material element (policy) arises from strategies of political conflict and consensus (politics)."

---

8   In the Czech language, the term *politika* is a frequent source of confusion because it is used, without an accompanying definition, to refer to both policy and politics. While politics is typically driven by struggle for power, policy has, to paraphrase Wildavsky (1979), its own *raison d'être*. Thus, in Czech expert discourse, we recommend using the term *veřejná politika* whenever one refers to a substantive policy area, and reserving the term *politika* to matters of politics.

Exercise: Try to assign the following examples: introduction of tuition at universities; adoption of a new constitution; voting down a state budget bill by the Parliament.

Polity	
Policy	
Politics	

PUBLIC POLICY AS SOCIAL PRACTICE

Anderson (1975) defines public policy as "a purposive course of action followed by an actor or set of actors in dealing with a problem or matter of concern" – a public interest. He distinguishes between (policy) demands, decisions, statements, actions (outputs) and (intended or unintended) consequences (outcomes).

Sartori (1987) argues that a defining characteristic of public policy as social practice lies in collectivized decision making, whereby decision makers are simultaneously the makers and implementers of public policy. Such decisions are taken on behalf of communities (aggregates of individuals comprised of different types of organizations), no matter if by one, several or multiple individuals. Whoever decides does so for all. Thus, public policies are determined by the content and extent of the given decision and collective action.

Jenkins (1978) understands public policy as a "set of interrelated decisions taken by a political actor or group of actors concerning the selection of goals and the means of achieving them" in a given situation and under given constraints.

However, as far as dealing with problems is concerned, most authors do not limit the scope of public policy to government activities. Lindblom and Woodhouse (1993) assume that government officials are mere "mediators," and they point out that public policies are realized by means of a complex political system and cannot be understood primarily with regard to the actions of top government officials (Ibid: 3). They infer that public policy can be better understood as a product of broader societal factors (especially the dominant position of business in democratic capitalism), as it exists within the constraints of human capabilities, and as it is affected by the discrepancy between rational judgment and political power.

In short, **public policy as social practice** refers to practical uses of public policy in pursuing and satisfying public interests. As mentioned above, the ambition to become a useful tool and source of information for better solving social problems has been the central factor behind the emergence of **public policy as a scientific discipline**.[9] However, this defining characteristic can be its advantage as well as its Achilles heel. On the one hand, the practical relevance of public policy inspires the effort of students and researchers to better understand society and policy, and to make their results immediately applicable. On the other hand, scholars from other disciplines may frown upon public policy as a craft that lacks scientific explanation and builds upon feeble theoretical premises.

With regard to securing public interest, one can distinguish between liberal and paternalist types of public policy:

Liberal public policies intervene only as far as a recognized public interest is jeopardized by the pursuit of individual/group interests. Their fundamental view of the state is that of a "night watchman."

Paternalist public policies often pursue a recognized public interest irrespective of the changing nature of social problems or harm to individual interests… More specifically, in an authoritarian regime, there is an increased risk that particular policies will be pursued under the disguise of public interest.

There is a number of differentiated policy areas such as the economic, social, education, health, family, foreign, energy, media, transportation, or security policies.[10]

For example, if the opinion prevails in a society that good family functioning is a matter of public interest, then family policy is instituted to respond to social problems caused by the occurrence of family dysfunction or breakdown.

Important distinctions of public policy as social practice – case of family policy:

- **active versus reactive** (family planning advice versus v. foster/residential care);
- **by regulatory principles or instruments applied** (family law, child benefits, tax relief, preschool establishments, parenting education);
- **global/European/national/local** (family policy is mostly implemented at the national level, sometimes at the regional or municipal level; recommendations are also formulated by organizations such as the EU or the OECD);
- **by actors involved** (departments, civic sector service providers, churches, schools, police, courts, family members);
- **by target group** (future families, families with dependent children, families with handicapped members, lone-parent families).

---

9   A social problem becomes a policy problem if something can be done about it. Cf. Chapter A6 for more details.
10   Chapter A6 provides a more detailed list of policy areas.

Permanent tension between theory and practice is the key productive factor behind the development of public policy. On the one hand, there is an autonomous theoretical and methodological evolution of public policy as a discipline. On the other hand, there are the ever-shifting demands of public policy as a social practice. Public officials and politicians tend to reject more abstract theories as they make little difference in everyday problems. In contrast, scholars may refuse to pursue the practical applicability in their studies because such a goal makes little difference in theory testing and generalization.[11]

FOUNDING FATHERS AND FOLLOWERS

Sociologists have traced the origins of their discipline back to the works of Auguste Comte. For public policy, such an effort to identify a single founding father is most likely futile. The discipline rather has a number of founding fathers and even one mother, namely Elinor Ostrom, co-recipient of the 2009 Nobel Prize for economics.

Table A1.2 Authors who made a major contribution to public policy theory

Author	Contribution
Arrow, Kenneth J.	The logic of collective action
Axelrod, Robert	Cooperative and noncooperative behaviour
Dahl, Robert A.	Theory of democracy, polyarchy
Dahrendorf, Ralf	Individual rights and social commitments; social liberalism
Dror, Yehezkel	Rational policy model; strategic governance
Dunn, William	The concept of *policy analysis*
Easton, David	Political system
Etzioni, Amitai	Ethics in the economy; communitarianism
Fischer, Frank; Forrester, John	Argumentative turn in policy analysis
Heclo, Hugh; Hughes, Owen E.	Issue networks, policy networks
Kingdon, John W.	Theory of agenda setting; three streams theory
Lasswell, Harold	The concept of *policy sciences* as comprised of *policy studies* and *policy analysis*; the "stages" model of the policy cycle

11 Unfortunately, policy analysis is sometimes misused in the pursuit of particular interests. For example, certain think-tanks do their research with a view to deliver the results expected by their clients or donors. The ideological bias of such works is often not reflected critically.

Lindblom, Charles E.	Incremental model of public policy; relationship between market and government
Lowi, Theodore J.	Model of arenas of power
Ostrom, Elinor	Institutional Analysis and Development Framework
Peters, Guy	Institutionalism; horizontal governance
Rose, Richard	Citizens in public policy; policy programs implementation
Sen, Amartya	Goal and function of public policy; human potential; models of development
Sabatier, Paul A.	Advocacy Coalition Framework
Simon, Herbert	Bounded rationality; human aspect of the workings of bureaucracy
Schneider, Anne L.; Ingram, Helen M.	Social construction of target groups
Weimer, David L.; Vining, Aidan R.	Methodology of policy analysis, relationship between market, government and civic sector
Wildavsky, Aaron	Policy analysis as science and art; implementation; the ethics of the relationship between policy advisors and politicians
Wilenski, Harold	Comparative analysis; corporatism

Exercise: As you study public policy, continuously expand the table above by adding new authors and their contributions to advancing the theory of public policy.

FUTURE PERSPECTIVES OF THE DISCIPLINE

Public policy is an independent, rapidly developing and self-confident scientific discipline. Its explanatory frameworks, analytical capacities and practical proposals for solving problems are more and more in demand by responsible political representatives and administrative officials. Approaches to public policy range on a scale from basic research (at a high level of abstraction) to elaborate empirical studies (often with an important comparative element) to practical applications that immediately intervene in policy and administrative communication and decision-making in the public space (often referred to as policy analysis). Depending on the perspective of choice, each item on this scale has its specific function throughout the discipline. [12]

---

12 There are two focal points of academic instruction and research in the field of public policy in the Czech Republic: the Faculty of Social Sciences at Charles University in Prague (with

REVIEW QUESTIONS

Chronicle the emergence, formation and implementation of a specific public policy up to the point of recognizing and securing the public interest.

Are efforts to regulate the Internet in the public interest?

What are the foundations of a theoretical approach that denies the existence of public interest?

Exemplify the consequences of politicians' failure to acknowledge a public interest.

What are the differences between political science and public policy – and what do they have in common?

Why does public policy cover a broader array of topics than public administration?

Exemplify[13] the difference between active and reactive public policies.

SOURCES

Anderson, J. E. 1975. *Public Policy Making.* New York: Praeger Publishers.

Council of Europe. 1950. *European Convention on Human Rights and Fundamental Freedoms.* Retrieved May 23, 2016 (http://www.echr.coe.int/Documents/Convention_ENG.pdf).

Dunn, W. N. 1981. *Public Policy Analysis.* Englewood Cliffs, NJ: Prentice Hall.

Dunn, W. N. 2012. *Public Policy Analysis.* 5th edition. Boston: Pearson.

Fiala, P., K. Schubert. 2000. *Moderní analýza politiky* [Modern Policy Analysis, in Czech]. Brno: Barrister & Principal.

Jenkins, W. I. 1978. *Policy Analysis.* Oxford: Martin Robertson.

Kinkor, J. 1996. *Trh a stát: k čemu potřebujeme filozofii* [Market and State: what Philosophy is for, in Czech]. Prague: Svoboda.

Lane, J.-E. 1993. *The Public Sector. Concepts, Models and Approaches.* London: Sage.

Lasswell, H. 1936. *Politics: Who Gets What, When, How.* New York: Whittlesey House, McGraw-Hill.

Lindblom, C. E., E. J. Woodhouse. 1993. *The Policy-Making Process.* Englewood Cliffs, NJ: Prentice Hall.

Lippman, W. 1955. *Essays in the Public Interest Philosophy.* Boston: Little, Brown and Co.

---

the Department of Public and Social Policy of the Institute for Sociological Studies, and the Center for Social and Economic Strategies), and the Faculty of Social Studies (with its Department of Social Policy and Social Work) and Faculty of Economics and Administration (with its Department of Public Economics) at Masaryk University in Brno. Both were well represented at the first two international conferences on public policy in Grenoble (2013) and Milan (2015). *Policy Analysis in the Czech Republic* (Veselý, Nekola, Hejzlarová 2016) was published as one of the world's first national monographs on the history and state of the art. Public policy readership can draw on a number of textbooks and other comprehensive volumes (see commented bibliography below), as well as on Charles University's *Central European Journal of Public Policy* (http://www.cejpp.eu). The School of Public Policy, Central European University in Budapest, Hungary represents an important focal point of public policy research and teaching in Central and Eastern Europe.

13   Do not use the case of family policy.

Martenas, S. J. 1991. "Beyond Scandals & Statutes: Ethics in Public Administration." *University of Virginia News Letter* 67 (9): 1–8.

McCool, D. C. 1995. *Public Policy Theories, Models, and Concepts: An Anthology.* Englewood Cliffs, NJ: Prentice Hall.

Nagel, S. 1994. *The Encyclopedia of Policy Studies.* New York: St. Martins.

Novotný, V. 2012. *Vývoj českého studia veřejných politik v evropském kontextu* [Development of the Czech Study of Public Policies in European Context, in Czech]. Prague: Karolinum.

Peters, B. G. 1993. *American Public Policy.* Chatham: Chatham House.

Potůček, M. 2007. "Czech Public Policy as a Scientific Discipline and Object of Research." *Central European Journal of Public Policy* 1 (1): 102–121.

Potůček, M., L. LeLoup, G. Jenei, L. Váradi. 2003. *Public Policy in Central and Eastern Europe: Theories, Methods, Practices.* Bratislava: NISPAcee.

Potůček, M. et al. 2005 (new edition 2010). *Veřejná politika.* [Public Policy, in Czech]. Prague: Sociologické nakladatelství (SLON).

Publications Office of the European Union. 2012a. "Consolidated Version of the Treaty on European Union." *Official Journal of the European Union* C326/13, October 26. Retrieved February 2, 2016 (http://eur-lex.europa.eu/legal-content/EN/TXT/PDF/?uri=CELEX:12012M/TXT&from=EN).

Publications Office of the European Union. 2012b. "Consolidated Version of the Treaty on the Functioning of the European Union." *Official Journal of the European Union* C326/47, October 26. Retrieved February 2, 2016 (http://eur-lex.europa.eu/legal-content/EN/TXT/PDF/?uri=CELEX:12012E/TXT&from=EN).

Roebroek, J. M. 1992. *The Imprisoned State.* Tilburg: Tilburg University.

Sartori, G. 1987. *The Theory of Democracy Revisited – Part One.* New Jersey: Chatham House Publishers.

United Nations. 1948. *The Universal Declaration of Human Rights.* Retrieved May 23, 2016 (http://www.ohchr.org/EN/UDHR/Documents/UDHR_Translations/eng.pdf).

Veselý, A., M. Nekola, E. Hejzlarová (eds.). 2016. *Policy Analysis in the Czech Republic.* Bristol: Policy Press.

Wildavsky, A. 1979. *Speaking Truth to Power: The Art and Craft of Policy Analysis.* Boston: Little, Brown and Co.

/**A2**/
Values in Public Policy

Social sciences and values are like identical twins. One who attempts to sell the results of his/her research under the disguise of impartial scientific truth, whether a sociologist, an economist or a political scientist, one who believes his/her research may escape the grip of values, is rather a slave to yesterday's fads… However, if this is true, does it make any sense to strive for learning the unknown? My answer is a definitive yes, with only two caveats. Not only do we have to abide by all the rules, respect all the limitations, and make the best possible use of the options science provides, but we must also be aware of the background value of our scholarly work and be prepared to disclose it whenever necessary.

This is especially important in public policy, whether as social practice or as a scientific discipline. Values are omnipresent in public policy as social practice, and every policy practitioner is forced to work in the context of conflicting values (Theodoulou, Cahn 1995). The concluding section is going to elaborate on this.

Values are reflected in the definition of social problems and public interests related to them, in the content of ideologies, policy doctrines, policies, programs and norms. They influence the choice and ways of utilization of policy instruments. They shape institutions, they guide actors' actions. They determine the processes of education, indoctrination or persuasion.

The **value background of public policies** reflects more general human communities' need to coordinate the actions of individuals and groups and foresee the reactions of other actors involved (... and thus minimize the transaction cost of such actions, an economist might say). While public policies must respect the different involved actors' value fields, they often transcend them, for example in order to meet general criteria such as quality of life or human rights. In public policy as a scientific discipline (and even more so in policy practice), one can observe the coexistence of and competition between overlapping specific normative models that are inspired by the works of social philosophers, by political ideologies, or directly by the involved actors' interests. Some light can be shed on this complex matter by the analytical distinction between **polity**, **policy** and **politics**[14]. Each of those levels is associated with values closely and in its own way.

VALUES IN POLITY

Shared values have been involved in human behavior since time immemorial. In the era of hunters and gatherers 30–20 thousand years BC, people abode by general norms with regard to the ways of getting food, moving in space, protection from forces of nature and external threat, sex life, and family life. Later these rules and values became codified (albeit not everything was written explicitly).

EXAMPLE CODIFICATIONS OF VALUE SYSTEMS:

Code of Hammurabi (1686 BC), Talmud, Bible, Quran, *Magna Carta Libertatum* (1215), Declaration of the Rights of Man and of the Citizen (French Revolution, 1789), Universal Declaration of Human Rights (UN, 1948), Charter of Fundamental Rights of the EU (2000, 2009).

HUMAN RIGHTS

Europe has been shaped by the evolution of values from the culture of Mesopotamia through classical antiquity, Christianity, the Enlightenment, up to the modern age. In comparison with the Middle Ages, modernity, the Enlightenment, and liberalism – inspired by renaissance humanism – marked

---

14   Cf. Chapter A1.

a fundamental turn to the recognition of the universality of human rights. That concept, which by the 20th century had begun to be used with more frequency, has its ancestry in the concept of natural rights. The first theorists of natural rights such as Grotius, Hobbes and Locke, emphasized in particular the right to freedom and property. The concept of natural rights was first incorporated into political documents in 1776, when the American Declaration of Independence stated:

"We hold these truths to be self-evident, that all men are created equal, that they are endowed by their Creator with certain unalienable Rights, that among these are Life, Liberty and the pursuit of Happiness."

At the same time, the French Declaration of the Rights of Man and of the Citizen of 1789 spoke of inherent/natural, irrevocable/imprescriptible and unalienable rights. "Liberty, Equality, Fraternity" – there is a direct link between the French Revolution's motto and various declarations of human rights, and above all the Universal Declaration of Human Rights adopted by the United Nations General Assembly in December 1948.

Marshall (1963) proposed the following account of the evolution of rights in modern states: There is an elementary form of human equality that relates to the full participation of the individual in the life of his/her community. That equality is not incompatible with economic inequality. It is therefore necessary to broaden the concept of the rights of the citizen to include three components: civil, political and social rights. **Civil rights** are associated with individual freedom – protection of personality rights, freedom of speech, thought and religion, the right to property and to conclude contracts, and equality before the law guaranteed through the right to due process. **Political rights** allow the individual to share in the decision making about the life of his /her community. For instance, in well-functioning systems of representative democracy, citizens elect their deputies or themselves stand for election to representative bodies. **Social rights** cover equal opportunities, and especially the right to share in the use of a given society's social inheritance, and the right to live in dignity, i.e., on a level corresponding to the standards prevalent in that society. Marshall argues that civil rights formed during the 18th century, political rights in the 19th century, and the 20th century saw the emergence of social rights.

Table A2.1 Evolution of rights

Formative period of nation-states	18th century	19th century	20th century	21st century
Content of human rights	* civil rights	+ political rights	+ social rights	+/– ?

Source: Marshall (1963), adapted.

Nevertheless, the very Universal Declaration of Human Rights also included on its list of human rights certain **cultural rights** guaranteeing equal access to culture and the opportunities for active involvement in it.

Since the end of World War II, the concept of human rights and its application in public policy has exhibited a tendency to diversify and specialize. A typical example of such specialization, gender equality has been defined to ensure equal opportunities for men and women. Minority rights have grown into an extensive agenda, with specific rights covering ethnic, religious, sexual and other minorities. At another level, specific rights have been defined for different conditions of life – for example, that of a child, a patient or a consumer.

Nowadays, human rights are clearly codified in the constitutional and legal systems of all democratic countries; among others, the Council of Europe and the European Union have placed strong emphasis on both declaring human rights and enforcing them in practice. In this way, human rights have become a set of criteria in which the practical implementation of a number of public policies is grounded. However, numerous authors[15] have "rightfully" raised the concern about a one-sided emphasis on rights without the corresponding attention paid to the other side of the coin – responsibilities.

At the level of polity, an important contribution to the debate about the orientation of European civilization was made by Czech environmentalist, management scientist and the first Minister of the Environment of post-communist Czechoslovakia Josef Vavroušek. Shortly before his tragic death (he and his daughter perished in March 1995 under an avalanche in the High Tatra Mountains), he formulated ten values linked to unsustainable trends in development and juxtaposed them with ten alternative value positions that were compatible with a sustainable way of life. See Table A2.2.

POLITICAL IDEOLOGIES

Naturally, there is a diversity of opinions about where societies should be going and what they should strive for. Such diversity is reflected in various **value orientations** and expressed in competing **political ideologies**.

Our societies are characterized by a plurality of opinions about what is and what is not right or desirable – and I have many reasons to believe that it is this plurality which enables us to conceive of a broad diversity of options and to better adapt to difficult situations. On the other hand, every society needs a common denominator, a set of shared fundamental criteria, to facilitate communication and draw a line between what is and what is not in the common good or public interest; to make sense of the different choices citizens

---

15   Giddens (1998), for instance.

Table A2.2 In search of human values compatible with a sustainable way of life

	European civilization's fundamental values related to unsustainable development trends (values A)	Alternative value positions compatible with a sustainable way of life (values B)
1. Man's relationship with nature	Exploitative relationship with nature	Awareness of belonging to nature
2. Relationship between individual and society	Extreme attitudes: a. one-sided emphasis on individualism and competition (typical of "real capitalism"), b. one-sided emphasis on collectivism (typical of "real socialism")	Balanced emphasis on individual and collective, competition supplemented by cooperation
3. Relation to the flow of time and the meaning of history	Obsession with the notion of quantitative growth	Emphasis on qualitative development of human society
4. Relation to meaning of one's own life	Hedonistic orientation and consumerist way of life	Quality of life, voluntary modesty and avoidance of nonessential goods
5. Relation to freedom and responsibility	One-sided emphasis on human rights and freedoms, eroded awareness of shared responsibility for the course of events	Respect for the symmetry of human rights and freedoms with responsibility
6. Relation to level of our knowledge	"Arrogance of reason"	Carefulness in all interactions with nature and society
7. Relation to one's own life	Alienation from one's own life, weakened self-preservation instinct and feedback for correcting wrong or unsuccessful actions	Restored self-preservation instinct in people
8. Relation to future generations	Preference of short-term interests over long-term and permanent ones	Respect for long-term results of human activity
9. Relation to alternative opinions and other civilizations	Intolerance of others' opinions	Mutual tolerance
10. Relation to public affairs	Giving up on shared decision making on public affairs	Development of participative democracy

Source: Vavroušek (1993).

and political leaders are faced with; and after all, to guide them in everyday decision-making situations. Otherwise, society might fall apart.

> "Finally, political ideas and ideologies can act as a form of social cement, providing social groups, and indeed whole societies, with a set of unifying beliefs and values."
> (Heywood 2012: 3)

Not only every society, but also every public policy as social practice necessitates a comprehensive value background of public interest. **Political ideologies** provide such comprehensive value systems. Gramsci (1994) characterizes ideologies as mediators between abstract philosophical concepts and real-life political environments. Mannheim (1936) sees them as systems of values and preferences that arise and come to be used as different social groups strive to assert their interests in practical politics. Bauman (1999, as paraphrased by Schwarzmantel 2008) defines ideology as a "set of ideas which is normative, setting out an ideal, aiming at arousing support on a mass basis for those ideas…" What these authors have in common is the conclusion that ideologies are relatively general and comprehensive accounts of society's problems, their causes and their possible solutions that are linked with a diversity of people's interests. At the same time, they embrace, to some extent, what one might refer to as the interests of a community as a whole, i.e., **public interests**.[16]

Political ideologies are a necessary component of communication in political discourse. They facilitate identification of political standpoints and priorities. However, they are at the same time a framework that significantly simplifies the understanding and interpretation of social realities. As such, they are a potential instrument of both misunderstanding as well as justification for decisions and acts that are unreasonable *vis-à-vis* the nature of the problem situation[17]. It is in this situation that we clearly see the advantages of a pluralistic political process, one which allows the possibility of a free exchange of opinions, while also allowing for the identification, before the genie is out of the bottle, of biases or deformations which had previously not been perceived by their supporters. Also, it is here where space opens up for making changes and corrections to existing ideologies that have been made necessary by the emergence of new problems or of ones that were previously unknown or, for various reasons, ignored.

Different political ideologies coexist, compete and intermix in policy practice, inspired both by the works of influential social philosophers and by social practice itself.[18] They operate in a field generated by the sum of key problems

---

16 For example, Weiss (1983) proposed three explanatory factors that influence policy decisions: ideologies, interests and information. Hence his contribution is referred to as "I-I-I theory." Cf. Chapter A8 for more on this.

17 See Mannheim (1936) for more.

18 Cf. Weimer & Vining (1992), Lane (1993).

of contemporary societies. Each ideology proposes certain ways of balancing the tension between economic growth, wellbeing, an emphasis on market and deregulation, individual growth and limited government, on one hand, and social justice, equal opportunities, social cohesion and a welfare state, on the other hand. Even if such tensions and ways of solving them are constantly on the policy agenda of every contemporary society, they are not the only items on that agenda. Policy discourses[19] have also come to be dominated by environmental, security, family, migration issues *et cetera*.

There is a vast body of literature on political ideologies (Kiss 1998, Heywood 2012, Stankiewicz 2006, Lupták & Prorok 2011). Here I am only providing a brief introduction to those ideologies that have made a difference in modern history, including different variants thereof.

Table A2.3 Characteristics of influential political ideologies

Liberalism	Emphasis on individual freedom, civil and political rights, negative freedom (freedom from…), the night-watchman state, private property is inviolable.	
	Social liberalism	Recognizes the importance of positive freedom (freedom to become…) and the role of government in managing the economy (Keynesianism).
	Neoliberalism	Minimizes government intervention, maximizes the regulatory role of the market.
Conservatism	Prefers traditional, time-tested institutions, hierarchies and authorities: government, church, family; private property is inviolable.	
	Authoritarian conservatism	An authoritarian political system.
	Paternalist conservatism	Treats institutions as mediators between citizens and government; social corporatism; principles of subsidiarity and decentralization.
Socialism	Human emancipation, positive freedom (freedom to become…), social /collective ownership of means of production.	
	State socialism	An authoritarian political system, planned economy.
	Democratic socialism/ communitarianism	Accepts the system of representative democracy, mixed economy.
Environ-mentalism	The ethics of reverence for life (Albert Schweitzer), a democratic system, mixed economy.	
Nationalism	Political and economic self-determination of a national community.	

Sources: Berlin (1958), Hayek (2006), Heywood (2012), Schwarzmantel (2008).[20]

---

19   For more details, see Chapter A5 on public policy instruments.
20   Thinkers who examine humanity's fate in depth and consistently have concluded that the concept of sustainable life cannot cover merely our species. One of them, Albert Schweitzer, formulated the concept of reverence for life, i.e. respect for all life on our planet. According

Table A2.4 Characteristics of now marginal political ideologies

Totalitarianism	Social whole is superior to individuals, who must submit to it	
	Nazism	Racial supremacy, loyalty to the *Führer*
	Fascism	Extreme nationalism, submission of corporations to government
	Communism	Classless society, "to each according to his needs"

Sources: Griffin (1995), Heywood (2012).

HOW INSTITUTIONS ARE SHAPED BY POLITICAL IDEOLOGIES:

THE CASE OF THE WELFARE STATE

Political ideologies have been and are going to remain instruments of political struggle, the outcome of which shapes institutional frameworks and public policies. This can be exemplified in the different types of welfare states.

DEFINITION:

A **welfare state** is a polity which asserts itself into various laws, people's consciousness and attitudes, into institutions' activities and practical policy; the idea that the social conditions people live in aren't just the concern of individuals or families but are public issue as well. Every citizen is given a certain approved minimal level of support and help in different life situations which could be a (potential or real) threat to them or to their families (Potůček 1995: 35).

Esping-Andersen (1990) proposed a distinction between several types of welfare states, namely liberal, conservative and social democratic ones. What are their basic characteristics? See Table A2.5.

Based on numerous critical responses, his typology has been expanded to include other types of welfare states as well. For example, the **Latin Rim Model** is characterized by the absence of a clearly formulated subsistence minimum, high demands on care provision by family members (especially women) and a fragmented social structure; the model is better suitable for Southern European countries. Furthermore, welfare states can be differentiated according to the role in service provision they ascribe to the public sector,

---

to Schweitzer, humanity is acting not only unethically but also irrationally by pursuing activities that effectively exterminate an ever larger part of the existing gene pool of Earth's biosphere, one that has been evolving for hundreds of millions of years.

Table A2.5 Characteristics of major types of welfare states

Characteristic → Type ↓	Decommodification (extent of free provision of social services)	Basis/ determinants	Key criterion for access to services	Consequences	Social structure
Liberal/ Anglo-Saxon	Stingy benefits, selectivity with means testing	Bourgeois hegemony, strong liberalism	Need	Polarized growth of employment with shrinking middle class; accentuation of class differences	Segmentation of society – public provision for the "truly" needy – private self-provision for middle classes
Conservative/ Continental European	Generous, wide access, but based on contributions	Class compromise without clear hegemony; strong Catholicism	Work performance and membership in an occupational category	Employment problems: "welfare without work"; support for families; segmentation insiders/outsiders	Status-specific fragmentation (status barriers between various occupational groups)
Social Democratic/ Scandinavian	Very generous, universal access	Dominance of labor movement & social democracy	Citizenship	Expansion of public social services; support for individuals	Universal-egalitarian (promoting solidarity)

Source: Author.

the family assisted by government, or the family alone. The **Radical Model** guarantees income through market regulation (regulation of wages, labor security), social care for marginal groups only, and a strong role of means testing (Australia, New Zealand). **Feminist movements**, too, have presented their perspectives on the welfare state, attempting to make existing typologies more sensitive to gender issues.

The exact state of a country's social policy typically resembles a mosaic – its social system consists of different elements inspired by different types of the Welfare State.

EXAMPLE:

Health care in the United Kingdom is organized by the (tax-funded) National Health Service and provided to all people equally. The NHS represents a social-democratic element in the overwhelmingly liberal Anglo-Saxon welfare state.

Nevertheless, even in such a complex mosaic, it is usually not difficult to identify some characteristic traits or traces of political ideologies that was used to dominate a country in the past years and decades…

In addition to political ideologies, the shape of welfare states can also be affected by more specific documents. As an important and frequently mentioned historical example, in the year 1891, Pope Leo XIII issued an encyclical, *Rerum Novarum*, devoted to social issues with respect to the rights and responsibilities of capital and labor. Recently, in 2001, an academic policy paper entitled, *Social Doctrine of the Czech Republic*, was proposed to political leaders as a value background for a long-term, strategically developed social policy with a view to reducing the risk of unnecessary fluctuation of policies as governments come and go (Social Doctrine 2002).

VALUES IN POLICY

A recent trend, especially in relation to the global crisis of the 2000s, has been to turn away from the most frequently used indicator of economic and social progress, the Gross Domestic Product (GDP) of a given country. The so-called Stiglitz Report commissioned by French President Nicolas Sarkozy concluded that GDP is not suitable for assessing individual countries' success, and recommended replacing it with indicators encompassing a broader complex of people's living conditions (Stiglitz, Sen, Fitoussi 2009).

EXAMPLE:

In international comparison, the UN-sponsored **Human Development Index** (HDI) has been applied. The HDI is based on a set of particular criteria including the Gross National Income (GNI – instead of GDP), average life expectancy at birth, and level of education in a country's population. The Human Development Report (2010) relies on an even more sophisticated indicator, adding to the coverage of the HDI also a general measure of inequality in individual countries, a measure of gender inequality or a multidimensional index of poverty.

EXAMPLE:

The government of Bhutan applies the indicator of **Gross National Happiness** (GNH) in its decision making. This approach is based on the philosophy of Buddhism and on the political determination of HM Jigme Singye Wangchuck, King of Bhutan, who declared in 1972: "Gross National Happiness is more important than Gross Domestic Product." The indicator is built upon four pillars: sustainable development, cultural values, natural environment, and good governance. It encompasses eight general contributors to happiness:
* physical, mental and spiritual health;
* time balance between paid/unpaid work and rest;
* active community life;
* cultural diversity and vitality;
* education;
* living standards;
* good governance;
* living in and with the nature.

This measurement method has all the necessary traits of serious scientific examination. The governments of Nepal and Singapore have chosen to follow a similar direction.

THE CRITERION OF QUALITY AND SUSTAINABILITY OF LIFE

The Center for Social and Economic Strategies at the Faculty of Social Sciences, Charles University in Prague, studied a set of criteria in which public policies in the Czech Republic were grounded *vis-à-vis* the country's future threats and developmental opportunities. In its works it proposed the criterion of **quality and sustainability of life** (Potůček, Musil, Mašková 2008).

Quality of life represents people's objective living conditions and, at the same time, their subjective perceptions of those conditions. It is a multidimensional concept covering all important aspects of human life that are related to the well-being of individuals living in a society[21]. In contrast, science cannot associate **sustainability of life** with the fate of mortal individuals, but rather with the future life and living conditions of human society as a whole. In this sense, the concepts of sustainability of life and sustainable development are similar or almost identical in their meanings.

EXAMPLE:

The relationship between quality and sustainability of life can be exemplified in a hypothetical case of a group of people stranded on a small island in complete isolation from the rest of the civilization. These people are able to considerably increase the quality of their present life by unrestrained consumption of all available resources (especially those of vegetable, animal, and mineral origin). Nevertheless, such a course of action would have fatal consequences for their ability to survive in the long term (primarily due to the extinction of vitally important species of plants and animals). Unless the small island civilization can limit their consumption at present time and avoid undercutting the reproductive capacity of their environment, it will sign its own death warrant for a near or more distant future.

In this approach, the criterion of quality and sustainability of life can be measured using several dimensions: economic, social, environmental and security. Those are also referred to as pillars upon which the quality and sustainability of life rest. Of course, forecasting and strategic efforts should also take into consideration the interrelations and interdependencies between the pillars.

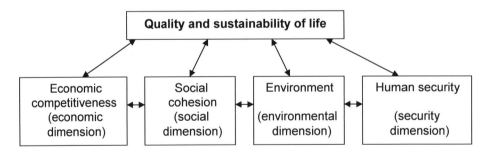

Figure A2.1 The criterion of quality and sustainability of life
Source: Potůček, Musil, Mašková 2008.

---

21 Recent approaches to quality of life define it as a combination of objective conditions for human life and the ways these are perceived subjectively by people.

VALUES IN POLITICS

After November 1989, a lot of Americans came to work in the Czech Republic because they were fascinated by the country's social transformation and sought to offer their knowledge and experience altruistically. One of them, Brack Brown, worked at the Faculty of Social Sciences, Charles University in Prague, became one of the founders of the first program in Public and Social Policy, and co-authored the very first policy textbook in Central and Eastern Europe (Potůček, LeLoup, Jenei, Váradi 2003).[22] It contains the following words of B. Brown:

"The ethics of public policy refers to much more than whether politicians finally make choices based on ethical considerations. Every facet and stage of public policy can involve ethics and all the actors involved must address ethical questions. Advisors, analysts, decision makers, administrators, and evaluators are ethically accountable. They are accountable for their behavior as agents of the public, for the methods they use, the content they focus on, and the outcomes of the policy." (Brown 2003: 196).

While the reader is kindly referred to Brown's text at this point, let us merely add two examples of value conflicts in which two different types of policy actors can be involved: elected representatives and policy consultants /analysts.

EXAMPLE: ELECTED REPRESENTATIVES

The value contexts that may shape the decisions of a Member of Parliament:
- own conscience (internalized values);
- public interests, e.g., as articulated in general programmatic documents (government policy statement, election programs of political parties);
- group interests (lobbying, corruption);
- benefiting one's own political party and/or harming others;
- private self-interest.

EXAMPLE: POLICY CONSULTANTS/ANALYSTS

Consultants may perform different (complementary or conflicting) roles:
- independent experts, policy technicians striving to identify the best solution based on objective scientific evidence[23];

---

22 His chapter on ethics in public policy was later translated and included in the first Czech textbook for the field (Potůček et al. 2005: 353–383).
23 We already know that this is an illusory approach. It is always necessary to define the underlying values in which a policy analysis or policy proposal is grounded.

- solvers of social problems as they perceive them;
- client advocates serving their clients' interests and goals.

Therefore, it comes as little surprise that the same piece of information can be interpreted in radically different ways, depending on one's values. If a value conflict arises between the client and the consultant, they can talk it through and try to find a mutually acceptable solution, they can terminate their contract, or the policy analyst might even "betray" the client by disclosing any facts that the client sought to keep secret.

Individual experts, and public think-tanks even more so, need to be aware of the fact that a reputation for competence and credibility is hard to get but easy to lose.

Neither public officials are, of course, immune from value conflicts of this or another kind, as suggested by the frequent occurrence of corruption in public administration. Such cases attest to the ethical failure of concrete individuals. However, oftentimes, corruption also arises from errors in the ways people were selected for their offices or from legal loopholes. **Codes of ethics** are a type of instrument used to counter corruption in public administration. Similar sets of rules are codified for members of different professional unions (attorneys-in-law, medical professionals, journalists).

EXAMPLE THEORY: HISTORICAL INSTITUTIONALISM

This theory is best applied in the study of long-term and macro-level social processes. It works with the assumption of path dependency, i.e., the generalized experience that once established, an institution (whether formal organizations or laws, or informal norms that influence actors' behavior) is marked by the genetic code it obtained from its creator and does not automatically adapt to changes; any change is indeed extremely difficult to effect (Pierson 2000). The theory relies primarily on case studies (Tilly 1984). Its proponents believe that "a specific model or method cannot capture the spirit of the larger enterprise, which is to pay closer attention to 'historicity' or 'temporalities'" (Immergut 2005).

The theory of historical institutionalism studies:
- what factors (including institutions in general, and political institutions in particular) shape actors' definitions of their interests and political situation, political goals, and assessments of the best course of action;
- how actors interpret the workings of these institutions and adjust their behavior according to these interpretations (including acting in ways to change the institutions or create new ones);
- how definitions of preferences, interests and issues change over time or vary across societies (Immergut 2005).

Hall and Taylor (1996: 938–942) define the following characteristic traits of the theory of historical institutionalism:

- it conceptualizes the relationship between institutions and individual behavior in relatively broad terms;
- it emphasizes the asymmetries of power associated with the operation and development of institutions, i.e., the ways institutions distribute power across social groups;
- its view of institutional development is centered upon path dependence and unintended consequences;
- it identifies factors other than institutions that can contribute to political outcomes.

Historical institutionalism views institutions as more than just intervening variables: institutions also determine the broader context of political action (they affect the goals and preferences of actors who are influenced not only by rational calculation but also by social norms). This is the way institutions shape policy development.

Pierson (1996: 127) states that historical institutionalism, in its effort to account for the evolution of institutions, behaves like film, rather than photography.

The school of **evolutionary institutionalism** analyses policy development from an even broader perspective than historical institutionalism. It draws inspiration from the works of Herbert Spencer and later sociobiology, population ecology, evolutionary economics and the theory of memes (units of cultural information) (Thelen 2004).

REVIEW QUESTIONS

Give examples of changes in the value background of public policies following major historical traumas (wars, revolutions).

Why is the Gross Domestic Product (GDP) gradually losing its status as a key indicator of a nation's progress?

What are the differences between the value contexts of a polity, a policy, and politics?

What are the strengths and weaknesses of using ideologies in the policy process?

Characterize various streams within influential political ideologies: liberalism, conservatism, socialism.

What was in the center of critical responses to Esping-Andersen's typology of welfare states?

What indicators of a nation's progress are available as alternatives to the Gross Domestic Product (GDP)?

What is the relationship between quality of life and sustainability of life?

What kind of value conflicts do Members of Parliament possibly face in their decision making?

At what level and timeframe is it suitable to apply the theory of historical institutionalism – and why?

SOURCES

Bauman, Z. 1999. *In Search of Politics*. Cambridge: Polity Press.

Berlin, I. 1958. *Two Concepts of Liberty*. Oxford: Clarendon Press.

Brown, B. 2003. "Ethics and Public Policymaking: An Incomplete Transition in Central and Eastern Europe." Pp. 175–200 in *Public Policy in Central and Eastern Europe: Theories, Methods, Practices*, by M. Potůček, L. LeLoup, G. Jenei, L. Váradi. Bratislava: NISPAcee.

Esping-Andersen, G. 1990. *The Three Worlds of Welfare Capitalism*. New Jersey: Princeton University Press, 1990.

Giddens, A. 1998. *The Third Way. The Renewal of Social Policy*. Cambridge: Polity Press.

Gramsci, A. 1994. *Pre-Prison Writings*. Cambridge: Cambridge University Press.

Griffin, R. 1995. *Fascism*. Oxford: Oxford University Press.

Hall, P. A., C. R. Taylor. 1996. "Political Science and the Three New Institutionalisms." *Political Studies*, XLIV: 936–957.

Hayek, F. 2006. *Constitution of Liberty*. London: Routledge.

Heywood, A. 2012. *Political Ideologies: An Introduction*. 5th ed. Basingstoke: Palgrave Macmillan.

Human Development Report 2010. *The Real Wealth of Nations: Pathways to Human Development*. New York: Palgrave Macmillan.

Immergut, E. M. 2005. "Paradigms of Change in Political Science: Historical-Institutionalism in Political Science and the Problem of Change." Pp. 237–259 in *Understanding Change: Models, Methodologies, and Metaphors*, edited by A. Wimmer, R., Kössler. Basinngstoke: Palgrave.

Kiss, J. (ed.). 1998. *Současná politická filosofie* [Contemporary Political Philosophy, in Czech]. Prague: Oikoymenh.

Lane, J.-E. 1993. *The Public Sector. Concepts, Models and Approaches*. London: Sage.

Lupták, M., V. Prorok. 2011. *Politické ideologie a teorie od starověku po rok 1848* [Political Ideologies and Theories from Antiquity to 1848, in Czech]. Plzeň: Vydavatelství a nakladatelství Aleš Čeněk.

Mannheim, K. 1936. *Ideology and Utopia*. New York: Harvest Books.

Marshall, T. H. 1963. *Sociology at the Crossroads and Other Essays*. London: Heinemann.

Pierson, P. 1996. "The Path to European Integration: A Historical-Institutionalist Analysis." *Comparative Political Studies* 29 (2): 123–163.

Pierson, P. 2000. "Increasing Returns, Path Dependence, and the Study of Politics." *American Political Science Review* 94 (2): 251–267.

Potůček, M. 1995. *Sociální politika* [Social Policy, in Czech]. Prague: Sociologické nakladatelství (SLON).

Potůček, M. et al. 2005 (new edition 2010). *Veřejná politika* [Public Policy, in Czech]. Prague: Sociologické nakladatelství (SLON).

Potůček, M., J. Musil, M. Mašková (eds.). 2008. *Strategické volby pro Českou republiku: teoretická východiska* [Strategic Choices for the Czech Republic: the Theoretical Foundations, in Czech]. Prague: Sociologické nakladatelství (SLON).

Potůček, M., L. LeLoup, G. Jenei, L. Váradi. 2003. *Public Policy in Central and Eastern Europe: Theories, Methods, Practices.* Bratislava: NISPAcee.

Schwarzmantel, J. 2008. *Ideology and Politics.* London: SAGE Publications.

Social Doctrine of the Czech Republic. 2002. Retrieved May 19, 2016 (http://martinpotucek.cz /index.php?option=com_rubberdoc&view=doc&id=503&format=raw).

Stankiewicz, W. J. 2006. *Hledání politické filosofie. Ideologie na sklonku dvacátého století* [Searching for Political Philosophy. Ideology in Late Twentieth Century, in Czech]. Brno: Centrum pro studium demokracie a kultury.

Stiglitz, J. E., A. Sen, and J.-P. Fitoussi. 2009. *Report by the Commission on the Measurement of Economic Performance and Social Progress.* Paris: Institut national de la statistique et des études économiques. Retrieved April 17, 2016 (http://www.stiglitz-sen -fitoussi.fr/documents/rapport_anglais.pdf).

Thelen, K. 2004. *How Institutions Evolve.* Cambridge: Cambridge University Press.

Theodoulou, S. Z., M. A. Cahn. 1995. *Public Policy. Essential Readings.* Englewood Cliffs, NJ: Prentice Hall.

Tilly, C. 1984. *Big Structures, Large Processes, and Huge Comparisons.* New York: Russel Sage Foundation Press.

Vavroušek, J. 1993. "Závod s časem. Hledání lidských hodnot slučitelných s trvale udržitelným způsobem života" [Race Against Time. Searching for Human Values Compatible with a Sustainable Way of Life, in Czech]. *Literární noviny* IV (49), (9 Dec): 1, 3.

Weimer, D. L., A. R. Vining. 1992. *Policy analysis: Concepts and practice.* 2nd ed. Englewood Cliffs, NJ: Prentice Hall.

Weiss, C. H. 1983. "Ideology, Interests and Information." Pp. 213–245 in *Ethics, The Social Sciences, and Policy Analysis*, edited by D. Callahan, B. Jennings. New York: Plenum Press.

Recommended sources for the theory of historical institutionalism:

Hall, P. A., C. R. Taylor. 1996. "Political Science and the Three New Institutionalisms." *Political Studies*, XLIV: 936–957.

Immergut, E. M. 2005. "Paradigms of Change in Political Science: Historical-Institutionalism in Political Science and the Problem of Change." Pp. 237–259 in *Understanding Change: Models, Methodologies, and Metaphors*, edited by A. Wimmer, R., Kössler. Basinngstoke: Palgrave.

Peters, B. G. 2004. "The Legacy of the Past: Historical Institutionalism." Pp. 71–86 in *Institutional Theory in Political Science: The New Institutionalism*, by G. B. Peters. London: Continuum.

Pierson, P. 1996. "The Path to European Integration: A Historical-Institutionalist Analysis." *Comparative Political Studies* 29 (2): 123–163.

Pierson, P. 2000. "Increasing Returns, Path Dependence, and the Study of Politics." *American Political Science Review* 94 (2): 251–267.

Pierson, P., Skocpol, Theda. 2002. "Historical Institutionalism in Contemporary Political Science." Pp. 693–721 in *Political Science: State of the Discipline*, edited by I. Katznelson, H. V. Milner. New York: W. W. Norton.

Steinmo, S., K. Thelen F. Longstreth (eds.). 1992. *Structuring Politics: Historical Institutionalism in Comparative Analysis*. New York: Cambridge University Press.

Tilly, C. 1984. *Big Structures, Large Processes, and Huge Comparisons*. New York: Russel Sage Foundation Press.

/**A3**/

<u>Governance</u>

"This public office (or: this ministry, that government, the European Union…) is not working the way it should." Too often do we hear such remarks (or much harsher ones). In short, we complain about the ways our affairs are governed – and we are often right.

    The fact that we are not alone in this is probably not too comforting. This problem is indeed affecting mankind as a whole: humanity cannot govern itself. It has unleashed such a dynamic of uncontrollable civilization changes that attested ways of governance are falling behind hopelessly. In this way, dangerous "pockets" of conflicts and tensions are created, revolts arise, and destructive potentials are nurtured. Does this problem have a solution? A general solution is unknown – and we can hardly expect it to ever be discovered. Even a large-scale humanitarian disaster might possibly occur. Here, the presence of sufficient or, conversely, insufficient capacities for governance may become the critical factor of the outcome (Dror 2001).

Public policy – both as a discipline and as social practice – is gradually creating tools for taking account of and responding to this trend. Thus, a **global public policy** is arising (Potůček 2009, Kaul, Grunberg, Stern 2009).

THE CONCEPT OF GOVERNANCE

Problems of governance have stimulated thinkers of all times. We may recall the classic works of Plato, Campanella, Francis Bacon, Thomas Moore, Bernard Bolzano, Niccolò Machiavelli, or Clausewitz. Despite the rich tradition these classics represent, there is a clear demand for a new approach which could respond to the profound changes of governing processes during the past decades. Government is not able to pursue all tasks and functions, necessary for the development of societies, alone. ... Bovaird (2005: 217) put it in a rather provocative way: "... are we moving to a future in which government remains the key player in public governance or is it realistic to assume that we might move (...) to (...) 'governance without government'?"

The concept of governance is of key significance. From an abundance of existing definitions, let me pick two that help us best grasp today's approach to the phenomenon. One of them is rather general: **governance** means the "... collective capacity to influence the future for the better" (Dror 2001: xi). The other one is more specific: "Governance is a system of values, policies and institutions by which a society manages its economic, political and social affairs through interactions within and among the state, civil society and private sector. It operates at every level of human enterprise" (Cheema, Maguire 2001). An important quality of governance is its strategic dimension (Potůček et al. 2009). In the following text, I am going to outline the above mentioned basic dimensions of the entire complex of governance.

DIMENSIONS OF GOVERNANCE

Governance cannot be reduced to the level of nation-states; one must take into regard not only its supra-national level (for most European states, this is especially true of the EU), but also its regional level (regions and municipalities in the Czech Republic). This is the so-called **multi-level governance** approach (MLG).

Contemporary public affairs are rarely **governed** exclusively **by the state and public authorities. One must consider** other regulators, and in particular **the market, the civic sector and the media**.[24] According to Kooiman (2003: 5), governance is the collective responsibility of the state, the business, and the civic sector, which is not carried out "in isolation, but as a shared set of responsibilities." In addition, there is the mass media which nowadays represents another indispensable regulator in governance.

Governance cannot rely solely on hierarchies, and consists of **horizontal ties and informal networks as well**. Kooiman (2003: 5) argues that interactions among policy actors "are a rich source for analyzing and synthesizing insights into many facets of governance."

Let me now pay more detailed attention to each of these three dimensions of the complex of governance.

MULTI-LEVEL GOVERNANCE

The age of sovereign nation-states is over. Although governance is still to a large extent executed at the national level, increasing shares thereof go either upward to the supra-national level or downward, especially to the regional level (Zürn, Leibfried 2005: 25; Pierre, Peters 2000). The need to cope with these changes gives rise to the concept of multi-level governance (Bovaird 2005: 219). We are in a situation of structural uncertainty. However, the term *post-national* defines the new constellation only in the negative sense, as something that has ceased to exist (Zürn, Leibfried 2005: 26). Marks (1993: 392) characterizes multi-level governance as "a system of continuous negotiation among nested governments at several territorial tiers."

This tendency can be exemplified by the European integration process, in which member states transfer part of their sovereignty to Brussels, but in which some of the responsibilities of central governments are also transferred to regional governments and groupings (the case of Euroregions). "European economic integration has significantly reduced the range of policy instruments available, and the range of policy goals achievable, at the national level. To that extent, the effectiveness as well as the responsiveness of governments, and hence democratic legitimacy, are seen to have been weakened" (Scharpf 2001: 360).

---

24 Refer to Potůček (1999, 2003) for an extended analysis of their regulatory capacities, specificities and mutual relations.

GOVERNMENT, MARKET, THE CIVIC SECTOR – AND THE MEDIA

Governance is concerned with creating general rules and specific frameworks for collective action. It cannot do without "governing mechanisms – grants, contracts, agreements – that do not rest solely on the authority and sanctions of government" and that involve agents from the private and nonprofit sectors as well (Milward, Provan 1999: 3).

Josef Ludvík Fischer, an important yet perhaps half-forgotten Czech sociologist, described the general mechanisms of regulation in somewhat archaic terms. His concept of societal regulators "includes all facts of a social origin that determine the behavior of associated individuals" (Fischer 1969: 7). In

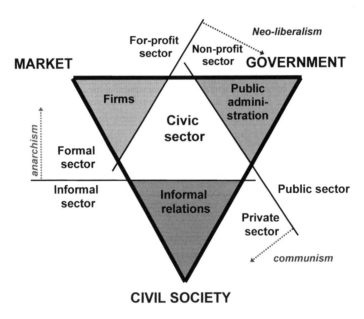

Figure A3.1 The relationship between market, government, and the civic sector as regulators of social life

Source: Abrahamson (1995), adapted.

---

25 The Visegrad Group, or V4, is an alliance of four Central European states – Czech Republic, Hungary, Poland and Slovakia – with a view to furthering their European integration, as well as to advancing cooperation with one another.

today's language, the definition can be formulated as follows: **Regulators influence the agency of individuals and organizations in desired directions by shaping the social conditions of their existence.**

As we know already, governments cannot fulfill their tasks alone, without engagement of the market and the civic sector (Potůček, 1999, 2003). The impact of their mutual interactions – sometimes synergic, sometimes contradictory – is carefully studied by many social scientists.

In the past couple of decades, the media has exerted growing influence on public affairs. Some authors even think that their agenda-setting power is larger than that of political leaders. Therefore, the media, too, satisfy the definition of a regulator – at least as far as some of their functions are concerned.

In the following, I am going to describe each of these regulators in more detail.

GOVERNMENT

Note: *The following section is limited to general remarks about the role of government in societal regulation. In Chapter A4 on "Actors and Institutions," I will return to the role of government in policy formulation and implementation.*

Government provides an established general framework for the functioning of society. At the same time, it mediates the formation and exercise of political power. It makes and enforces laws, while relying on public administration. The goals society pursues in different areas require that attention is paid to managing and coordinating divergent interests and to streamlining decision making about the order of such preferences and tasks that are deemed public. It is above all – and sometimes exclusively – government that can play such a role efficiently and harmoniously (Holländer 1995). What only states and states alone are able to do is aggregate and purposefully deploy legitimate power. This power is necessary to enforce the rule of law domestically, and it is necessary to preserve world order internationally (Fukuyama 2004). This brings us to the dual roles of government in regulation. First, government defines, maintains and enforces general conditions for the actions of other regulators. Second, government regulates on its own, namely by administrative, judicial and financial instruments (Dunleavy, O'Leary 1987).

Any specific control through political power is wielded either by direct coercion, or by establishing rules which must be obeyed. Political power as a means of regulation is relatively simple, and governmental control need not be costly. However, establishing and maintaining power is costly in and of itself.

Political power is applied through public administration: rules are implemented through which this power is delegated to diverse units of government. The risks of exerting political power through government administration become visible when power is abused. Therefore, it is desirable to equip politics and public administration with an effective built-in system of checks and balances.

MARKET

> *"The market resembles fire: it is a good servant, but a cruel master."*
> *(Potůček 1999: 11)*

The market is a self-regulating system in which supply and demand, profit and loss, within certain limits, allocate resources (goods and services) more effectively than any other regulator. The market mechanism is based on a voluntary agreement between seller and buyer to exchange a particular resource for money. Balanced price systems, which regulate both production and consumption, are created on the basis of millions of such exchanges.

Economic theory assumes that prices generated by the market are signals used by actors involved as guides to maximize the sum of utility for the minimum expenditure of available resources. Therefore, actors only pursue their own self-interest. The magic of the invisible hand of the market is, according to interpretations of Adam Smith who coined the metaphor, based on the belief that collective satisfaction is attained through the pursuit of purely selfish interests by each and every one of these self-interested individuals.

The ideal model of a market economy is balanced: in the uncomplicated world of the market with its perfectly competitive environment, price levels evolve such that distribute firms' inputs and the goods sold to buyers in a way that no other combination of inputs and outputs could possibly increase the profit of one or more participants of the market exchange without decreasing someone else's profit. This maximizes the potential attainable wealth of society – and at the same time, such prices of inputs and outputs of production and such consumer prices are established that the supply of all goods is equal to the demand for them.[26] Keep in mind that the distribution of wealth among the participants of market exchange is neutral in the context of public policy. Hence, it bears no relation to the total wealth distributed among the members of a given society. In other words, were the market given free reign, the circular and cumulative processes brought about by repeated acts of supply and demand would make those who already have a large amount of resources at their disposal even wealthier, and the poor would lose even the modest amount with which they entered the market.[27] (Myrdal 1968, Barry 1987)

---

26 Economists refer to this as Pareto-efficient distribution.
27 Regulation by means of a free market differentiates participants of market exchange in a way that is familiar to every fan of the *Monopoly* game: the wealthy get even wealthier and

The civic sector grows out of the grassroots of civil society, which itself is empowered by certain attitudes and actions that are characteristic of responsible civility.

Civility is defined by Etzioni (1988: 56) as the moral obligation of individuals to take an interest in the community in which they live. This obligation drives people to do something for others: when the concept of civility is "introduced at home, cultivated in schools, fostered by the news media, enhanced by voluntary associations, and extolled from Presidential and other civic leaders' 'pulpits,' citizens of a nation feel obliged to contribute to the well-being of the community they share" (Ibid).

Civil society therefore may be understood as "the independent self-organization of society, the constituent parts of which voluntarily engage in public activity to pursue individual, group, or national interests within the context of a legally defined state-society relationship" (Weigle, Butterfield 1993).

Civil society propagates itself through constantly emerging, functioning, and dissolving social interactions between citizens; it creates opportunities for citizens to collectively express and act upon their opinions and values. Keep in mind that situations may arise when society has the potential for citizenship, but government does not create the necessary institutional framework for its cultivation and application. Citizens are, therefore, left with no choice but to find alternative means of association in order to realize this potential. These may grow into civil unrest or revolutions.

Civic sector is the institutionalized expression of the life of civil society. The sector is made up of non-profit organizations which are voluntary associations of citizens who share common values and are willing to work together.

While government depends on political processes and manages through legislation and public budgets, the private sector uses the market to optimize decisions about production and the exchange of goods. The civic sector needs information about human needs if it is to satisfy them in areas where they are not being (adequately) satisfied by either the business sector or government. The civic sector is formally independent of the government; in this sense, it is a part of the private sector. Its activities are not motivated by profit, but rather by the desire to satisfy the interests of a specific community or society as a whole; in this sense, then, it is like the public sector.

Analysts of civic sector development call attention to the fact that civic sector organizations tend to form where neither the market nor the government are effective. They cannot replace the market or government in their

---

become winners (the centripetal effect of market regulation), while the poor get even poorer (the centrifugal effect of market regulation) and eventually become losers.

primary functions; yet, they are able to complement them adequately and, in many cases, indispensably.

A variety of organizations tend to be subsumed under the civic sector.[28] The following table categorizes organizations depending on whether they focus on issues of an exclusive group or rather society as a whole, and whether they provide services or rather advocate for an interest.

Table A3.1 Types of civic sector organizations

Interest pursued → Type of activity ↓	Mutual benefit	Public benefit (possibly limited to an exclusive group or territory)
Service activities	1. Mutual benefit service non-profit organizations *sports* *recreation* *community development* *leisure clubs*	2. Public benefit service non-profit organizations *social work and healthcare* *education* *humanitarian aid, charity*
Advocacy activities	3. Mutual benefit advocacy non-profit organizations *trade unions* *employer unions* *professional associations (unions)*	4. Public benefit advocacy non-profit organizations *environmental protection* *human rights protection* *civic (consumer) rights protection*

Source: Frič, Angelovská, Goulli (2009), modified.

Generally speaking, the civic sector exists to fulfill two basic purposes. Through it, people implement activities in which they are interested and through which they want to realize themselves (the social function); at the same time, political cohesion is strengthened and the political culture of a society is developed (the political function). However, the civic sector's contribution to economic life is also growing – as a consumer, a producer of goods and services, as well as an employer (the economic function).

The specific characteristics of each of the three regulators are summarized.

---

28 Some authors include churches and political parties as well, yet given their specific role, this tends to be disputed by the scholarly mainstream.

Table A3.2 Basic characteristics of government, market and civic sector

Regulators → / Characteristics ↓	Government	Market	Civic sector
Principal mechanisms	Public administration	Market exchange	Voluntary associations
Decision makers	Politicians, bureaucrats and citizens	Owners of the means of production, financial institutions, producers, consumers	Leaders and members
Guides for behaviour	Laws, regulations	Supply and demand	Agreements
Criteria for decisions	Policy goals, ways of implementation	Maximization of profit	Interests of members, public interests
Sanctions	Government authority backed by coercion	Financial loss	Social pressure
Basic mode of operation	Top-down	Horizontal contract	Bottom-up

Source: Uphoff (1993), adapted.

The theory of corporatism is one of the frameworks that help us to understand the relations between government, market and the civic sector.

EXAMPLE THEORY: CORPORATISM[29]

The theory of corporatism studies and explains the specific relations of cooperation between government as a representative of public interest, on the one hand, and organizations as representatives of group interests, on the other. It analyzes the arrangements through which these entities engage in the process of formulation and implementation of public policies in ways that reconcile competing group interests and make them compatible with public interests. It also evaluates the effects of such arrangements. It explicates situations where government transfers some of its responsibility for identifying and satisfying public interests to nongovernmental organizations – namely when the interests pursued by such organizations can be expected to largely overlap with those public interests. It builds on the assumption that "there is a certain range of policy areas for which institutions of group self-regulation may produce more socially adjusted and normatively acceptable results than either communal self-help, free trade, or étatisme" (Streeck, Schmitter 1985).

---

29   See Potůček (1999) for more details.

"Corporatism is more than a peculiar pattern of articulation of interests. Rather it is an institutionalized pattern of policy formation in which large interest organizations co-operate with each other and with public authorities not only in the articulation and even 'intermediation' of interests, but also – in its developed forms – in the 'authoritative allocation of values' and in the implementation of such policies" (Lehmbruch 1979: 150).

Corporatist policies are characterized by strategic interdependence of participants: government depends on nongovernmental (for-profit and not-for-profit) organizations, and those cannot do without well-functioning government and other nongovernmental organizations involved. The actors involved are motivated to conclude relatively stable contracts because such contracts also contain guarantees for better securing their particular interests.

The central scholars behind this theory, Streeck and Schmitter, are also aware of the risks of such a solution: "It is only to the extent that the state – by a combination of procedural, instead of substantive, regulation with a credible threat of direct intervention – can hold private governments at least partially accountable to the public, that the associative-corporative mode of social order can become a legitimate alternative to communitarianism, étatisme and market liberalism" (Streeck, Schmitter 1985: 26).

In the Czech Republic, the Tripartite represents a concrete example of a corporatist institution.

EXAMPLE CORPORATIST ARRANGEMENT: THE TRIPARTITE

The Council of Economic and Social Agreement of the Czech Republic (RHSD, "Tripartite") was established in 1990 and brings together:

1. representatives of government (as a rule, the government is represented and the Tripartite headed by the Prime Minister, often substituted by the Minister of Labor and Social Affairs);
2. representatives of labor (major trade union associations); and
3. confederations of employers.

It is an institutionalized means of negotiation between representatives of government, labor, and employers. The parties agree to respect joint decisions (concerning not only economic and social policy, and specifically, employment issues, wage policy, working conditions, industrial relations, social security, but also education or equal opportunities) and agree to implement the approved policies within their scope of responsibilities. RHSD activities are governed by its Statute and Rules of Procedure, not by law.

Similar tripartite arrangements operate at the EU level, in some other countries (e.g., Germany, Austria) and at some regional levels as well.

As we know, the different regulators do not act in isolation. They exist in a complex web of relations that is shaped by the specifics of their roles and by the variety of the tasks they face. In the following, I will focus on the most important relation that affects both individual people's lives and the activities of organizations – the market-government relationship.

Are there any general reasons to maintain the role of government in market regulation? Ernest Gellner (as quoted in Musil 1996: 31) had the following view: "The side effects of unlimited economic activity would destroy everything – the environment, cultural heritage, and human relations. These powers simply must be politically restricted, though the control should be gentle, camouflaged, and negotiated. The economy must be strong enough to create pluralistic institutions, but not strong enough to destroy our world."

EXAMPLE 1: MARKET FAILURES IN THE ABSENCE OF PARETO-EFFICIENT DISTRIBUTION[30]

Possible reasons:
- existence of public goods,
- existence of externalities,
- natural monopoly of supply or demand,
- information asymmetry between seller and buyer,
- changing preferences of market participants,
- unregulated competition (*tragedy of the commons*),
- discounting (neglecting) the future.

EXAMPLE 2: MARKET FAILURES BASED ON CRITERIA OTHER THAN PARETO-EFFICIENT DISTRIBUTION[31]

Examples of such criteria:
- reducing inequalities in the distribution of wealth,
- maintaining institutional values,
- human dignity,
- cultivating and utilizing human potential,
- sustainable way of life.

30 See, for example, Samuelson, Nordhaus (2010) for more details.
31 For more details, see Potůček (1999).

The regulatory role of government in relation to market is not at all simple. Government depends on the private sector in many respects. Since the public functions of business (employment, prices, production, growth, standard of living, and the economic security of individuals) are often performed by private owners and businesspeople, government cannot be indifferent to how they achieve their goals. Therefore, businesspeople in general, and corporate management in particular, are in such privileged positions *vis-à-vis* government and are incomparable to any other group. The risk of government failure grows as decision makers find themselves controlled by coalitions of economic interest groups (Mlčoch 1996: 157). A noteworthy symbiosis occurs between government and business, in which neither side would gain from threatening the basis of the relationship. Although business does not get everything it would like from government, it does receive, according to Lindblom (1977), a large part of it.

The market cannot function without competition. Competition is, however, a form of conflict. Government is the only institution than has the power to create specific control mechanisms to keep this conflict within certain boundaries. If government fails, according to Etzioni (1988), this otherwise productive and constructive conflict may escalate to the point that it destroys the social ties that are a precondition of market exchange (such as trust between the participants of market exchange).

MEDIA

It took centuries after the invention of the printing press until the media came to play an essential role in politics – due to widespread use of newspapers, and especially radio, television and the internet (Heywood 2013). Relatedly, there is a useful analytical distinction between the role of mass media as a regulator, as they actively intervene in the policy process, and their role as an "independent" mediator of information and facts. In the former role, the media filter, sort and select information, acting as a gatekeeper who holds the audience at a distance from reality (McQuail 2010). "The press may not be successful much of the time in telling people what to think, but it is stunningly successful in telling what to think about" (Cohen 1963: 13). Yet the media also mediate information about what goes on around us, reflecting happenings like an open window that provides us with a specific view of the world outside.

Media as a regulator
In the 1870s, Chancellor Otto von Bismarck coined the term "seventh power" when he stated that the press exerts influence as strong as any of Europe's six powers of that time (Great Britain, France, Austria, Russia, Italy and Germany) (Hvížďala 2000: 42). "Whether directly or indirectly, the media

influence recipients' ideas, beliefs, attitudes, values and behaviors" (Burton, Jirák 2001: 347).

For many years, media's influence on governance was neglected or under-estimated by political science and public administration theories; and till present day, there have not been many theories that include them, along with the government, market, and civic sector, as the regulators of public affairs. Thompson's social theory of the media is an important contribution to under-standing the interlinked roles of government, market and the media. Thompson (2013) believes that due to media activities, the tendency to provide biased information might possibly grow into uncontrolled informational deforma-tion of the public space at all levels of government – whether due to political interests (public service media) or economic interests (private media). Cur-ran (2000: 127) and similarly McQuail (2010) state that the vigilance of com-mercial media may be undermined by economic interests and partisanship, and that of public media by constant pressure from governments. Jakubowicz (2011) presumes that there is a danger of "mediatized politics" in a reversal of the traditional roles of both entities: the media becomes independent of politi-cal institutions, and political organizations in their activities follow the media logic instead of that of politics. Politics has transformed itself by adapting to the media logic.

Media as a mediator

In modern democracies, the media is also indispensable in their role as medi-ators between actors, especially between politicians, officials, and citizens (Jirák 2001). The media is also an influential source of input for public opinion and political decision. Politicians use television, press, radio, news servers, and the Internet to keep being informed about their political opponents and about the needs and attitudes of the public (Schulz 2004).

The Internet put an end to the traditional dominance of hierarchical structures of information dissemination. **New media** has entered the stage as a new actor of public policy. Online social networks such as Facebook or Twitter, along with mobile telephony, provide horizontal networks of action and communication that possess a high potential for mobilizing participants. "Stone age" political institutions are forced to adapt to the new situation and use new media for their communication in the public space as well.

According to Hagen (2004), there are three general criteria of information quality: **relevance** (how important a message is), **veracity** (validity of infor-mation in the message) and **comprehensibility** (potential of the message to be understood).

REGULATORS UNDER CHANGE

Contemporary forms of governance cannot be understood without grasping the specifics of government, market, civic sector and media as regulators, including the links between them.

That, however, represents an enormous challenge for social scientists: "The problem of mapping influence patterns now seems even greater with the growing behavior of 'complex adaptive systems' in which intensive and ever-changing system interactions, with non-linear characteristics, give rise to non-predictable but self-organizing outcomes, although it is still unclear how well such models apply to decision making in the public domain" (Bovaird 2005: 218).

There is an obvious imbalance between the entrenched character of the nation-state and the global operations of the market, the media, and to a non-negligible extent, the civic sector as well (Thompson 2013). "The Club of Rome-esque approach emphasizes alternatives in which global democracy, the global market economy, and a harmonious global civilization (instead of hierarchy of any type) form the only sustainable basis for a politics of humanity. So far these kinds of social limits have been successfully set up only on the level of the nation state and, as such, with limited results. These achievements alone have required several centuries to emerge. What would be the means and joint efforts that could hasten similar progress on global level?" (Neuvonen 2005: 18)

ACTORS' NETWORKS

Networking and the ensuing actors' networks are the third and indispensable dimension of the concept of governance. Networks enable and facilitate broad cooperation of a large number of independent actors to help them attain their goals. Governance through networks tends to rely on informal understandings, motivation and effective cooperation skills, on an "agreement to agree" (Gibson, Goodin 1999). According to Rhodes (1997: 15), inter-organizational networks rely on mutual dependence, exchange of resources, self-steering, respect for rules of the game, and a high level of autonomy from government.

The term **networked governance** is also used in this context (Heclo 1978, Rhodes 1997, Castells 2000). Kooiman (2003), too, views networks as a special type of governance.

Actors' networks extend across the horizontal and vertical boundaries set by the former two dimensions of governance. Some are comprised of actors from two or more levels of governance, and some are even transnational in their nature (Císař 2004). They often bring together actors from the public, business and civic sectors as well as from the media. The capacity and operability of this dimension of governance is greatly enhanced by the influence of new information and communication technologies, and above all by the network of networks – the Internet.

When networks are formed in relation to certain policy issues, they are referred to as **policy networks**. The lifespan of a policy network may vary.

EXAMPLE THEORY: POLICY NETWORKS

A **policy network** is described by its boundary, its actors, and by their linkages. It includes a relatively stable set of mainly public and private corporate actors. The linkages between the actors serve as communication channels and for the exchange of information, expertise, trust and other policy resources. The boundary of a given policy network is not primarily determined by formal institutions but results from a process of mutual recognition dependent on the functional relevance and structural embeddedness" (Kenis, Schneider 1991: 41). A later definition by Schneider (1992) specifies policy networks as "clusters of relatively autonomous but interdependent actors that are incorporated into the process of public policy making."

Policy networks are spaces in which groups of actors are linked freely and interact with one another in order to formulate and implement policies. The function of such a space can also be understood as a set of rules delimiting/restricting the universe of involved actors' decisions and actions. Policy networks differ by the level of formalization of these rules; level of network accessibility from outside; and level of stability. At one pole, there are *ad-hoc structures* emerging around an issue. Referred to as **issue networks** (Heclo 1995: 46), they are alliances of interest groups and individuals formed around certain policy issues; they are in fact alliances of interest groups and individuals sharing the goal to bring policymakers' attention to the issue at hand and push for its solution. At the opposite pole, there are stable "clusters of individuals that effectively make most of the routine decisions in a given substantive area of policy" (Ripley, Franklin 1981: 8) – typically politicians, officials and interest group representatives. In the United States, these occur in the form of **iron triangles** between government officials, congress committee members, and interest group representatives (Ripley, Franklin 1981). Somewhere in the middle, **policy networks** operate in specific policy areas. Finally, **epistemic communities** (Haas 1992) are a special type of network.

Analysts have been using a proven set of three criteria in order to better grasp the different types of policy networks and their characteristics (various actors, ties and network boundaries). First, the level of institutionalization serves as a measure of network stability; when this criterion is applied, one can identify both relatively stable structures of participants and ad-hoc groupings of diverse actors. The second criterion tells us whether the policy process is centered upon a given policy area or takes place across areas. According to the third criterion, some policy networks are restricted to an exclusive circle while access to others is relatively easy or open to practically any actor.

SOCIALLY PATHOLOGICAL FORMS OF REGULATION

Thus far, I have dealt with such forms of governance that are not usually expected to have negative effects on society. In public policy, though, there are also certain structures that persistently burden and disintegrate society (especially corruption and the mafia) or that regulate ineffectively (primarily the structural imbalance between global markets and nation-states). Such socially pathological forms of regulation are signs of parasitism on the public interest, or even the domestication thereof by private or group interests.

EXAMPLE: THE MAFIA[32]

Mafia activity can be compared with that of a firm which produces, promotes, and sells protection. It can do so when government is unable to fully employ its legitimate power monopoly to effectively intervene when laws are violated. The second necessary condition for the mafia to emerge is the absence or lack of mutual trust among market actors. Protection is necessary in such a situation, though it is an insufficient – and expensive – replacement for trust. The mafia offers to protect its clients; from an economic point of view, payment for such protection is a rational course of action. In places where the market functions without government and without mutual trust, the mafia offers protection that no one else could provide. The mafia can, of course, artificially stimulate the need for protection. In its activity, the mafia uses confidential information; like other business entities, it maintains its reputation and uses advertising; and, if necessary, it is prepared to use violence.

EXAMPLE: GLOBAL MARKETS VS. NATION-STATES

Globalized financial markets follow a rent maximization strategy *vis-à-vis* individual states. The global players in these markets speak the universal language of money. In contrast, as nation-states strive for understanding, cooperation and policy harmonization, they are hindered by a Babel of cultures, languages, values and, more generally, civilizations – and above all, by the natural differences between their interests. In order to support economic development and employment, governments often resort to social dumping (pushing down the price of labor) or tax exemptions for large multinationals. As a result, the resources available for the public sector are shrinking, public social services are retrenching, and polarization between poor and rich is growing both within national communities and across the globe.

CAPACITIES OF GOVERNANCE IN THE CONTEMPORARY WORLD

Globalization, regionalization, the establishing of horizontal cooperation networks, and the intertwining of the market, administration, and the media make responsibility for the consequences of political and administrative decisions increasingly unclear. In this way, irresponsible attitudes and actions are facilitated in politicians and citizens. "Globalization is radically changing both the nature of power and the ways it operates – by fragmenting it and by making it increasingly impersonal, invisible and difficult to locate in any unambiguous scheme of hierarchy. Democracy is corroding with the shrinking of

---

32   For more details, see, for example, studies by Gambetta (1993) or Potůček (1999).

the scope governed by institutions related to politics in the traditional sense" (Staniszkis 2009: 13). According to Jakubowicz (2011), a model is emerging that relies on a reconfiguring of institutions and political procedures. Instead of yesterday's centralized, vertical and hierarchical structures that operated on the basis of a strictly defined order of decision making or supervision, the system emerging today is multi-layered, less centralized and based on increasingly multilateral cooperation. Such a system of governance also relies on new (information) technologies in order to make its work more transparent and facilitate citizen involvement in different kinds of debates.

Held and McGrew (2002) define global authority as follows:
- it is configured between various infrastructures of governance: supra states (e.g., United Nations, Organization for Economic Cooperation and Development, International Monetary Fund, World Bank, G8, G20), regional (e.g., EU or ASEAN), transnational (corporations, global civil society organizations such as Greenpeace), and substate (municipalities, local civil society organizations); sandwiched between these layers is national government;
- it is pluralistic – there is no single center of decision making;
- it has a variable geometry: the part of governance that belongs to each infrastructure strongly varies from issue to issue, in time, and between places;
- it is structurally complex, embracing diverse actors and networks.

However, the capacity and effectiveness of global governance is falling far behind the importance of the problems humanity is facing; such as global warming, the growing gap between poor and rich, or the proliferation of weapons of mass destruction. "Because of the ongoing global transformation, governmental efforts to influence the future significantly are essential for preventing the bad and achieving the good – governmental passivity constituting not only a denial of democratic responsibility but a failure leading in all probability to very undesirable and perhaps catastrophic futures outcomes" (Dror 2001: 10). The need to provide global governance with the knowledge necessary to overcome that deficit gives rise to a new subdiscipline of public policy – **global public policy** – as mentioned in the beginning of this chapter (Potůček 2009). See Table A3.3.

Table A3.3 Major challenges to global governance and possible solutions

Major governance challenges	Possible solutions
Disproportion between the regulatory power of global markets and the absence of supranational level of governance.	Organic tendencies of European integration, especially those centered upon the EU, and similar efforts at the level of global organizations and summits.
Insufficient coordination of the global, supranational, national, regional and local levels of governance.	Networks of actors supported by modern information and communication technologies; encouraging new modes of governance based on responsibility sharing.
Insufficient coordination between government departments.	Goal-oriented programming, horizontal and matrix management.
Differentiation of conditions and styles of living brings about destruction of organic forms of social cohesion; market liberalization weakens the institutions that maintain social cohesion – the welfare state.	Faster adaptation of the welfare state, civic sector institutions and informal assistance to changing conditions is the only way to counter these challenges (yet one rather defensive up to now).
In spite of noble slogans about environmental friendliness and respect for the criterion of sustainable development, individuals' and corporations' narrow and short-term profit maximizing interests prevail over respect for other forms of life and the fate of future generations.	Only strict regulation to secure public interests, along with voluntary simplicity as a style of living, can bring about a change of course in the long term.
The unaccountability of political representatives for public affairs is reinforced by the unaccountability of citizens and vice versa.	This negative relationship can be eliminated through education and by treating the forms and frameworks of participative, deliberative, corporatist and direct democracy equally as the traditionally more advanced (yet insufficient) representative democracy.

Source: Author.

REVIEW QUESTIONS

Why does government still have an exclusive position vis-à-vis other regulators (market, civic sector, media)?

Characterize the forms and effects of corporatist relations between government and organized representation of group interests.

Name the different levels of governance that are usually distinguished. How do they interact? And what kind of organizations operate at each level?

What kind of role is the public sector suitable for? Where is the business effective and where the civic sector? Why?

How did the position of nation-states change over the past fifty years?

Why, and in what roles, did the media become an essential actor of public policy?

What are the reasons behind the argument that the market cannot be the single universal regulator of social life?

Characterize the different types of actors' networks in public policy, including the principles and effects of their operation.

Outline the key dimensions of the concept of governance, and describe how they interact.

Clarify the conditions for the emergence of the mafia, its work patterns, and its instruments.

Why are some countries affected by extreme corruption while others remain mostly corruption-free?

SOURCES

Abrahamson, P. 1995. "Welfare Pluralism: Towards a New Consensus for a European Social Policy." *Current Politics and Economics of Europe* 5 (1): 29–42.

Barry, N. 1987. "Understanding the Market." Pp. 161–171 in *The State or the Market*, edited by M. Loney. London: SAGE Publications.

Bovaird, T. 2005. "Public Governance: Balancing Stakeholder Power in a Network Society." *International Review of Administrative Sciences* 71 (2): 217–228.

Burton, G., J. Jirák. 2001. *Úvod do studia médií* [Introduction to Media Studies, in Czech]. Brno: Barrister a Principal.

Castells, M. 2000. "Materials for an Exploratory Theory of the Networked Society." *British Journal of Sociology* 51 (1): 5–24.

Cheema, G. S., L. Maguire. 2001. *Governance for Human Development. Public Administration and Development* 21: 201–209. Retrieved June 24, 2016 (http://onlinelibrary.wiley.com/doi/10.1002/pad.178/pdf).

Císař, O. 2004. *Transnacionální politické sítě* [Transnational Policy Networks, in Czech]. Brno: Masarykova univerzita, Mezinárodní politologický ústav.

Cohen, B. C. 1963. *The Press and Foreign Policy*. Princeton, NJ: Princeton University Press.

Curran, J. 2000. "Nový pohled na masová média a demokracii" [A New Perspective on Mass Media and Democracy, in Czech). Pp. 116–164 in *Politická komunikace a média* [Political Communication and the Media, in Czech], by J. Jirák, B. Říchová. Prague: Univerzita Karlova.

Dror, Y. 2001. *The Capacity to Govern*. London: Frank Cass.

Dunleavy, P., B. O'Leary. 1987. *Theories of the State. The Politics of Liberal Democracy*. Basingstoke and New York: Macmillan.

Etzioni, A. 1988. *The Moral Dimension: Towards a New Economics.* New York: The Free Press.

Fischer, J. L. 1969. *Pokus o nástin systému sociologie* [The Attempt to Outline the System of Sociology, in Czech]. Unpublished manuscript. Retrieved April 18, 2014 (http://www.insoma.cz/fischer.pdf).

Frič, P. 2002. "Bez korupce nejsou koláče" [No Corruption, No Gain, in Czech]. Prague: *Lidové noviny,* 13. 7. 2002.

Frič, P. et al. 1999. *Korupce na český způsob* [Corruption in a Czech Style, in Czech]. Prague: G plus G.

Frič, P., O. Angelovská, R. Goulli. 2009. *Revitalizace a konsolidace neziskového sektoru v ČR po roce 1989* [Revitalization and Consolidation of the Nonprofit Sector in the Czech Republic after 1989, in Czech]. Prague: Agnes.

Fukuyama, F. 2004. *State Building, Governance and World Order in the 21st Century.* Ithaca: Cornell University Press.

Gambetta, D. 1993. *The Sicilian Mafia. The Business of Private Protection.* Cambridge and London: Cambridge University Press.

Gibson, D. M., R. E. Goodin. 1999. "The Veil of Vagueness." Pp. 357–85 in *Organizing Political Institutions: Essays for Johan P. Olsen,* edited by M. Egeberg, P. Laegreid. Oslo: Scandinavian University Press.

Haas, P. M. 1992. "Epistemic Communities and International Policy Coordination." *International Organization* 46 (1): 1–35.

Hagen, L. 2004. "Informační kvalita a její měření" [Information Quality and its Measurement, in Czech]. Pp. 51–70 in *Analýza obsahu mediálních sdělení* [Analyzing the content of media communication, in Czech], edited by W. Schulz, I. Reifová. Prague: Karolinum.

Heclo, H. 1978. "Issue Networks and the Executive Establishment." Pp. 88–124 in *The New American Political System,* edited by A. King. Washington, DC: American Enterprise Institute.

Heclo, H. 1995. "Networks and the Executive Establishment." Pp. 46–58 in *Public Policy. Essential Readings,* by S. Z. Theodoulou, M. A. Cahn. Englewood Cliffs, NJ: Prentice Hall.

Held, D., A. McGrew. 2002. *Governing Globalization. Power, Authority and Global Governance.* Cambridge: Polity.

Heywood, A. 2013. *Politics.* 4th edition. London: Palgrave Macmillan.

Holländer, P. 1995. *Základy všeobecné státovědy* [Foundations of the General Theory of State, in Czech]. Prague: Všehrd.

Hvížďala, K. 2000. *Média a moc* [Media and Power, in Czech]. Prague: Votobia.

Jakubowicz, K. 2011. *Nowa ekologia mediow. Konwergencja a metamorfoza* [New Media Ecology. Convergence and Metamorphosis, in Polish]. Warszawa: Wydawnictwo Poltext.

Jirák, J. 2001. "Medializace jako strašák politiky [Medialization as a Scarecrow of Politics, in Czech]." Pp. 203–209 in *Institucionalizace (ne)odpovědnosti: globální svět, evropská integrace a české zájmy I.* [Institutionalization of (Ir)responsibility: Global

World, European Integration and Czech Interests I, in Czech], by J. Kabele, M. Mlčoch. Prague: Karolinum.

Kaul, I., I. Grunberg, M. A. Stern (eds.). 2009. *Global Public Goods*. Oxford: Oxford University Press.

Kenis, P., V. Schneider. 1991. "Policy Networks and Policy Analysis: Scrutinizing a New Analytical Toolbox." Pp. 25–59 in *Policy Networks: Empirical Evidence and Theoretical Considerations*, edited by B. Marin, R. Mayntz. Boulder, Frankfurt: Campus Verlag, Westview Press.

Kooiman, J. 2003. *Governing as Governance*. London: SAGE Publications.

Lehmbruch, G. 1979. "Liberal Corporatism and Party Government." Pp. 147–184 in *Trends Towards Corporatist Intermediation*, edited by P. C. Schmitter, G. Lehmbruch. Beverly Hills/London: SAGE Publications.

Lindblom, C. E. 1977. *Politics and Markets*. New York: Basic Books.

Marks, G. 1993. "Structural Policy and Multilevel Governance." Pp. 402–403 in *The State of the European Community: The Maastricht Debates and Beyond*, edited by A. Cafruny, G. Rosenthal. 2nd ed. Harlow: Longman.

McQuail, D. 2010. *Mass Communication Theory: An Introduction*. 6th edition. London: Sage.

Milward, H. B., K. G. Provan. 1999. *How Networks are Governed*. Unpublished paper.

Mlčoch, L. 1996. *Institucionální ekonomie* [Institutional Economics, in Czech]. Prague: Karolinum.

Musil, J. 1996. "Nový pohled na občanskou společnost" [A New Perspective on Civil Society, in Czech]. *Nová přítomnost* 2 (1): 31.

Myrdal, G. 1968. *Asian Drama: An Inquiry into the Poverty of Nations*. Harmondsworth: Pelican Books.

Neuvonen, A. (ed.). 2005. *Hostages of the Horizon. The twin challenge of ignorance and indifference. Review on issues raised in the Club of Rome 2004 Annual Conference*. Helsinki: Finnish Association for the Club of Rome.

Pierre, J., G. Peters. 2000. *Governance, Politics, and the State*. New York: St. Martin's Press.

Potůček, M. 1999. *Not Only the Market. The Role of the Market, Government and Civic Sector in the Development of Postcommunist Societies*. Budapest: CEU Press.

Potůček, M. 2009. Will Global Public Policy Arise from Global Crisis? *Central European Journal of Public Policy*. 3(2): 4–21.

Potůček, M. et al. 2009. *Strategic Governance and the Czech Republic*. Prague: Karolinum.

Potůček, M. 2003. "Policy Coordination: Government, Markets, and the Civic Sector." Pp. 77–102 in *Public Policy in Central and Eastern Europe: Theories, Methods, Practices*, by Potůček, M., L. LeLoup, G. Jenei, L. Váradi. 2003. Bratislava: NISPAcee.

Rhodes, R. A. W. 1997. *Understanding Governance: Policy Networks, Governance and Accountability*. Buckingham: Open University Press.

Ripley, R., G. Franklin. 1981. Congress, the Bureaucracy and Public Policy. Homewood, Il.: Dorsey Press.

Samuelson, P., W. D. Nordhaus. 2010. *Economics*. 19th ed. Boston: McGraw-Hill Irwin.

Scharpf, F. W. 2001. "Democratic Legitimacy under Conditions of Regulatory Competition: Why Europe Differs from the United States." Pp. 355–376 in *The Federal Vision: Legitimacy and Levels of Governance in the United States and the European Union*, edited by K. Nicolaidis, R. Howse. New York: Oxford University Press.

Schneider, V. 1992. "The Structure of Policy Networks." *European Journal of Political Research* 21 (1–2): 109–129.

Schulz, W. 2004. "Proces politické komunikace: vymezení problémů a kladení otázek" [Political Communication as a Process: Defining Problems and Asking Questions, in Czech]. Pp. 9–27 in *Analýza obsahu mediálních sdělení* [Analysing the content of media communication, in Czech], edited by W. Schulz, I. Reifová. Prague: Karolinum.

Staniszkis, J. 2009. *O moci a bezmoci* [On Power and Powerlessness, in Czech]. Brno: Centrum pro studium demokracie.

Streeck, W., P. C. Schmitter. 1985. *Private Interest Government. Beyond Market and State.* London: SAGE Publications.

Thompson, J. B. 2013. *The Media and Modernity*. Cambridge: Polity.

Uphoff, N. 1993. "Grassroots Organizations and NGOs in Rural Development: Opportunities with Diminishing States and Expanding Markets." *World Development* 21 (4): 607–622.

Weigle, M. A., J. Butterfield. 1993. "Civil Society in Reforming Communist Regimes." *Comparative Politics* 25 (2): 1–23.

Zürn, M., S. Liebfried. 2005. "Reconfiguring the National Constellation." *European Review* 13 (1): 1–36.

Recommended sources for the theory of corporatism:

Goldthorpe, J. H. 1984. *Order and Conflict in Contemporary Capitalism*. Clarendon Press.

Hunold, C. 2001. "Corporatism, Pluralism, and Democracy: Toward a Deliberative Theory of Bureaucratic Accountability." *Governance* 14 (2): 151–167.

Schmitter, P. C. 1974. "Still the Century of Corporatism?" Pp. 85–131 in *Trends toward Corporatist Intermediation*, edited by P. C. Schmitter. Beverly Hills: SAGE.

Streeck, W., P. C. Schmitter. 1985. *Private Interest Government. Beyond Market and State.* London: SAGE Publications.

Lehmbruch, G. 1979. "Liberal Corporatism and Party Government." Pp. 147–184 in *Trends Towards Corporatist Intermediation*, edited by P. C. Schmitter, G. Lehmbruch. Beverly Hills/London: SAGE Publications.

Recommended sources for the theory of policy networks:

Compston, H. 2009. *Policy Networks and Policy Change*. Palgrave Macmillan.

Enroth, H. 2011. "Policy Network Theory." Chapter 2 in *The SAGE Handbook of Governance*, edited by M. Bevir. SAGE Publications.

Haas, P. M. 1992. "Epistemic Communities and International Policy Coordination." *International Organization* 46 (1): 1–35.

Heclo, H. 1978. "Issue Networks and the Executive Establishment." Pp. 88–124 in *The New American Political System,* edited by A. King. Washington, DC: American Enterprise Institute.

Cheema, G. S., L. Maguire. 2001. *Democracy, Governance and Development. A Conceptual Framework.* New York: United Nations. Available at http://unpan1.un.org/intradoc /groups/public/documents/un/unpan005781.pdf

Kenis, P., V. Schneider. 1991. "Policy Networks and Policy Analysis: Scrutinizing a New Analytical Toolbox." Pp. 25–59 in *Policy Networks: Empirical Evidence and Theoretical Considerations*, edited by B. Marin, R. Mayntz. Boulder, Frankfurt: Campus Verlag, Westview Press.

Rhodes, R. A. W. 2006. "Policy Network Analysis." Pp. 425–442 in *Oxford Handbook of Public Policy,* edited by M. Moran, M. Rein, R. E. Goodin. Oxford: Oxford University Press.

Ripley, R., G. Franklin. 1981. Congress, the Bureaucracy and Public Policy. Homewood, Il.: Dorsey Press.

Schneider, V. 1992. "The Structure of Policy Networks." *European Journal of Political Research* 21 (1–2): 109–129.

Waarden, Frans van. 1992. "Dimensions and Types of Policy Networks." *European Journal of Political Research* 21: 29–52.

/**A4**/

Actors and Institutions

"It is certain that the institutional structure of society is the key variable which encourages and underpins the adaptability, ability, and willingness of society to experiment, search, creatively enterprise, undergo inevitable risks, and learn from its mistakes."
Mlčoch (1996)

THE RELATIONSHIP BETWEEN ACTORS AND INSTITUTIONS

Effecting change requires a sufficient amount of willingness and activity on the part of those involved – **actors**. Their actions do not take place in a vacuum, but rather are confronted with obstacles raised by other actors. Those can be either individuals or collectives. Actors of both types are further confronted with the forms and characteristics of **institutions**, which exist independently of what they want and which must be respected.[33] And both can be either formalized (such as organizations or explicit rules of behavior) or non-formalized (such as unwritten norms or customs actors follow). Finally, organizations can be (and often are) both institutions and actors.

Individuals and groups pursue their own interests.[34] The ways they interpret and assert them are shaped by institutional factors – and some institutional environments are more advantageous for effective policymaking than others (Stoker 1989, May 1993).

All that is summarized in the table below.

Table A4.1 Formalized and non-formalized policy actors and institutions

Level of formalization	Actors		Institutions
	Individual	Composite	
Formalized	Political leaders Bureaucrats Policy analysts	Political parties Government, public administration bodies Firms Civic sector organizations Think-tanks Media	Constitutional-legal system Territorial and administrative structure /division of the state Administrative procedures
Non-formalized (unwritten)	Opinion leaders Policy entrepreneurs	Interest groups Policy networks Epistemic communities	Ethical norms, social norms, expectations, customs

Source: Author.

In the following, I am going to pay more detailed attention to the actors (and subsequently institutions) and their roles in policy making and implementation.

Actors are individuals or collectives (composite actors) involved in the policy process that may initiate it or influence its course or outcome. They are characterized by their preferences (which may change through persuasion), their perceptions of the problems they seek to address (which may change through learning), and their capabilities – the resources at their disposal. Their action is motivated by their interests (Scharpf 1997: 43).

Political leaders may have (and often have) more room for effecting policy than other actors. Of course, they, too, are restrained by their constitutional

---

33 Compare the theory of historical institutionalism in Chapter A2.
34 This kind of behavior is postulated by Rational Choice Theory, which is presented in Chapter A9 below.

roles; yet they do not always abide by those roles. In contrast, **political activists** take a bottom-up approach to the policy process. At the same time, those more successful may eventually rise to top political offices.

History knows a large number of significant political personalities that made a difference in the world. True leaders do more than merely adapt to the situation (Schumpeter 1939). They conceive original ideas, violate the status quo, innovate, and think in the long-term perspective. According to Frič (2008), leaders are people who have a vision (shaping the collective action of themselves and their followers), strive for real change in line with that vision, and manage to mobilize their followers to work together and make that change a reality.

EXAMPLES OF SIGNIFICANT POLITICAL PERSONALITIES:

Mahatma Gandhi, Winston Churchill, Martin Luther King, Nelson Mandela, Edward Snowden.

Policy work can rarely be done without **policy analysts** these days. This is caused by two factors: the demand for analysis is growing steeply with the complexity of society's functioning, and policy work itself has become so time-demanding that one can hardly perform both roles simultaneously.

Opinion leaders are unable to directly participate in policy making. In an era of electronic media, though, they are in a better position than ever to influence the ways people perceive social problems and the policy options people consider. Sometimes they are the ones who initiate an issue on the agenda.[35]

As the concept of governance shows, this set of actors can be extended to include those operating at the supra-national, European, regional and local levels as well (see previous chapter). Nevertheless, the main center of public policymaking is still typically located at the level of **nation-states**. The regulatory roles of government in society have been outlined in the previous chapter; here I am going to deal with its basic roles in the formulation and implementation of specific public policies.

POLITICAL PARTIES

Political scientists identify a "vibrant tension" between political parties' aspirations to articulate and secure the public interest on one hand, and the typically narrower scope of their own interests on the other. One cannot

---

35   See the section on agendas further below in this chapter.

understand their active role in public policy merely by studying their programmatic documents; rather, it is revealing to analyze what kind of policies political parties actually push for.

Various **interest groups** assert themselves in the policy process as well. When looking at the systems of political parties more closely, it becomes obvious that the boundary between interest groups and political parties is both unclear and permeable. Political parties as well as interest groups reflect the diversity of people's needs, attitudes and interests at different levels of governance and to varying degrees of intensity. As shown by Duverger, political parties traditionally arose out of existing interest groups such as trade unions, business associations, intellectual circles, etc.

GOVERNMENT, PUBLIC ADMINISTRATION[36]

Government performs the following key functions:
- develops the constitutional-legal framework of social life and enforces it among other actors;
- guarantees internal and external security;
- sets the institutional framework of economic activity;
- ensures the provision of public social services (social security, health care, education, culture, physical education and sport, public transport, research and development, public service media, etc.);
- protects the environment.

In recent decades, important changes to the position of governments and bodies of public administration, as agents of public authority, have been associated with a gradual shift from a positive state – which governs authoritatively, is based on hierarchy, and strives for a monopoly of power – to a **regulatory state** (Majone 2006: 234) – which delegates an increasing part of its traditional agendas either to other levels of governance or to business /civic sector actors, and at the same time, expands its traditional policy scope to cover social and environmental issues.[37]

In public policy, the terms **fragile states** or **failed states** refer to nation-states that are unable to perform their basic functions, and in particular to ensure the safety and basic vital needs of their citizens or to enforce the law at some elementary level. The government loses its legitimacy, society falls apart, and internal conflicts abound (Rotberg 2002). Successor states may be established or perhaps an outside aggressor uses the situation to his advantage.

---

36 Refer to Jenei, Hoós & Vass (2003) for a more extensive discussion about the role of the government and bureaucracy in public policy making.
37 Compare the concept of governance in previous chapter.

THINK-TANKS

The mission of think-tanks is to analyze public policies. They exist in the form of flexible networks at the intersections of research, education, politics, public administration, the business sector, and the civic sector. They engage in the policy process by critically appraising how effective the workings of government and public institutions are (Malíková 2003: 24). However, it is often difficult for think-tanks to set a boundary between producing expertise (which is governed by the strict rules of academic research), on the one hand, and furthering the interests of their financial and political sponsors, on the other (Peters 1999: 64). They have a tendency towards blurring that boundary, especially when analyzing complex interrelations using highly specialized expertise (Malíková 2003: 37).

Other types of composite actors – **businesses, civil society organizations and the media** – are discussed in the previous chapter.

INSTITUTIONS[38]

The category of formalized institutions includes the constitutional-legal system and organizational structures.

When a polity is formed, its constitution is written to define the fundamental values and functions of government and its different bodies, thus creating the foundation of its political system. **Along with the country's laws and regulations, a constitution forms an intricately structured and constantly evolving hierarchical system.** Policy analysts and policy makers must either respect it or – as long as it stands in the way of any legitimate goals defined – try to modify it.

It is impossible to formulate or implement public policies without the mediating role of government's **organizational structures.** In this respect, at least the following aspects have to be taken into consideration:
- governmental administration rests on the tiers of legislature, executive and judiciary, complemented by an ombudsman and independent audit bodies;
- the state is divided into territorial units (the capital, regions, municipalities, or if necessary, other administrative territorial units such as Euroregions or associations of local authorities);
- public administration exists at the levels of central, regional and local government, professional self-regulation, and participatory governance;

---

38 Contemporary public policy can avail itself of a number of existing theories to explicate the role of institutions in policymaking. For example, compare Chapter A2 for the theory of historic institutionalism, this chapter for the theory of actor-centered institutionalism and neo-pluralist theory, or Chapter A5 for the theory of discursive institutionalism.

- government administration consists of functionally specialized bodies, and in particular ministries, with formally set up fields of competences and specific responsibilities.

Public administration serves as the main instrument for the implementation of government's public roles. Authored by German sociologist and economist Max Weber a century ago, the theory of bureaucracy has been criticized frequently and rightfully. Nevertheless, after late-20th century enchantment with new "managerial" approaches such as New Public Management or New Public Administration, there has been a humble, yet not uncritical turn back to Weber, both among theorists and among practitioners.[39]

Organizational structures of firms, civic sector organizations as well as the media constitute another important factor shaping public policies. Complex organizations are divided into units amongst which they distribute labor and responsibilities.

Compared to formalized institutions, the study of non-formalized or **unwritten institutions** (ethical norms, social norms, expectations, and customs) is more demanding.

EXAMPLE:

It is the nature of unwritten institutions that may ultimately determine the success or failure in public policies proposed. Brown (2003) considers them as one of the main causes of the transitional flaws in post-communist countries. While these countries introduced the same formal institutions that typically exist in market economies and democratic political systems, they were not accompanied by informal institutions such as ethical and social norms, expectations and customs, all of which had been inherited from the era of central planning and authoritarian regimes.

As shown in the introduction to this chapter, individual and composite actors pursue their own interests in the policy process, while government is expected to defend the public interest. The ways actors interpret and assert such divergent interests is, as we know, strongly influenced by institutional factors. The theory of actor-centered institutionalism studies the interrelations between actors and institutions.

---

39 Chapter A8 gives a detailed account of the evolution of bureaucracy theory. Also, Potůček (2008) analyses the relationship between Neo-Weberian thought in public administration and the theory of global governance.

EXAMPLE THEORY: ACTOR-CENTERED INSTITUTIONALISM

This theory explains how actors formulate and implement policies by way of politically feasible measures and/or institutional change. It is based on the assumption that actors' actions are strongly (but never fully) determined by the ways existing institutions (whether formalized or unwritten ones) influence their perceptions, preferences and capabilities. Institutions have such a strong effects on actors' actions because actors expect one another to act in conformity with the institutions. Individuals working in formalized institutions are, too, assumed to follow their internal rules: "Rules and systems of rules in any historically given society not only organize and regulate social behavior but make it understandable – and in a limited conditional sense – predictable for those sharing in rule knowledge" (Burns, Baumgartner, Deville 1985: 256).

The theory operates with two specific concepts. A **constellation** is a structure of involved actors, their strategic choices, and the effects of the different combinations of actors' strategies and preferred outcomes. When taking account of a constellation, one inquires about potential conflicts and ways of overcoming them, and whether actors are able to attain their preferred solutions through mutual coordination or rather through competition (Ovseiko 2002: 23). According to Scharpf (1997: 44), such coordination /competition can be conceptualized as different game situations, based on game theory. However, the concept of constellations provides us merely with a snapshot, not a dynamic account of the actual interactions through which actors accomplish policy action. Therefore, a wide range of **modes of interaction** are distinguished, including unilateral action, negotiated agreement, majority voting, or hierarchical direction. In the latter mode, an actor positioned higher in the hierarchy determines the strategies of other actors (Scharpf 1997: 46). The following figure shows how the theory is applied.

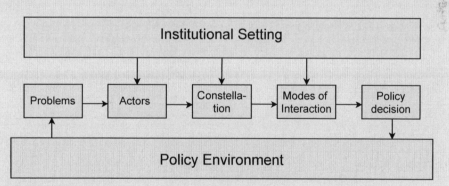

Figure A4.1 Policy research on the relationship between actors and institutions
Source: Scharpf (1997: 44).

STUDY TIP: Refer to **Chapter B3** for a case study which applies the Theory of actor--centered institutionalism.

At this point, one must bring attention to the **neo-pluralist theory,** which holds that formalized institutions are able to influence interest representation by giving preference to some interests over others. They may support and offer privileged treatment to an under-represented public interest (Hix 1999: 190). This occurs, for instance, when businesses have a stronger influence over the policy process than non-governmental organizations.

ARENAS

Policy arenas (also referred to as policy venues) are specifically delimited spaces in which different policy actors engage one another in a relationship of cooperation/consensus or competition/conflict.

Three types of arenas were traditionally distinguished: the legislature, the executive, and political parties. Later on, Jordan and Richardson (1987) added three more types: the public arena, the bureaucratic arena, and the arena of interest groups. The three traditional arenas in which public policies come to be initiated and implemented are institutionalized in a firm and transparent way. Not only are the different actors bound by established rules, but their interactions and communication links are also governed by stable institutional frameworks, both within and between arenas. In contrast, the arenas of general public and interest groups are not fundamentally institutionalized (the forms and contents of interactions therein may or may not be governed by clearly defined rules).

However, what is missing in this typology, from today's perspective, are the media and the judiciary with their increasing role in public policy making.

There is yet another typology of policy arenas, as shown by Fiala and Schubert (2000: 67-75) based on Lowi (1972) and Salisbury (1968). The original distinction between distributive, redistributive and regulative arenas was later extended to include three more types, namely constitutive, auto-regulative and persuasive arenas. Clearly, this perspective on arenas has to do with the different types of instruments applied in public policy.[40]

AGENDAS

Agendas are areas characterized by long-term struggles between varying combinations of public and group interests. Defined by Cobb and Elder (1983: 14) as "specific sets of political controversies," agendas represent formulated, solved, or postponed social problems; as well as, the ways they are perceived and communicated by actors in given institutional environments. They

---

40 See the following chapter for more on policy instruments.

consist of ever-changing sets of specific policy issues. Agendas are constantly developed, modified and complemented by such specific issues, which in turn reflect both long-term interests and the fluctuating political urgency thereof. The specific sets of issues on a given agenda are constantly reassessed not only by actors, along with the evolution of their needs and interests, state of knowledge, but also irrational factors.

EXAMPLE:

The agenda of public health care provisions constantly evolve in all countries as the set of issues on the policy agenda come and go. In the past, this agenda included a public, non-profit or for-profit ownership of hospitals, or waiting times for operations. Among the other issues debated were patient co-payments, the wording of a healthcare payment regulation, the salaries of healthcare professionals, price and taxation of drugs, etc.

EXAMPLE THEORY: ACTORS GENERATING AGENDAS IN ARENAS (A-A-A MODEL)

This approach stems from the concept of policy arenas as coined by Jordan and Richardson (1987). It contextualizes the policy process in an interactive field with mutual links and dynamics among three segments, namely policy Arenas, policy Actors, and policy Agendas. It started to be referred to shortly as the A-A-A model, which was applied in the design of various case studies (Potůček, Vass, Kotlas 2005).

Through mutual interaction in arenas, actors establish and maintain different kinds of relations with one another, not only within but also across arenas. This results in a multitude of flows of communication within each arena as well as in liaisons between actors from different arenas (ranging from positive cooperation to sharp confrontation, whether on policy goals or on preferable methods of attaining them, with regard to one or several issues on a given agenda).

One can give the following rough account of the process: an actor from any arena "brings to life" a new issue on the policy agenda. He/she tables the issue, initiates it and problematizes it, but also suggests the ways to address it. Issue definition changes throughout the different forms and stages of "problem-solving coalitions," and an articulated issue gets onto the policy agenda when actors with a threshold potential of influence are mobilized. Of course, the resulting form of the new issue on the policy agenda may differ substantially from the way it was initiated (a social problem in the eyes of one actor may represent an economic problem in the eyes of another; the temporal dimension of a problem may vary from short-term to long-term; and last but not least, actors may have divergent perceptions of the importance of a problem).

The interactive A-A-A model helps us keep track of the permanent, perhaps volatile processes of agenda setting. An issue goes through different "reincarnations," some of them closer to and others more distant from the original impulse. Finally, the concentrated effort of actors involved moves the issue toward a certain solution. Then the level of communication among actors subsides and the issue "implodes," drifting away to the margins of policymakers' attention.

REVIEW QUESTIONS

Policy arenas/venues: define them and name different types.

Go back to the table on "Formalized and non-formalized policy actors and institutions" and fill in examples for the global level of governance.

What do political leaders, policy entrepreneurs and opinion leaders have in common – and how do they differ?

Can non-formalized institutions play a more important role in policy implementation than formalized ones? Try to find examples of supporting evidence.

Name the key functions of government and its authorities; what are the possible consequences of its failure to secure each function?

On various examples, document the difference between non-formalized and formalized actors.

Characterize Weber's ideal model of bureaucracy and critical responses to it.

What are think-tanks? Can they be trusted?

What are the different theories that study the relationship between actors and institutions? Name some original concepts applied in the field.

Give an example of a policy agenda and its issues.[41]

Explain why politicians may tend to focus on petty issues while neglecting more important ones.

Go back to the table on "Formalized and non-formalized policy actors and institutions" and fill in examples for the regional level of governance.

SOURCES

Brown, B. 2003. "Ethics and Public Policymaking: An Incomplete Transition in Central and eastern Europe." Pp. 175–200 in *Public Policy in Central and Eastern Europe: Theories, Methods, Practices*, by M. Potůček, L. LeLoup, G. Jenei, L. Váradi. Bratislava: NISPAcee.

Burns, T. R., T. M. Baumgartner, P. DeVille 1985. *Man, Decisions, Society: The Theory of Actor-System Dynamics for Social Scientists*. Milton Park: Gordon and Breach Science Publishers.

---

41   Not in the field of public health.

Cobb, R. W., C. D. Elder. 1983. *Participation in American Politics: The Dynamics of Agenda-Building*. Baltimore: Johns Hopkins University Press.

Fiala, P., K. Schubert. 2000. *Moderní analýza politiky* [Modern Policy Analysis, in Czech]. Brno: Barrister & Principal.

Frič, P. 2008. *Vůdcovství českých elit* [The Leadership of Czech Elites, in Czech]. Prague: Grada.

Hix, S. 1999. *The Political System of the European Union*. New York: St. Martin Press.

Jenei, G, J. Hoós, L. Vass. 2003. "Public Policy Institutions: The State and Bureaucracy." Pp. 105–119 in *Public Policy in Central and Eastern Europe. Theories, Methods, Practices*, by Potůček, M., L. T. Leloup, G. Jenei, L. Varadi. Bratislava: NISPAcee.

Jordan, A. G., J. J. Richardson. 1987. *British Politics and The Policy Process – An Arena Approach*. London: Allen Unwin.

Lowi, T. J. 1972. "Four Systems of Policy, Politics, and Choice." *Public Administration Review* 33: 298–310.

Majone, G. 2006. "Agenda Setting." Pp. 225–250 in *The Oxford Handbook of Public Policy*, edited by M. Moran, M. Rein, R. E. Goodin. Oxford: Oxford University Press.

Malíková, L. 2003. *Verejná politika. Aktéri a procesy* [Public Policy. Actors and Processes, in Slovak]. Bratislava: Univerzita Komenského.

May, P. 1993. "Mandate Design and Implementation: Enhancing Implementation Efforts and Shaping Regulatory Styles." *Journal of Policy Analysis and Management* 12 (4): 634–63.

Mlčoch, L. 1996. *Institucionální ekonomie* [Institutional Economics, in Czech]. Prague: Karolinum.

Ovseiko, P. 2002. *The Politics of Health Sector Reform in Eastern Europe: the Actor-Centered Institutionalist Framework for Analysis*. Budapest: Center for Policy Studies. IPF Working Paper No. 2002-01.

Peters, B. G. 1999. *American Public Policy: Promise and Performance*. New York, London: Chatham House Publishers, Seven Bridges press, LLC.

Potůček, M. 2008. "The Concept of the Neo-Weberian State Confronted by the Multi-Dimensional Concept of Governance." *NISPAcee Journal of Public Administration and Public Policy* 1 (2): 83–94.

Rotberg, R. 2002. "The New Nature of Nation States Failure." *Washington Quarterly* 25 (3): 85–96.

Salisbury, R. H., 1968. "The Analysis of Public Policy: A Search of Theories and Roles." Pp. 151–175 in *Political Science and Public Policy*, edited by A. Ranney. Chicago: Markham.

Scharpf, F. W. 1997. *Games Real Actors Play. Actor-Centered Institutionalism in Policy Research*. Boulder: Westview Press.

Schumpeter, J. 1939. *Business Cycles: A Theoretical, Historical and Statistical Analysis of the Capitalist Process*. New York: McGraw-Hill.

Stoker, R. P. 1989. "A Regime Framework for Implementation Analysis." *Policy Studies Review* 9 (1): 29–49.

Recommended sources for actor-centered institutionalism:

Maarse, H. 2008. *The Politics of European Union Health Policy-Making: An Actor-Centered Institutionalist Analysis*. Maastricht: Universitaire Pers Maastricht.

Ovseiko, P. 2002. *The Politics of Health Sector Reform in Eastern Europe: the Actor-Centered Institutionalist Framework for Analysis*. Budapest: Center for Policy Studies. IPF Working Paper No. 2002-01.

Potůček, M., L. Vass, P. Kotlas. 2005 (new edition 2010). "Veřejná politika jako proces." [Public Policy as a Process, in Czech]. Pp. 61–84 in *Veřejná politika* [Public Policy, in Czech], by M. Potůček et al. Prague: Sociologické nakladateství (SLON).

Scharpf, F. W. 1997. *Games Real Actors Play. Actor-Centered Institutionalism in Policy Research*. Boulder: Westview Press.

Recommended sources for the theory of actors generating agendas in arenas (A-A-A Model):

Jordan, A. G., J. J. Richardson. 1987. *British Politics and the Policy Process: An Arena Approach*. London: Allen Unwin.

Potůček, M., L. Vass, P. Kotlas. 2005 (new edition 2010). "Veřejná politika jako proces" [Public Policy as a Process, in Czech]. Pp. 33–60 in *Veřejná politika* [Public Policy, in Czech], by M. Potůček et al. Prague: Sociologické nakladatelství (SLON).

Vos, M., H. Schoemaker, V. Luoma-aho 2014. "Setting the Agenda for Research on Issue Arenas." *Corporate Communications* 19 (2): 200–215.

/**A5**/

Public Policy Instruments

Just like a carpenter, a blacksmith or any other tradesman, a politician has a whole range of tools at his or her disposal. In contrast to them, though, the politician's improper use of those tools does not translate into visible damage at first sight. Sometimes it may take decades before a policy failure becomes apparent – and that is when he or she can no longer be made accountable. Moreover, the failure is possibly not only the politician's fault because he/she is never the lone player in the field of decision making. There is a multitude of actors pursuing their goals, sometimes complementary, often competing or contradictory ones. Policies might be co-created by the involvement of collaborating actors; other actors may pose obstacles to the intended policy. After all, a policy may well be jeopardized by unexpected events that could not be foreseen in any policy design.

However, the politician can increase the likelihood of attaining the goals of his/her policy by adequately selecting, combining and applying the instruments for its implementation. This was noted for the first time by Harold Lasswell, one of the founding fathers of public policy, in his 1936 book, *Politics: Who Gets What, When, How.* This chapter is going to follow in his footsteps.

For example, Peters (1999) differentiates between law, services, money, taxes, other economic instruments, and suasion. Bardach's (2000) typology contains as many as eleven items. In addition to these and other lists, as commented and reviewed by Veselý and Nekola (2007, p. 259), I take into consideration **inquiry** and **policy documents**. The latter two instruments are typically applied in the initial stages of the policy process – problem delimitation and recognition, and policy decision-making.[42] Among the instruments applied in the following stages, I distinguish **law, public administration, public social services, instruments of power, and means of information and communication**.

Here I am going to follow a general distinction between the most fundamental categories of instruments, namely: inquiry, policy documents, law and public administration, economic instruments, public social services, instruments of power, and means of information and communication. This typology relies on experience from dozens of public policy projects I was able to participate in. With a high degree of simplification, then, I am going to compare these instruments to different parts of a society's body or "social organism."

Table A5.1 Comparing public policy instruments to body parts

Instrument	Part of the "social organism"
Inquiry	Sensory system
Programming documents	Brain
Law	Skeleton
Public administration	Muscular system
Economic instruments	Circulatory system
Public social services	Specialized organs
Instruments of power	Immunity system
Information and communication instruments	Nervous system

Source: Author.

---

42 Cf. Chapter A6 for more details.

INQUIRY

Good inquiry is a necessary but not sufficient condition of the effective application of other policy instruments. **The ultimate success of public policies depends on a thorough inquiry about the environment in which they are to be implemented.** A carpenter cannot work with just a set of sharpened tools, but also needs to know a lot about the wood worked by him /her. *Inquiry can be likened to sensory perception, informing the "social organism" about the environment in which it exists.* Many public policies are "blind" and "deaf" because their makers simply do not understand the problems they intend to solve. If inquiry is taken seriously, one can, on the other hand, speak about **evidence-based policy making**.

Not only history but also various other scientific disciplines can participate in the **inquiry process**. Moreover, such a process should cover not only **past development but also the present state**. Credible public policies tend to rely on **attempting to foresee possible futures**,[43] too. The reason is apparent: the conditions of their implementation may, and will, change with the situation in the field, and one should know how.

Academia is the most suitable environment for inquiry. This is the home environment of think-tanks and policy analysts, as mentioned in the previous chapter, and their products – policy analyses and forecasts, research reports, and policy briefs. Finally, members of the general public, too, should get involved in policy inquiry – for example by means of public discourse.[44]

PROGRAMMING DOCUMENTS[45]

No public policy can be implemented without preparation. One must first clarify the policy's goals, outline the ways of attaining them, identify the available resources, consider modifying existing institutions, and coordinate the actions of the actors involved. *Programming documents are seen metaphorically as the brain of the "social organism."* They include visions, strategies, white papers, programs, plans, doctrines, and road maps.[46]

In a **vision**, the community of a nation or a country not only cultivates, by means of democratic discussion, a set of ideas about the threats and opportunities of its development, but also, in keeping with generally shared values,

---

43 The challenges of inquiring about the future are discussed by Potůček et al. (2009).
44 For more details on public discourse, see further below in this chapter.
45 With regard to these type of instruments, Veselý, Nekola (2007: 50) talk about strategic, declaratory or advocacy documents. Programming documents are merely one of a number of types of policy documents that deserve a policy analyst's attention. In addition, Veselý distinguishes between legislative and research documents.
46 They are also applied as instruments of strategic governance (Potůček et al. 2009).

about the ways of minimizing threats and making the best possible use of the opportunities identified.

Strategies guide an effort to providently minimize developmental threats and maximize developmental opportunities of an entity (supra-national organization, country, region, bureau, firm, policy area) in the mid-term and long-term perspective, while economizing on available resources.

White papers facilitate the implementation of the different strategic goals of an entity (supra-national organization, country, region, bureau, firm, policy area) and help define the means of attaining those goals. As a rule, they are more specific and more determinate than strategies.

EXAMPLE:

The European Commission prepares its White Papers on the basis of Green Papers. First, a Green Paper provides an introduction to the subject matter and formulates questions for public debate. Subsequently, the Commission reviews the debate along with other available information and drafts a White Paper to specify the direction in which the entire European Community and its member states should follow, and the instruments they should utilize.

Programs specify the steps towards attaining defined goals. They set the instruments, conditions of implementation, and possibly also implementation responsibilities and deadlines. Programs of political parties constitute a special category of programs that can be long-term, medium-term or "tailor-made" for a single electoral campaign.

EXAMPLE:

A government policy statement is an important document guiding the future actions of a country's executive, as presented in some countries to the Parliament before its vote of confidence.

Plans are narrowly focused documents that specify the desirable future state of an area and define measurable targets accordingly. There are either directive plans (where meeting the target values is strictly required) or indicative plans (where such values serve for orientation only). This type of document is applied, for instance, in community development planning at the local or regional levels.

Doctrines are typically brief documents that define a general set of guiding principles for a policy area. In contrast to the previous types of programming documents, they do not set specific goals or responsibilities for different actors.

A **road map** sets out the way towards a defined long-term objective. It consists of a scheduled set of stages followed to attain the objective. With a certain degree of freedom, it provides a platform for different actors to forge consensuses between their competing interests and to coordinate their activities.

LAW AND PUBLIC ADMINISTRATION

A country's **legal system** *can be envisaged as a skeleton that holds the "social organism" together, delimits the functions of different organs and helps them, both individually and collectively, to find orientation in their environment and adapt to changing external and internal conditions in which they exist.* **Legislation** serves to adapt a country's legal system to social change – albeit such adaptation tends to be delayed, which causes problems. Political leaders who intend to change laws are bound by the complex rules of the legislative process which reserve an opportunity for other actors to intervene (above all, political opposition and opposing interest groups). From the moment a legislative intent is formulated, it may take years to become law.

If the legal system is the skeleton of the "social organism" then public administration can be imagined as its muscular system, responsible for the movement or "life" of the bones.

of public administration. This means that the central government delegates the implementation of some of its legal responsibilities to regional and municipal governments while reimbursing them for the expenses incurred.

However, existing structures of public administration may pose obstacles to newly formulated public policies. Besides **robust constitutional changes** (such as the establishment or the abolition of regional governments), policy makers seeking to adapt public administration to new demands have several other instruments at their disposal.

EXAMPLES:

Centralization or decentralization – responsibility for an agenda is transferred vertically from one level of public administration to another.

Concentration or deconcentration – in a hierarchical system of public administration, responsibility for some agendas is transferred from several lower-level or same-level organizational units to a single unit, or vice versa.

Reorganization – public administration adapts to new needs and possibilities by changing the scope of responsibilities of a body, establishing a new body, or merging several bodies. Reorganization may have important effects on the policy process and on interactions between governmental and non-governmental actors (Peters 1992).

Coordination – bodies or rules are established to facilitate the cooperation between several units of public administration with regard to a shared agenda. Interdepartmental committees or ad-hoc task forces are typical examples of such bodies. They differ in terms of formalization, lifespan, and scope of responsibility. What they have in common is involving selected stakeholders and giving them additional rights in the policy process.

Procedural change – one formulates a new way of solving public tasks or defines new roles for the actors involved (e.g., new building regulations).

Public administration also creates **specialized regulatory agencies** in order to supervise non-governmental actors and inspect their activities within a framework prescribed by law. Their fields of authority vary and may comprise, among others, drug control, water or nuclear management, energy, media and telecommunication, labor or trade inspection, or transport.

ECONOMIC INSTRUMENTS

Having likened the legal system to the skeleton of the "social organism" and public administration to its muscular system, one can view economic instruments as its circulatory system. Just as the circulatory system oxygenates the blood and transports oxygen to all parts of the human body, so the economy distributes money that is vital for the existence and evolution of the "social organism."

PUBLIC REVENUES

Taxes as an economic instrument have been used since dark antiquity. The law commits natural or legal persons to mandatory payments to defined recipients. Not only do taxes channel the resources necessary for public spending, but also the structure of taxes and the effectiveness of tax collection determine the relative tax burden imposed upon the resources of different categories of persons or institutions.

EXAMPLE:

Progressive income taxation means that a heavier tax burden in both absolute and relative term is imposed on higher-income individuals.

As one of the instruments associated with the use of taxes, **tax rebates or exemptions** are applied to encourage desirable or discourage undesirable behavior among taxpayers.

User fees, penalties are payments for a defined type of conduct (waste disposal, traffic transgressions, etc.)

Revenue from business activities comprises primarily the profits of state-owned enterprises.

PUBLIC EXPENDITURES

PUBLIC BUDGETS

Many years ago, one of the founding fathers of public policy, Aaron Wildavsky (1974: 3), noted: "Perhaps the 'study of budgeting' is just another expression for the 'study of politics'; yet one cannot study everything at once, and the vantage point offered by a concentration on budgetary decisions offers a useful and much neglected perspective from which to analyze the making of policy."

Public budgets copy the structure of public administration. The central government formulates the **government's budget** (which is structured into items for each ministry or other central body). The following section is limited to central-level budgeting, albeit the principles and instruments outlined here can be applied *mutatis mutandis* at the regional and local levels as well.

Certainly the most important policy tool that public administration has, **government budgets** are used to distribute a constantly limited amount of money to support prioritized policy areas and institutions. They "reflect general public consensus about what kinds of services governments should provide and what citizens are entitled to as members of society" (Theodoulou, Cahn 1995: 185). Government budgets may also work as instruments to stabilize the economy.[47]

Political debates and policy practice evolve around itemized annual budgets that divide the total available amount into a large number of detailed appropriations for individual departments. In addition to such budgets, other, more effective methods of budgeting have been used internationally as well (Högye 2003). Decision-making about extremely expensive long-term objectives is more rational with medium-term budgeting. "Programmatic allocation of resources is a type of allocation of resources that 'places' available resources according to defined allocation objectives – referred to as 'purposes' – whereas the objective's priority rank is the criterion for allocating limited resources. The allocation criterion is optimized if an expected output is achieved at minimum cost, or if maximum utility is achieved for given expenditure" (Ochrana 2005: 23).

SUBSIDIES, GRANTS, BENEFITS, LOANS, ALLOWANCES, COUPONS

Defined objectives are promoted through all forms of financial or non-financial transfers from public budgets to eligible beneficiaries (the latter include allowances and coupons, which entitle people to pre-defined amounts of goods or services). "They are often applied to promote activities that are not provided in sufficient quantity and quality either by markets or by non-profit and voluntary activities" (Beblavý et al. 2002: 87). They are distributed under certain terms and conditions that beneficiaries must follow to avoid penalties.

From time to time, ownership change becomes a legitimate economic instrument of public policy making. **Privatization** takes place when government-owned assets are transferred to private owners, whereas the reverse process is called **nationalization**.

Different methods of collecting and allocating public resources, as well as operations with national currency, are viewed as relatively autonomous public policies – fiscal policy and monetary policy, respectively.

---

47 The relevance of government budgets is further underlined by the fact that in most European countries, the rejection of a draft government budget by the legislature has the effects of a no-confidence vote, forcing the national government to resign.

Fiscal policy pursues policy priorities by manipulating the level and structure of taxes and other public revenues on one hand, and public spending on the other. In addition, it uses fiscal incentives or restrictions to influence the country's economic development.

> **EXAMPLE:**
>
> A member state of the EU is required to meet the Maastricht convergence criteria as a precondition to adopt the common currency (the Euro). In the area of public finance, the ratio of public debt relative to gross domestic product (GDP) must not exceed 60%, and the government budget deficit must be lower than 3% of GDP.

Monetary policy seeks to attain policy and economic goals not only by influencing monetary magnitudes such as total money supply and interest rates, but also currency exchange rates. One of its goals is to keep inflation under a defined limit; at the same time, it can have both positive and negative effects on economic development. A country's monetary policy is implemented by its central bank, which is typically independent of the national government.

PUBLIC SOCIAL SERVICES

Over the past century, all developed countries have dramatically raised the extent of publicly financed social, health and education services as well as activities in the fields of culture, physical education & sports, transport, and research & development. This trend was importantly shaped by the growth of factors such as the productivity of labor, economic output, average life expectancy, length and difficulty of educational pathways, and technological development. It was also accompanied by an expanding scope of government authority and responsibility in regulating and providing these services. Each of these fields (collectively referred to as human development) has its specifics and requires a tailored set of management and administration instruments, with important differences from instruments applied in fields that are primarily regulated by the market.

> **EXAMPLES:**
>
> **Employment policy:** unemployment benefits, a range of instruments of active employment policy: retraining, socially beneficial jobs, subsidized jobs for people with disabilities, community service, etc.

Health policy: public health insurance, fee-for-service, per-capita or episode healthcare payments, or medicines reimbursement caps based on the strength of active substance.

Social policy: social insurance schemes, universal provision versus means testing, social assistance in the form of welfare benefits or social services, general subsidies ("per brick," supporting each service provider as a whole) versus per-capita payments (spent by eligible beneficiaries on any social services they deem necessary).

Education policy: per-student subsidies, program-based subsidies (e.g., to enhance schools' access to communication and information technologies), individualized subsidies based on the demands of one's education pathway, different subsidies for different education programs, school rankings.

*The different **public social services** can be pictured as organs of the "social organism," specialized to perform its diverse vital functions.*

Nevertheless, the state's primary responsibility for public social services does not mean that governments or public organizations have to provide them directly. As pointed out in Chapter A3 above, government may, wherever it deems adequate, delegate service provisions either to civil society organizations (as it does throughout the field of human development, especially in the social services) or to the business sector (e.g., private schools, healthcare establishments, or contractors providing employment services or social services).

INSTRUMENTS OF POWER

Over the past couple of decades, there has been an apparent shift from a positive to a regulatory state.[48] In spite of that, government has retained some of the traditional roles of feudal lords.[49] Specialized bodies of public administration monitor and enforce compliance with laws (to name the most important examples: **Public Prosecutor's Office, Police, Customs Administration, tax offices, courts, Prison Administration**). The **military** is a special instrument of power with primary, but not always exclusive, responsibility for the external security of a country.

*These **instruments of power** can be imagined as the immune system of the "social organism," specialized to protect its vital functions.*

---

48   Compare previous chapter.
49   These roles are reserved for government only – they are monopolized by the state.

INFORMATION AND COMMUNICATION INSTRUMENTS

Information alone is powerless, merely a quantity of zeroes and ones. Only communication empowers it. On one hand, struggles in public policy are above all information struggles. On the other hand, cooperation between actors must be based on communication as well. Formalized institutions cannot exist without an exchange of information, without communication from both inside and outside.

Information and communication instruments thus can be seen as the nervous system of the "social organism."

Some of these instruments are employed (whether in overt or covert ways) to influence the preferences, and in turn behaviors, of selected actors and institutions. These include **propaganda, indoctrination and lobbying,** and also **public relations,** which operates on the same principle yet less explicitly. A role is played by **awareness campaigns** and **political education,** which tend to be less one-sided in terms of interests and values. Finally, the instrument of **public discourse** is best suited to facilitate the interplay of divergent interests and opinions.

One-sided in terms of interests and values, **propaganda** is employed primarily in the hands of authoritative or totalitarian regimes that restrict the access of citizens to independent sources of information. However, liberal democracies have their more covert forms of propaganda as well. Political and economic elites form alliances with media elites in order to moderate the flow of information in both public service and private media in ways that benefit their individual or group interests.

EXAMPLE:

Silvio Berlusconi – a media tycoon, businessman, long-term prime minister of Italy, and eventually a convicted criminal – built his stunning political career on massive influence over the content of the media he owned (especially TV stations) to serve his political movements and goals. After two decades, Berlusconi was convicted for tax fraud and prohibited by the court from running in future elections.

Lindblom (1977) treats **indoctrination (persuasion)** as the third regulator of the life of people and their communities (along with the market and government). Its possible motives are either economic (to promote sales of goods and services) or political (as guided by a given political ideology). Both producers and mediators of information may find it in their interest to provide incomplete or biased information.

A legitimate yet somewhat flawed part of pluralist democracy, **lobbying** serves to promote specific group interests in any stage or segment of policy formulation or implementation. Charles P. Taft offered, in 1974, a simple and relatively broad definition: lobbying is presentation of group interests to legislative, executive or judicial authorities at any level of governance. Encyclopedia Britannica (2014) defines lobbying as "any attempt by individuals or private interest groups to influence the decisions of government; in its original meaning it referred to efforts to influence the votes of legislators, generally in the lobby outside the legislative chamber." I am going to complement this definition by stating that advocacy non-profit organizations, which are private by nature, can assert not only group interests (mutual benefit non-profit organizations) but also public interests (public benefit non-profit organizations).

EXAMPLES: REGULATED AND UNREGULATED LOBBYING

In the United States, lobbying has been regulated by law since 1946. Relatively strict limits are imposed on the numbers of lobbyists and lobbying agencies and the behaviors allowed or forbidden in their contact with politicians. Other, especially European countries followed the American example later. For example, in the UK, the behavior of Members of Parliament *vis-à-vis* lobbyists is governed by law, while lobbying activities are regulated by the Association of Professional Political Consultants Code of Conduct. Extensive activities of lobbying groups are also apparent at the level of the EU and its bodies. The Czech general public perceives lobbying with a high degree of mistrust (and the "lobbyist" label has strongly negative connotations). In spite of that, several draft laws to regulate lobbying have failed to pass through the parliament. Are there interests of both those lobbying and those lobbied involved in such reluctance? Without regulation, lobbying tends to influence decision-making processes in illegitimate and uncontrolled ways which harm the public interests.

Indoctrination, persuasion and lobbying in the hands of competing advocacy coalitions may serve as means to controlling the public space. The Advocacy Coalition Framework has more to say about those processes.

EXAMPLE THEORY: ADVOCACY COALITION FRAMEWORK

The Advocacy Coalition Framework (hereinafter as "ACF") is an influential theory of the policy process which is based on the idea that interest groups are organized in policy communities within policy domains (Birkland 2005: 226).

A single sentence perhaps best expresses the gist of this theory: "The concept of an 'advocacy coalition' assumes that it is shared beliefs which provide the principal 'glue' of politics" (Sabatier 1995: 351). In order to increase their chances of success, actors seek allies with similar basic beliefs ("policy core beliefs"), coordinate their actions with them and thus form a kind of policy communities – advocacy coalitions. "Policy core beliefs" are defined as a set of value orientations, causal assumptions and perspectives on problems (Sabatier, Hunter, McLaughlin 1987; Sabatier, Jenkins-Smith 1999).

Advocacy coalitions have different resources and tools to achieve their goals:

1. access to formal authority to make political decisions (legislators, judges), or directly to the membership of such an actor in the coalition (e.g., political parties in power[50]);
2. public opinion and public support;
3. information, knowledge;
4. mobilizing sympathizers and supporters;
5. funds;
6. the presence of charismatic leaders (Kingdon 1994, Mintrom, Vergari 1996).

The ACF explicates change in the state of latent or explicit conflicts between diverse actors from different levels of government, interest groups, research organizations, and the media in a defined policy subsystem (Hoppe, Peterse 1993). Competing advocacy coalitions assert competing policy conceptions. Due to the nature of advocacy coalitions, a radical change inside the subsystem is extremely unlikely. ACF therefore studies external direct or indirect shocks as agents of change. The theory assumes learning within the coalition and between allies as well as opponents, with policy change typically facilitated by mediators between competing coalitions and occurring in the longer term (around ten years).

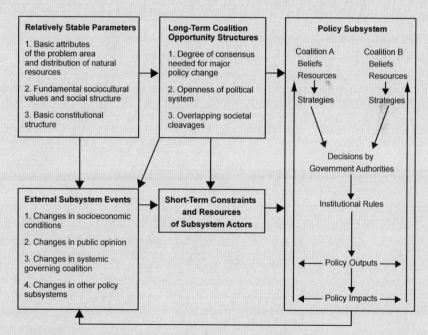

Figure A5.1 Modeling advocacy coalitions
Source: Veselý, Drhová, Nachtmannová (2005) following Sabatier, Jenkins-Smith (1999), adapted.

---

50 One characteristic feature of dominant coalitions is the number of actors in the category of formal authority (possessing the right to make political decisions).

STUDY TIP: Refer to **Chapter B4** for a case study which applies the theory of Advocacy Coalition Framework.

The business sector has almost perfected the art of **public relations,** and the number of specialized PR agencies on the market is growing. Political parties, major civil society organizations, ministries, state-owned enterprises, regional administrations and other public sector organizations, too, have been learning how to communicate with the general public, establishing their own PR departments, and formulating and implementing their communication strategies.

A special type of instrument, **information (education, awareness) campaigns** spread the word about the content or methods of provision of specific public social services, both existing and newly planned ones. Public sector or civil society organizations undertake these campaigns to help citizens make better-informed decisions. In an effort to popularize a public policy, one should consider the ways to communicate its content and goals to the public; a desirable policy image tends to be linked to widely accepted values (Jordan 1981). It is often extremely difficult to give a comprehensive, brief and distinct outline of the complex structures, relations and linkages that exist in a given policy area.

Political education is another important information and communication instrument. Whether targeted at members of political parties, public officials, political representatives or citizens themselves, it helps better understand social, political and economic problems and their possible solutions. It cultivates political communication and promotes its application in policy decision-making.

EXAMPLE:

In Germany and Austria, the state promotes political education of members of all important political parties by subsidizing their educational foundations from the government budget. While the activities of each foundation rest on the ideological roots of its mother party, they are obliged to abide by the goal of disseminating expert knowledge about the workings of law, economics, the social system, the political system, international relations, etc. German federal government supports six foundations named after important leaders of different political streams and affiliated with six political parties: the Rosa Luxemburg Foundation (the Left), the Friedrich Ebert Foundation (the Social Democracy), the Heinrich Böll Foundation (the Greens), the Friedrich Naumann Foundation (the Liberals), the Konrad Adenauer Foundation (the Christian Democrats), and the Hans Seidel Foundation (the Christian Socials).

It is common sense that "two heads are better than one." Since policy analysis is no exception, a policy analyst is usually better off taking into account an additional source of knowledge, **public discourse**, namely in the form of **public hearings** or **panel discussions**.[51] Many might object that such forums are misused by their participants by asserting the narrow views and interests of particular groups or organizations. This is indeed partially the case, yet whenever such a discourse is well moderated and guided by a search for the best ways to secure the public interest, its strengths (as the level of general knowledge grows so does the quality of the solutions adopted) tend to prevail over the threat of dominance by the limited perspectives of politicians' or one-sided special interests. This approach opens the space for a more robust co-production, co-creation of policy design (Howlett 2014, Howlett 2016). There is yet another positive aspect of opening up space for co-decision: it engages actors. Those who actively debate a given public policy as early as in the preparation stage will be more likely to identify with it, become a proponent, and keep supporting it throughout the implementation stage.

EXAMPLE THEORY: DISCURSIVE INSTITUTIONALISM

Discursive institutionalism theory explains the role of ideas and debates in politics. In comparison with other institutionalist theories, it also offers a dynamic approach to the analysis of institutional change.

Discursive institutionalism uses the concept of discourse in two senses: to understand the role of ideas as the main ingredient of a debate, and to identify how ideas influence public policy making. We would be hardly able to identify how ideas move from individual to collective action without studying real discourse, including interactions and channels which are thought to interpret, share and later promote those ideas. Put simply, it is impossible to know what the actors think and why they act the way they act, unless they say it. In this conception of the term discourse, we do not examine ideas or thoughts only, but also how they are created and how they are suitable to persuade politicians, experts, and the public.

Discursive institutionalism distinguishes between cognitive and normative ideas. Cognitive ideas describe and try to identify "how and what works and what does not work" and "how and what can be accomplished." In contrast, normative ideas justify changes with reference to their suitability in the normative sense – "what is good, what is bad, what should be done" (Schmidt 2008, Campbell, Pedersen 2007).

Schmidt (2008) further distinguishes between coordinative discourse and communicative discourse. The first one is typical within societies/economies (mostly with proportional electoral systems) where there has been a consensual political tradition supported

---

51 See Chapter A3 for more information on the Tripartite as an institutional platform for negotiations between government, unions, and employers.

by the institutional framework of corporatism (e.g., in Germany, Austria or Belgium). In contrast, the second one prevails in societies/economies with a strong concentration of decision-making power, associated often with a majority electoral system (e.g., United Kingdom, USA). Political decision-making is often done "behind closed doors" and the communication of changes and political goals in order to gain political support is oriented towards the general public.

Discursive institutionalism criticizes other institutionalist theories for their static perception of institutional framework (historical institutionalism), or of the environment in which the actors interact and which promotes their interests (rational institutionalism).[52] In discursive institutionalism, institutions are not perceived as external variables. So not only do the institutions form the structure of the environment in which actors interact, but, at the same time, the institutions themselves are an element which actors have created and potentially also change. This means that actors have the ability to think critically about the institutions and to change the way we think about these institutions themselves or their surroundings – and in that case it is even right to change them, whether individually or collectively. This ability explains why unexpected institutional changes are sometimes effected. Institutions determine and limit actors, but institutions themselves are subjects on which actors operate. One can either substitute them with other institutional forms, or use them in a different way than originally intended.

Although discursive institutionalism has brought about new possibilities to explain institutional changes, it is still necessary to remember the risks that are associated with its application. Schmidt (2008) states that traditions and culture will always influence the presentation of ideas and guide the debate. Thus, for empirical research it is always a challenge to identify when, where and why ideas and discourses bring about institutional change and when they do not.

STUDY TIP: Refer to **Chapter B2** for a case study which applies the Theory of discursive institutionalism.

APPLICATION OF POLICY INSTRUMENTS – HARMONY, DISHARMONY, IMPROVISATION?

Let me once again use the – somewhat schematic – metaphor of policy instruments as parts of the "social organism" (see table above in this chapter). Just as no human body can function if its organs fail to cooperate with one another, so no policy action can achieve the desired goals unless it relies on a harmonic, coordinated application of different policy instruments.

---

52 Compare the theory of historical institutionalism in Chapter A2 or rational choice theory in Chapter A9.

A **policy design** represents a way of harmonizing and applying selected instruments in a way that best promotes the defined policy goal(s). It involves the engagement of different actors, it guides the preparation of different actions and coordinates both the activities of actors involved and the application of different instruments.

Problems arise if different policy instruments are applied irrespective of one another.

EXAMPLE:

In the past, ideology often fueled a policy struggle against "excessive government." In the name of fiscal responsibility or austerity, the budgetary allocations of all government departments were cut down by a certain flat percentage every year. This was, however, not supported by an analysis of the potential consequences of the cuts on the public roles performed by each department. As a result, most of the burden of austerity was borne not only by departments with responsibilities for an extensive range of entitlement-based public services (and in turn by the eligible individual beneficiaries), but also by a number of longer-term projects, no matter if they were promising and already approved.

PUBLIC POLICIES

The workings of contemporary societies are highly complex, relying on a wide range of interrelated, interdependent, synergic or contradictory policies that exist in evolving external and internal environments. Indeed, there is no such public policy that could be implemented irrespective of others. And the situation is even more complicated with regard to the overlaps between and hierarchies of public policies.

EXAMPLE:

Employment policy falls under the economic, social and education policies. There may be other overlaps as well, for example with migration, environmental and foreign policies.

Therefore, a level of simplification is necessary for any attempt to **categorize public policies at the national level systematically**. The following proposal distinguishes between five categories of related policies. See Table A5.2.

A number of analysts have paid attention to instances of disagreement or even contradiction between different public policies. There are two types of efforts to **reconcile public policies** with one another: **functional**

harmonization (between different public policies at the same level of governance) and **territorial harmonization** (between the same policies of different jurisdictions).

EXAMPLE:

The European Union strives for territorial harmonization of member states' public policies in instances where the decision-making responsibilities still lie within national political representations; but, the logic of European integration requires harmonization of taxation, social security systems, regulations, etc.

Table A5.2 Categorizing national-level policies

Policy category	Policy areas
Economic policies	Monetary policy Fiscal policy Industrial policy Agricultural policy Natural resource policy
Social policies	Social security policy (including pension policy) Policies against poverty and social exclusion Family policy Employment policy Housing policy Equal opportunities policy
Human development policies	Population policy Education policy Health policy Cultural policy Physical education and sports policy
Infrastructural policies	Policy of public administration Transport policy Energy policy Research, development and innovation (RDI) policy Telecommunications policy Media policy Environmental policy
Foreign, security and human rights policies	Foreign policy Policy of country's actualization in international organizations Defence policy Homeland security policy Human rights policy Migration policy (including asylum policy)

Source: Author.

A policy may also consist of reluctance to articulate a public policy. In this way, some problems may be kept "under wraps" (Bachrach, Baratz 1970). Agents of strong group interests prevent a policy from being established and implemented if they assume they would lose some of their privileges. This is when they strive to avoid change at all cost.

EXAMPLE:

Repeated governmental attempts to tighten gun control have always been successfully prevented by the National Rifle Association in the USA.

REVIEW QUESTIONS

How can public policy as a scientific discipline learn about the past, present and future of its field of interest?

What are the different types of policy documents – and why are they so important in public policy? Name real-life examples.

Name the different types of structural change to public administration that are foreseen by public policy. What are some of the reasons for implementing each type?

Why is the preparation and approval of government budgets among the major topics analyzed by public policy as a scientific discipline?

Outline the structure and instruments of public social services provision in relevant policy domains.

Explain the difference between fiscal and monetary policy.

Information is power. What are the different tools that help exert that power?

Try to identify all public policies that are somehow related to education policy. Explain these relations.

Define advocacy coalitions. Describe how they are formed and what roles they play in the policy process.

Give an example of two or more conflicting public policies that are implemented simultaneously.

SOURCES

Bachrach, P., M. S. Baratz. 1970. *Power and Poverty*. New York: Oxford University Press.

Beblavý, M. et al. 2002. *Manuál pre tvorbu verejnej politiky* [Manual for Public Policy Making, in Slovak]. Bratislava: Inštitút pre dobre spravovanú spoločnosť.

Birkland, T. 2005. *An Introduction to the Policy Process: Theories, Concepts, and Models of Public Policy-Making*. 2nd ed. Armonk: M. E. Sharpe.

Campbell, J. L., O. K. Pedersen. 2007. "The Varieties of Capitalism and Hybrid Success: Denmark in the Global Economy." *Comparative Political Studies* 40 (3): 307–332. Retrieved May 24, 2016 (http://openarchive.cbs.dk/bitstream/handle/10398/7351/varieties_capitalism_hybrid_success_18.pdf?sequence=1).

Encyclopædia Britannica, Inc. 2014. "Lobbying." *Encyclopedia Britannica*. Retrieved May 24, 2016 (http://www.britannica.com/topic/lobbying).

Högye, M. 2003. Budgeting as a Political Process. Pp. 231–256 in *Public Policy in Central and Eastern Europe: Theories, Methods, Practices*, by Potůček, M., L. LeLoup, G. Jenei, L. Váradi. Bratislava: NISPAcee.

Howlett, M. 2014. From the "old" to the "new" policy design: design thinking beyond markets and collaborative governance. *Policy Sciences*, 47(3), 187-207.

Howlett, M. 2016. *Matching Policy Tools & Their Targets: Beyond Nudges and Utility Maximization in Policy Design*. Paper presented to the ECPR conference in Pisa, Italy. Retrieved November 7, 2016 (https://ecpr.eu/Filestore/PaperProposal/7aa0ca4c-c689-4f0f-bad1-12286042cd0c.pdf).

Hoppe, R., A. Peterse. 1993. *Handling Frozen Fire*. Boulder, CO: Westview Press.

Jordan, A. G. 1981. "Iron Triangles, Woolly Corporatism and Elastic Nets." *Journal of Public Policy* 1 (1): 95–123.

Kingdon, R. 1994. "The Genevan Consistory in the Time of Calvin." Pp. 21–24 in *Calvinism in Europe 1540–1620*, edited by A. Pettegree, A. Duke, G. Lewis. Cambridge: Cambridge University Press.

Lasswell, H. 1936. *Politics: Who Gets What, When, How*. New York: Whittlesey House, McGraw-Hill.

Lindblom, C. E. 1977. *Politics and Markets*. New York: Basic Books.

Mintrom, M., S. Vergari. 1996. "Advocacy Coalitions, Policy Entrepreneurs, and Policy Change." *Policy Studies Journal* 24: 420–35. doi: 10.1111/j.1541-0072.1996.tb01638.x.

Ochrana, F. 2005. *Veřejné rozpočty jako nástroj veřejné politiky a strategického vládnutí. Veřejná politika, veřejná volba, veřejný zájem* [Public Budgets as Instruments of Public Policy and Strategic Governance, in Czech]. Prague: CESES FSV UK. Retrieved May 24, 2016 (http://ceses.cuni.cz/CESES-20-version1-sesit05_06_ochrana.pdf).

Peters. B. G. 1992. "Government Reorganization: A Theoretical Analysis." *International Political Science Review* 13 (2): 199–218.

Potůček, M. et al. 2009. *Strategic Governance and the Czech Republic*. Prague: Karolinum.

Sabatier, P. A. 1995. "An Advocacy Coalition Framework of Policy Change and the Role of Policy-Oriented Learning Therein." Pp. 339–379 in *Public Policy Theories, Models, and Concepts: An Anthology*, edited by D. C. McCool. Englewood Cliffs, NJ: Prentice Hall.

Sabatier, P. A., H. Jenkins-Smith. 1999. "The Advocacy Coalition Framework: An Assessment." Pp. 117–166 in *Theories of the Policy Process*, edited by P. A. Sabatier. Boulder, CO: Westview Press.

Sabatier, P. A., S. Hunter, S. McLaughlin. 1987. "The Devil Shift: Perceptions and Misperceptions of Opponents." *Western Political Quarterly* 40 (3): 51–73.

Schmidt, V. A. 2008. "Discursive Institutionalism: The Explanatory Power of Ideas and Discourse." *Annual Review of Political Science* 11: 303–326.

Social Doctrine of the Czech Republic. 2002. Retrieved May 19, 2016 (http://martinpotucek
.cz/index.php?option=com_rubberdoc&view=doc&id=503&format=raw).

Theodoulou, S. Z., M. A. Cahn. 1995. *Public Policy. Essential Readings.* Englewood Cliffs,
NJ: Prentice Hall.

Veselý, A., M. Nekola (eds.). 2007. *Analýza a tvorba veřejných politik: přístupy, metody
a praxe* [Policy Analysis and Design: Approaches, Methods and Practices, in Czech].
Prague: Sociologické nakladatelství (SLON).

Veselý, A., Z. Drhová, M. Nachtmannová. 2005. *Veřejná politika a proces její tvorby. Co je
"policy" a jak vzniká* [Public Policy and the Policy Process. What Policy Is and How It
Arises, in Czech]. Studie CESES, vol. 8. Prague: CESES FSV UK.

Wildavsky A. 1974. *The Politics of the Budgetary Process.* Boston: Little, Brown & Co.

Recommended sources for the theory of discursive institutionalism:

Birkland, T. 2005. *An Introduction to the Policy Process: Theories, Concepts, and Models
of Public Policy-Making.* 2nd ed. Armonk: M. E. Sharpe.

Campbell, J. L., O. K. Pedersen. 2007. "The Varieties of Capitalism and Hybrid Success: Denmark in the Global Economy." *Comparative Political Studies* 40(3): 307–332.
Retrieved May 24, 2016 (http://openarchive.cbs.dk/bitstream/handle/10398/7351
/varieties_capitalism_hybrid_success_18.pdf?sequence=1).

Dudová, R. 2010. "The Framing of Abortion in the Czech Republic: How the Continuity
of Discourse Prevents Institutional Change." *Sociologický časopis/Czech Sociological
Review* 46 (6): 945–976.

Hašková, H., S. Saxonberg, J. Mudrák. 2013. *The Development of Czech Childcare Policies.*
Prague: Sociologické nakladatelství SLON.

Panizza, F., R. Miorelli. 2013. "Taking Discourse Seriously: Discursive Institutionalism
and Post-structuralist Discourse Theory." *Political Studies* 61 (2): 301–318.

Schmidt, V. A. 2008. "Discursive Institutionalism: The Explanatory Power of Ideas and
Discourse." *Annual Review of Political Science* 11: 303–326.

Schmidt, V. A. 2010. "Taking Ideas and Discourse Seriously: Explaining change through
discursive institutionalism as the fourth 'new institutionalism'." *European Political
Science Review* 2 (1): 1–25.

Recommended sources for the Advocacy Coalition Framework:

Hoppe, R., A. Peterse. 1993. *Handling Frozen Fire.* Boulder, CO: Westview Press.

Sabatier, P. A. 1995. "An Advocacy Coalition Framework of Policy Change and the Role
of Policy-Oriented Learning Therein." Pp. 339–379 in *Public Policy Theories, Models,
and Concepts: An Anthology,* edited by D. C. McCool. Englewood Cliffs, NJ: Prentice
Hall.

Sabatier, P. A., S. Hunter, S. McLaughlin. 1987. "The Devil Shift: Perceptions and Misperceptions of Opponents." *Western Political Quarterly* 40 (3): 51–73.

Sabatier, P. A., H. Jenkins-Smith. 1993. *Policy Change and Learning: An Advocacy Coalition
Approach.* Boulder, CO: Westview Press.

Sabatier, P. A., H. Jenkins-Smith. 1999. "The Advocacy Coalition Framework: An Assessment." Pp. 117–166 in *Theories of the Policy Process*, edited by P. A. Sabatier. Boulder, CO: Westview Press.

Sabatier, P. A., C. M. Weible. 2005. *Innovations in the advocacy coalition framework.* Paper presented at the American Society for Public Administration meeting, Milwaukee, WI.

Weible, C. M., D. Nohrstedt. 2012. "The Advocacy Coalition Framework: Coalitions, Learning, and Policy Change." Pp. 125–137 in *Handbook of Public Policy*, edited by E. Araral, S. Fritzen, M. Howlett, M. Ramesh, and Xun Wu. New York, NY: Routledge.

/A6/
Public Policy Process. The Stage of Problem Delimitation and Problem Recognition

PUBLIC POLICY AS A PROCESS

Actors of public policy should always keep in mind one famous quote of Heraclitus: "No man ever steps in the same river twice…" For public policy (as social practice) can be compared to a river: the only thing of permanence is that the water constantly gurgles, heaves, flows, and passes… However, a policy analyst would be better off with a longer version of the quote, as formulated by Seneca in one of his letters to Lucilius: "We do and do not enter the same river twice. The name of the river stays the same, the water has passed on." While the content of a specific policy area changes, the ways we name it and try to understand it remain the same. They crystallize into explanatory frameworks, models, hypotheses and theories that support our inquiry with generalized experience from the past. They, too, evolve, only at an incomparably slower pace.

Identifying the actors, institutions and instruments of a given policy area (see the previous two chapters) is merely the first of a series of steps towards better understanding that area. More needs to be done to grasp the processes taking place in it, its dynamics. As we know already, the policy process takes place at multiple levels, the relations between actors and institutions evolve and change – and a given public policy depends not only on other policies but also, often more strongly, on its external context. Therefore, one must make use of such explanatory frameworks that seek to take account of that change – even at the price of simplification. Stage models of the policy cycle are some of the oldest instruments for that purpose.

EXAMPLE THEORY: A STAGE MODEL OF THE POLICY CYCLE

The first theories of public policy were based on Easton's (1953) systemic approach. Easton believed that policy activity could be analyzed as a system with certain inputs, elements and outputs.[53] The policy process necessarily spans some period of time and comprises a number of particular processes. The purpose, goals and instruments of a policy are typically defined in the beginning of that process. When policy outcomes are achieved, the policy may or may not be discontinued. In fact, this can be a new beginning for the policy: either it is upheld in its original form, or, more typically, modified to take into account evolving needs, a changing environment, and a critical appraisal of the effects of the original policy. Such instances of a new beginning – when the process changes but repeats cyclically – were conceptualized at that time using what general systems theory (von Bertalanffy 1968) and cybernetics (Ashby 1956) referred to as **feedback**. Information about the system's outputs are fed back into the system, processed and used for any changes to the system's behavior necessary.

Lasswell (1956) divided the process of public policy into seven stages – a continuous series of distinct steps. Other authors followed up by proposing models which differed in the number, nature and content of the stages. Serious critics of this approach joined the debate as well. Lindblom (1968) was one of the first to underline the fact that the boundary between those stages is somewhat blurred. Later he went as far as to note that: "Policy making is a complexly interactive process without beginning or end" (Lindblom, Woodhouse 1993: 11)[54]. Yet such a statement may leave a policy researcher rather depressed.

In an optimization effort, Dror (1968) formulated a highly complex model of the policy cycle. He worked with a strong assumption that humanity is able to govern itself rationally. His model consisted of three stages (meta-policymaking, policymaking and post-policymaking) that were broken down into 18 phases. Dror considered all of those phases as

---

53 Systems theory was on the rise at that time, and social science, too, was enchanted by it.
54 This statement is basically in compliance with reality, yet it uncovers a fundamental paradox of policy inquiry: in order to learn something about policy, we have to allow an *a priori* simplification of the methods of our inquiry.

interconnected through a network of feedback.[55] So far, however, there is no evidence of policy practice in any country resembling that model closely.

Schlager (1999: 239) sees the utility of staging for students of the policy process in the distinction made between the categories of negotiation, decision-making, and action. Hupe and Hill (2006: 18) view the stage model as an explanatory framework, rather than theory. The traditional stage model helps us "capture a trend but is unable to analyze and explicate it" (Winkler 2007: 29). Importantly, the distinction between stages of the policy process is a helpful simplification for the purposes of teaching the discipline (John 2013; Howlett, Ramesh 2009), albeit it is precisely its "textbook-like" nature that the model is often criticized for (Nakamura 1987). In the following, I am going to work with an extremely simple model of four stages. It proves useful in public policy, for example, when one seeks to prepare and subsequently implement a strategy or a program.[56]

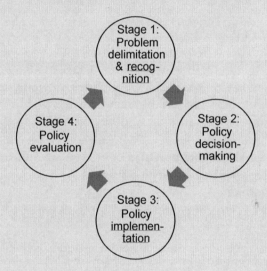

Figure A6.1 A stage model of the policy cycle
Source: Howlett, Ramesh (1995), adapted.

STUDY TIP: Refer to **Chapter B3** for a case study which applies the stage model of the policy cycle.

In the following parts of this publication, I am going to deal with the different stages in more detail. In this chapter I outline the initial stage of problem delimitation and recognition. Chapter A7 deals with decision-making in public policy, Chapter A8 with policy implementation, and Chapter A9 with evaluation.

---

55 For a scheme of the model, see Dror (1983: 163–164).
56 Management and planning theory works with an analogous explanatory framework.

THE STAGE OF PROBLEM DELIMITATION AND RECOGNITION[57]

Before one starts solving a problem, one should make sure it is well delimited. And this is often a stumbling block in public policy (both as a scientific discipline and as social practice). As noted by Dunn (1988: 720), "policy analysts fail more often because they formulate the wrong problem than because they choose the wrong solution."

The chapter continues with some reflections on problems as such, followed by a discussion of social problems, policy problems and the relations between them. I am going to conclude by characterizing the processes that result in the recognition of a policy problem as such.

WHAT IS A PROBLEM?

MacCrimmon and Taylor (1976) view a problem as a gap between an existing state and a desired state. Hoppe (2002: 38) defines it in similar, yet more specific terms: as an unacceptable gap between normative ideals or aspiration levels and present/future conditions. And Veselý (2014) adds that an actual problem arises if three additional conditions are met. The gap must:
- be perceived as important enough to get onto the "agenda of problems" and motivate thinking about possible solutions;[58]
- be difficult to overcome;
- and be manageable – to avoid mere "wishful thinking."

WHAT IS A SOCIAL PROBLEM?

Sociology should be the most qualified discipline to address this question, yet the answer it provides is not unambiguous. Traditional sociology has held that a **social problem** exists when there is a large gap between society's ideals and actual outcomes. More recently, social constructivism has seen a social problem where a significant number of people believe that a certain condition is in fact a problem (Kerbo, Coleman 2006: 363). Even if both approaches are difficult to integrate, "such integration is highly desirable from the practical perspective. Policy practitioners need to know how to differentiate between important and less important social problems, i.e., to what extent a given construction is substantiated by real situation in society. They need to know to what extent they should cover a given social condition by

---

57 In this section I draw on the works of Veselý (2010 etc.) and on the sources referred by him.
58 Here one can apply the theory of agenda setting (see below).

the policy process – make it a policy problem" (Veselý 2014). When working with the concept of social problems, policy analysts simply have to take both approaches into account.

The following scheme illustrates the evolution of social problems and how they mature into the stage where their solution becomes a part of the public policy agenda.

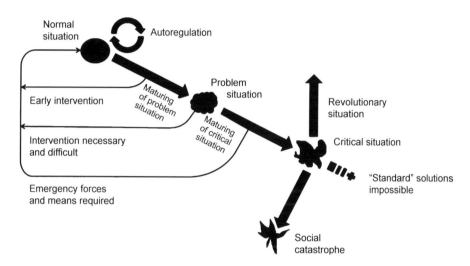

Figure A6.2 Maturing and solution of social problems
Source: Bestuzhev-Lada, 1984. Adapted.

In a "normal" situation, social actors themselves are able to find solutions to changing needs in a changing context. There is no need to define a policy problem and choose policies for solving it – and typically there is no room to do so either.

Maturing social problems are defined by Bestuzhev-Lada (1984) as areas of gross imbalance between what is desirable (necessary) and what really is, given that social conditions are changing as a result of some factors while existing institutions (established under previous conditions and driven by the force of social inertia) strive to solve newly emerged problems in old ways.[59] Tensions between real and desirable states are, however, nothing extraordinary. A maturing social problem only emerges when such tensions exceed socially acceptable limits, cause substantial difficulties in the vital activities of important social groups, or come to be recognized by large groups of people as important obstacles to their self-actualization. As we know, all this

---

59 A useful explanation of these situations is provided, among others, by the institutional theories mentioned in this book (historical institutionalism, discursive institutionalism, actor-centered institutionalism).

largely depends on how the situation is interpreted by the different social actors, the ways they view the world, their values, political ideologies, and programs.

When undertaken during the course of a maturing problem situation, early intervention tends to solve the problem while avoiding substantial social or economic damage. More mature problem situations can be solved through social reforms, which typically cannot do without changing the goals, organizational structures and roles of social institutions; in that process, some institutions may cease to exist and others may arise. If problem situations are not solved, critical situations arise. Ultimately, either the given social form quickly disintegrates and is replaced by an alternative arrangement, or a social catastrophe ensues in the form of a revolution, military conflict, a failed state, etc.

WHAT IS A POLICY PROBLEM?

At this point, social problems may, or may not, make a transition to **policy problems**: "A (public policy) problem is linked to a solution; a problem is a problem only if something can be done about it" (Wildavsky 1979). The perspective of Dunn (2003: 72) is similar: policy problems are "unrealized needs, values, or opportunities for improvement that may be pursued through public action." Dery (1984), too, views policy problems as problem situations or discrepancies – and more specifically, as solvable discrepancies or opportunities for improvement.

Table A6.1 Relationship between perceived urgency of a social problem and agenda setting in public policy

		As a social problem, the issue…	
		...is not perceived as urgent by the public	...is perceived as urgent by the public
As a policy problem, the issue…	**...is not on the agenda**	No problem, or only one burdening powerless groups	Growing social/political tension, may result in a crisis
	...is on the agenda	Low political legitimacy because tabled top-down; difficult to solve	The social problem can be solved by public policy if democratic institutions of interest representation are functional

Source: Author.

A social problem becomes a policy problem if one can do something about it using public policy instruments.

EXAMPLE:

As long as polio could not be treated, it continued to be an important health and social problem. However, it did not become a policy problem until an efficient vaccine was developed, making the disease preventable. Mandatory inoculation of all children in a given population became the main instrument of a newly introduced public policy (adapted from Birkland 2006: 71, and Veselý 2010: 79).

Landry (1995: 316) defines four conditions for the existence of a policy problem:
- a past, present or future occurrence is appreciated as negative by an actor or a group of actors (in other words: a social problem occurs);
- a preliminary judgement is made on the ability to act in order to solve the problem;
- a clear intention is expressed to do something about the problem and to commit resources in order to solve it;
- there is uncertainty as to the appropriate action and the ways of implementing it.

This opens up space for searching for the right policy instruments and policy measures to solve the social problem.

I have referred to the first stage of the policy cycle as problem delimitation and recognition. The effort to delimit policy problems is rather a cognitive exercise for analysts, while the quest to win recognition is primarily a politician's job (and in turn, one for the public). Although both tend to be connected in practice, just like the different engagements of actors involved, it is preferable to discuss one at a time.

PROBLEM DELIMITATION IN PUBLIC POLICY

To put things simply, a good problem definition is half the solution. However, the task of defining or delimiting policy problems is much more difficult than it might appear. This is what Polanyi (1958: 120) had in mind when he stated that "the recognition of a problem which can be solved and is worth solving is a discovery in its own right."

According to Veselý (2010: 65), the term **problem delimitation** refers to an "...intentional or unintentional process of naming, specifying and systemizing hitherto incoherent, diffuse or vaguely defined problem situations into statements about the existence of a problem that calls for a solution. Thus, problem delimitation (author's note: in public policy) is a process of creating and constructing problems based on objective evidence as well as subjective interpretations thereof."

In the process of problem delimitation, policy analysts also engage in problem structuring, mapping the different aspects of an area and the perspectives from which it can be seen. One strives to identify divergent or even conflicting views of the problem. As a result, one determines the nature of the problem and its level of complexity; sometimes even a structured set of problems is produced. Policy alternatives and instruments tend to be touched upon by the structuring exercise as well.[60] Actors often formulate solutions, rather than problems per se. Problem structuring is always highly subjective, and different sets of problems may be structured in different ways. That is why the exercise has to be done systematically and based upon empirical evidence (Veselý, Nekola 2007). The resulting problem structure reflects the ways reality is seen by different actors (Veselý 2007).

Some policy problems are easily structured, while others are strongly resistant to structuring efforts (see Table below).

Table A6.2 How structured are different policy problems?

		Consensus on relevant norms and values	
		Yes	**No**
Certainty about relevant knowledge	**Yes**	Well-structured problem (e.g., road maintenance)	Moderately structured problem (agreement on means of inquiry, disagreement on ends; e.g., abortion, euthanasia, migrant voting rights)
	No	Moderately structured problem (agreement on ends, disagreement on means of inquiry; e.g., traffic safety)	Unstructured problem (e.g., car mobility)

Source: Veselý, Nekola (2007) based on Hisschemöller & Hoppe 2001, adapted.

A policy analyst is faced with the challenge of formulating policy problems in the most brief, comprehensible and persuasive way possible, in order to spread the word about them among other actors, especially political leaders and the public (Veselý 2007; Veselý, Nekola 2007). This is one of the preconditions for the analyst's view to prevail in practice. Indeed, it is ultimately up to policy practice to decide whether that view will be accepted, at least taken into consideration, or outright ignored.

---

60 This creates the necessary conditions for moving on to the next stage of the policy cycle – decision-making.

PROBLEM RECOGNITION IN PUBLIC POLICY

There is no easy or direct avenue from awareness of a policy problem to recognition thereof. Politicians are often eager to focus on less urgent agendas, while neglecting or ignoring policy problems that are perceived as more important by the public, by experts, or both. How does that happen? The theory of agenda setting provides us with some tips on how to answer that question.

EXAMPLE THEORY: AGENDA SETTING

One of the conditions for an issue to move on to the policy agenda is that it is backed by the legal system and by corresponding structures of public administration. Also, influential actors have to exist to adopt the agenda[61] and the issue should have enough conflict potential. Perceptions of a policy problem and possible solutions are shaped not only by its urgency but also by the cognitive frames that influence the content and intensity of public discourse, and by the potentials and capabilities of actors involved. An agenda is actually set if all of the above is favorable (Theodoulou 1995: 88).

According to Kingdon (1984), agenda setting proceeds as follows: There is a set of public problems, existing constellations of political power, public policies in place, potential actors and policy options. Over years, policy ideas are developed and connected with one another in the context of epistemic and policy communities. Policy entrepreneurs such as elected representatives, public officials, lobbyists, academics or journalists strive to make those communities identify with such ideas and adopt them as their goals. A successful policy agenda also involves windows of opportunity that must be used by policy entrepreneurs before closing and that consist of random social and political factors that can be neither foreseen nor repeated (Birkland 2006).

Three subsystems are distinguished by the theory of agenda setting: the public, policymakers and the media. Agenda setting, too, takes place at three forums: the public, policy making and the media (Dearing, Rogers 1996). Public agendas are formed by public opinion. A policy agenda consists of what policymakers consider relevant, yet without necessarily being fully under their control (Majone 2006: 230). They have to take into consideration what public opinion says. Furthermore, both the public agenda and the policy agenda are strongly shaped by mass media content (Larson 1994). Connected by a dense network of bonds, the three subsystems may respond to the slightest movement in the network.

Once a policy problem is tabled, it becomes capable of being recognized. Recognition takes place in different arenas. It occurs routinely when political parties or governments adopt new strategies, programs or resolutions; when

---

61 The agenda may or may not be adopted by an existing advocacy coalition. See previous chapter for more on the Advocacy Coalition Framework.

new legislation is passed; when public institutions act; when budgetary measures are taken; or through a combination of any of these.[62]

The first stage of the public policy cycle (problem delimitation and recognition) is followed by the second stage – policy decision making. The next chapter deals with it in more detail.

REVIEW QUESTIONS

Why is the stage model of the policy cycle still used? What are its strengths and weaknesses?

Name the different stages of the policy process that are usually distinguished. What do they represent and how are they related to one another?

When does a social problem turn into a policy problem? Give an example.

Can a social problem be defined as a considerable gap between society's ideals and actual outcomes, or rather as something considered problematic by a significant number of people?

A social problem is becoming critical but no intervention is underway. What could be the reasons for this scenario – and what are its possible consequences?

Why is it often difficult to agree on what is a policy problem?

Which actors engage in problem delimitation and which ones in problem recognition?

What kind of relationship is there between problem structuring and policy alternatives, and why?

Under what conditions will a recognized and structured policy problem move on to the policy agenda?

What are the places where and the means by which policy problems are moved on to the agenda?

SOURCES

Ashby, W. R. 1956. *Introduction to Cybernetics.* London: Chapman and Hall.

Bertalanffy, von L. 1968. *General System Theory.* New York: George Braziller.

Bestuzhev-Lada, I. V. 1984. *Poiskovoe sotsiaľnoe prognozirovanie: perspektivnye problemy obshchestva: opyt sistematizatsii* [Exploratory social foresighting: future problems of society: systematization of experiences, in Russian]. Moskva: Nauka.

Birkland, T. A. 2006. "Agenda Setting in Public Policy." Pp. 63–78 in *Handbook of Public Policy Analysis*, edited by F. Fischer, G. J. Miller, M. S. Sidney. New York: Taylor and Francis Group.

---

62   Cf. Chapter A4 for more on policy arenas and Chapter A5 on policy instruments.

Dearing, J. W., E. M. Rogers. 1996. *Agenda-Setting.* Thousand Oaks, London, New Delhi: SAGE Publications.

Dery, D. 1984. *Problem Definition in Policy Analysis.* Lawrence, KS: University Press of Kansas.

Dror, Y. 1968. *Policy Making Reexamined.* San Francisco: Chandler Publishing Company.

Dror, Y. 1983. *Public Policy Re-examined.* New Brunswick and Oxford: Transaction Publishers.

Dunn, W. N. 1988. "Methods of the Second Type: Coping with the Wilderness of Conventional Policy Analysis." *Policy Studies Journal.* 7 (4): 720-737.

Dunn, W. N. 2004. *Public Policy Analysis: An Introduction.* 3rd ed. New Jersey: Pearson Prentice Hall.

Easton, D. 1953. *The Political System.* New York: Knopf.

Hisschemöller, R., R. Hoppe. 2001. "Coping with Intractable Controversies: The Case for Problem Structuring in Policy Design and Analysis." *Policy Studies Review Annual* 12: 47-52.

Hoppe, R. 2002. "Cultures of Public Policy Problems." *Journal of Comparative Policy Analysis* 4 (3): 305-326.

Howlett, M., M. Ramesh. 1995. *Studying Public Policy: Policy Cycles and Policy Subsystems.* Oxford: Oxford University Press.

Hupe, P. L., M. J. Hill. 2006. "The Three Action Levels of Governance: Re-Framing the Policy Process Beyond the Stages Model." Pp. 13-30 in B. G. Peters, J. Pierre. *Handbook of Public Policy.* London: SAGE Publications.

John, P. 1998. *Analyzing Public Policy.* London: Pinter.

Kerbo, H. R., J. W. Coleman. 2006. "Social Problems." Pp. 362-369 in *21st Century Sociology: A Reference Handbook,* edited by C. D. Bryant, D. L. Peck. Vol. 1: Traditional and Core Areas. CA, London: SAGE Publications.

Kingdon, J. 1984 (1995). *Agendas, Alternatives, and Public Policies.* Boston: Little, Brown.

Landry, M. 1995. "A Note of the Concept of 'Problem.'" *Organization Studies* 16 (2): 315-343.

Larson, C. U. 1994. *Persuasion.* 7th ed. Belmont, CA: Wadsworth.

Lasswell, H. D. 1956. *The Decision Process: Seven Categories of Functional Analysis.* College Park, MD: University of Maryland.

Lindblom, C. E. 1968. *The Policy-Making Process.* Englewood Cliffs (NJ): Prentice-Hall.

Lindblom, C. E., E. J. Woodhouse. 1993. *The Policy-Making Process.* Englewood Cliffs (NJ): Prentice-Hall.

MacCrimmon, K. R., R. N. Taylor. 1976. "Decision Making and Problem Solving." Pp. 1397-1453 in *Handbook of Industrial and Organizational Psychology*, edited by M. D. Dunnette. Chicago: Rand-McNally.

Majone, G. 2006. "Agenda Setting." Pp. 225-250 in *The Oxford Handbook of Public Policy,* edited by M. Moran, M. Rein, R. E. Goodin. Oxford: Oxford University Press.

Nakamura, R. 1987. "The Textbook Policy Process and Implementation Research." *Policy Studies Review* 7 (2): 142-154.

Polanyi, M. 1958. *Personal Knowledge. Towards a Post-Critical Philosophy.* London: Routledge.

Schlager, E. 1999. "A Comparison of Frameworks, Theories, and Models of Policy Process." Pp. 233–260 in *Theories of the Policy Process,* edited by P. A. Sabatier. Boulder: Westview Press.

Theodoulou, S. Z. 1995. "Making Public Policy." Pp. 86–96 in *Public Policy. Essential Readings,* by S. Z. Theodoulou, M. A. Cahn. Englewood Cliffs, NJ: Prentice Hall.

Veselý, A. 2005. *Metody a metodologie vymezení problému* [Methods and methodology of problem delimitation, in Czech]. Studie CESES, vol. 5. Prague: CESES FSV UK.

Veselý, A. 2010. *Vymezení a strukturace problému ve veřejné politice* [Problem Delimitation and Structuring in Public Policy, in Czech]. Prague: Karolinum.

Veselý, A. 2014. *Vymezení veřejně politických problémů. Učební text k veřejné politice* [Delimitation of Public Policy Issues. Lecture Notes on Public Policy, in Czech]. Prague: Univerzita Karlova. Unpublished manuscript.

Veselý, A., M. Nekola (eds.). 2007. *Analýza a tvorba veřejných politik: přístupy, metody a praxe* [Policy Analysis and Design: Approaches, Methods and Practices, in Czech]. Prague: Sociologické nakladatelství (SLON).

Wildavsky, A. 1979. *Speaking Truth to Power: The Art and Craft of Policy Analysis.* Boston: Little, Brown and Co.

Winkler, J. 2007. *Teorie rozhodování a dynamika sociální politiky* [Theory of Decision Making and the Dynamics of Social Policy, in Czech]. Brno: Masarykova univerzita.

Recommended sources for the stage model of the policy cycle:

Dror, Y. 1968. *Policy Making Reexamined.* San Francisco: Chandler Publishing Company.

Dror, Y. 1983. *Public Policy Re-examined.* New Brunswick and Oxford: Transaction Publishers.

Howlett, M., M. Ramesh. 1995. *Studying Public Policy: Policy Cycles and Policy Subsystems.* Oxford: Oxford University Press.

Hupe, P. L., M. J. Hill. 2006. "The Three Action Levels of Governance: Re-Framing the Policy Process Beyond the Stages Model." Pp. 13–30 in *Handbook of Public Policy,* by B. G. Peters, J. Pierre. London: SAGE Publications.

John, P. 1998. *Analyzing Public Policy.* London: Pinter.

Lasswell, H. D. 1956. *The Decision Process: Seven Categories of Functional Analysis.* College Park, MD: University of Maryland.

Lindblom, C. E. 1968. *The Policy-Making Process.* Englewood Cliffs (NJ): Prentice-Hall.

Lindblom, C. E., E. J. Woodhouse. 1993. *The Policy-Making Process.* Englewood Cliffs (NJ): Prentice-Hall.

Nakamura, R. 1987. "The Textbook Policy Process and Implementation Research." *Policy Studies Review* 7 (2): 142–154.

Schlager, E. 1999. "A Comparison of Frameworks, Theories, and Models of Policy Process." Pp. 233–260 in *Theories of the Policy Process,* edited by P. A. Sabatier. Boulder: Westview Press.

Recommended sources for the theory of agenda setting:

Birkland, T. A. 2006. "Agenda Setting in Public Policy." Pp. 63–78 in *Handbook of Public Policy Analysis*, edited by F. Fischer, G. J. Miller, M. S. Sidney. New York: Taylor and Francis Group.

Dearing, J. W., E. M. Rogers. 1996. *Agenda-Setting*. Thousand Oaks, London, New Delhi: SAGE Publications.

Kingdon, J. 1984 (1995). *Agendas, Alternatives, and Public Policies*. Boston: Little, Brown.

Maher, T. M. 2003. "Framing: An Emerging Paradigm or a Phase of Agenda Setting?" Pp. 83–94 in *Framing Public Life. Perspectives on Media and Our Understanding of the Social World*, edited by S. D. Reese, O. H. Gandy, A. E. Grant. Mahwah, New Jersey: Lawrence Erlbaum Associates.

Majone, G. 2006. "Agenda Setting." Pp. 225–250 in *The Oxford Handbook of Public Policy*, edited by M. Moran, M. Rein, R. E. Goodin. Oxford: Oxford University Press.

McCombs, M. E. 2004. *Setting the Agenda. The Mass Media and Public Opinion*. Cambridge: Polity Press.

Theodoulou, S. Z. 1995. "Making Public Policy." Pp. 86–96 in *Public Policy. Essential Readings*, by S. Z. Theodoulou, M. A. Cahn. Englewood Cliffs, NJ: Prentice Hall.

/**A7**/
<u>Policy Formulation, Decisionmaking</u>

People make choices throughout their lives, all the time – yet they do not always think in the process. Public policy is by no means an exception. One might even say that most of our personal decisions – as well as most policy decisions – are made on a routine basis, based on personal habits or institutional customs and framed by social conventions or stereotypes.

From time to time, both people as individuals and society as a whole arrive at a crossroads. That is where questions abound: Do we know where we are going? Do we know which way is best? Do we know what kind of obstacles might arise on the way? Do we know how much time and energy we will have to expend? Are we going to walk alone, or have company? And what can we expect when we arrive?

Cybernetics, management theory, game theory or administrative science are some of the scientific disciplines that specialize on the study of decision-making processes. Management theory also provides us with insights into decision-making at the level of organizational practice. In the following, I am primarily going to apply such perspectives that are helpful in solving policy problems.

DECISION-MAKING: RATIONALIST VERSUS INCREMENTALIST MODELS

Before discussing the basic explanations of the decision-making process involved in public policy formulation, I am going to dwell on a crucial choice – one between Lindblom's (1977) two competing models of public policy.

Model 1: Society can be governed by reason. This model builds on the optimistic assumption that a person's reason is a powerful skill. (It dates back to the Enlightenment's glorification of rationality and the Marxist vision of grasping at and using the motivational forces of social development.) The model is driven by the intellect of social elites, by analysis, by "science." Social conflict is suppressed. The fundamental question is: "What is best for society?" Enlightened government is the main underlying regulator.

Model 2: Limited knowledge causes incremental decision-making. This model is based on two concepts: **bounded rationality** and policy process **incrementalism**. Herbert Simon, who coined the former concept, holds that the rationality of decision-making is limited by available information, choice in the ways of thinking, and time. These limitations may have crucial effects on the outcome of the decision-making process. Another founding father of our discipline, Charles Lindblom, added the concept of **disjointed incrementalism** as the pluralistic interplay of actors' interests that takes place in mutual interactions. Negotiation between policy makers only begins when a policy problem occurs. Decision-making is based on actors' preferences and shaped by the social interactions between them. As a result, actors **"muddle through"**: aware of the inaccessibility of perfect knowledge about the problem, they advance their objectives through piecemeal measures, not major changes. Decision-making is characterized by extreme pluralism and decentralization. The diversity of individuals and groups is viewed positively. The market is the primary regulator, possibly (but not necessarily) complemented by democratic institutions of interest representation. The following table shows more details.

Table A7.1 Types of politico-economic systems

Political system → Economic system ↓	Democratic	Authoritarian
Market-oriented	Democratic capitalism (Model 2)	Countries with working markets but without guaranteed human/civic rights
Centrally planned	-----	Socialist countries (Model 1)

Source: Lindblom (1977: 161), adapted.

Public policy could never be a scientific discipline if it did not strive to bolster a rational effort to find the best solutions. Yet at the same time, it would (rightfully) be accused of escaping reality if it pretended that there are no limits to scientific knowledge, no limits beyond which we simply no longer know.

The method of **mixed scanning** is informed by the critique of the above approaches as one-sided – and combines both together (Etzioni 1967, Vickers 1965). "The incrementalist and rationalist approaches are complementary alternatives that help us understand the complex and multi-faceted character of the decision-making process" (Malíková 2003: 77).

POSSIBILITIES OF POLICY CHANGE

In short, there is no need to be either too optimistic or crushingly skeptical. History provides us with many examples of how enlightened reason (Model 1) was applied, for better or worse.

Positive examples: gradual extension of the human rights guaranteed by society, abolition of slavery, abolition of serfdom, universal suffrage, 8-hour workday, US President Roosevelt's New Deal as a response to the 1930's Great Depression, European Community (established 1957).
Negative examples: communism in cultural symbiosis with Tsarist autocracy: political prosecutions, failing five-year plans of economic development.

In the early 1990s, communism was defeated and Model 2, which relies primarily on the mechanisms of a market economy, became so predominant that Fukuyama (1992) was talking about an "end of history." He assumed that history would give no more chances for any other societal arrangement to survive. The subsequent commotion that eventually grew into the global financial crisis of the early 21st century brought Fukuyama (2004) to revise his position and contemplate government as a regulator of public affairs.

Let us now put emotions aside and take a look at real-world decision-making situations through the lens of both models, and more specifically the ways they depend on the level of available knowledge. See Table A7.2.

Table A7.2 Relationship between level of knowledge and decision-making models

Possibilities of policy change		Decision-making model	
		Incremental	Nonincremental
Knowledge of problem and alternative solutions	High	Rational decisionmaking is possible with regard to clear policy problems	Fundamental change possible. Low risk of failure.
	Insufficient	Most real-world problems	Fundamental change possible. High risk of failure.

Source: Hayes (2001), adapted.

STRUCTURE OF DECISION-MAKING

As we know, policy formulation and decision-making depend on problem delimitation (the ways we define one or more social problems). This is followed by a formulation of policy options for solving the problem(s).[63] "Policy formulation typically results from a combination of creative thinking, available evidence, available policy instruments and the experiences we and other people have" (Drhová, Veselý 2007: 256). Alternatively, one can anticipate the effects of different policy options and evaluate them in advance – often based on pre-defined criteria[64] – and finally choose the best option accordingly.

This notion alone is, however, a highly abstract one. Other important determinants include the social and situational context in which decision-making takes place, the level of available knowledge about the subject matter, the rules governing actors' responsibilities and behaviors, the existing composition of actors, the value conflicts between them, their negotiation styles, and their choice of instruments and implementation methods. When assessing the different policy options, one cannot merely consider whether or not they will lead to the defined goals and satisfy the defined public interest. Attention must also be paid to the political and practical feasibility of policy options (Majone 1975, 1989; Dror 1969).

---

63   See previous chapter. There is rarely just one solution available. However, decision-makers may either know nothing about other alternatives or reject them outright.
64   See detailed discussion in Chapter A9.

DECISION-MAKING IN POLICY SUBSYSTEMS

Decision-making tends to be limited to actors who are motivated to engage in solving the policy problem – and at the same time have access to a solution. On the one hand, the stage of problem delimitation is accessible to many other types of actors. On the other hand, actors who participate in decision-making tend to operate in a given **policy subsystem**.

EXAMPLE:

In the United States, such a policy subsystem is exemplified by the decision-making about health care reform. The main roles were played by the President, Congress and responsible committees thereof – and also by the American Medical Association, which had been blocking all attempts to adopt a universal health care system for all (such that exists in all other developed countries of the world). The reason was simple: the country's liberal health care system allowed medical professionals to maximize their profits. Eventually, after a major effort and a number of compromise deals, President Obama's reform was pushed through and became effective on January 1, 2014.

The effects of policy subsystems on decision-making have been elaborated in a number of studies (e.g., Kingdon 1984, Howlett 2002). According to Sabatier, such subsystems are important contributing or limiting factors of policy change. Marsh and Rhodes (1992) and Zahariadis and Allen (1995) talk about policy subsystems' cohesion and exclusivity as important conditions shaping the tendencies for innovation. The structure of a subsystem is fundamental: steady *status quo* maintenance suggests that the policy process has been driven by the same actors for a very long time. Scholars have studied policy subsystems' level of openness to new actors and new solutions (Howlett, Ramesh 2009).

Actors' ability to make a credible mutual "commitment" to certain acceptable forms of behavior in future plays a highly important role in the decision-making processes. This is because "habits, addictions, traditions, and other preferences that are directly contingent on past choices partly control, and hence commit, future behavior in predictable ways. Indeed, habits and the like may be very good substitutes for long-term contracts and other explicit commitment mechanisms" (Becker 1996). This, however, is neither easily done nor easily predicted. Therefore, the level of trust between decision-makers is of extreme (or even fundamental) importance here.

EXAMPLE DECISION-MAKING MODEL: PRISONER'S DILEMMA

The prisoner's dilemma decision-making model assumes a game between two gang members who are in custody, facing criminal charges. Each is given two options: either to betray the other by testifying that the other committed the crime, or to remain silent – and each prisoner must make his choice separately, without knowing the other's choice. The rules of the game are as follows: If both remain silent, both of them will only serve a lesser charge. If they betray each other, each of them will serve an equal part of the sentence. However, if one remains silent but the other betrays him, the latter will be set free and the former will serve the maximum sentence.

This dilemma exemplifies a way of analyzing and viewing different kinds of interactions between actors making choices, and especially the effects of cooperative versus non-cooperative behavior (Axelrod 1984, 1997).

EXAMPLE: ONE OF THE CAUSES OF THE "CHINESE ECONOMIC MIRACLE"

Fukuyama (1995) brought attention to the fact that small family businesses in China enjoy a low level of transaction costs because they conduct most of their internal transactions informally and rely on trust between family members. This gives them a competitive advantage over businesses from other cultures.

A policy decision typically includes the following:
- description of the goal(s) to be attained;
- definition of the target population;
- allocation of responsibility for implementation: who, what, when, how, with what resources and limitations;
- structure of implementation (choice of instruments[65] and ways of ensuring that the policy becomes reality);[66]
- justification of necessity.

Over the past couple of years, special methods to evaluate the impacts of policies have been applied increasingly (but not always).[67]

All decisions taken by public authorities must have a legal basis and their provisions must be in conformity with the law. A motion to adopt a new law or regulation is a kind of policy decision, too, insofar as it changes the rules of behavior for the actors involved. Any doubt that arises may be brought to an administrative court.

---

65 Cf. Chapter A5.
66 Cf. Chapter A8.
67 Cf. Chapter A9.

DECISION MAKERS

Most public policy decisions in democratic countries are taken by three types of actors: **politicians** (expected to represent people's diverse interests), **officials**, and **experts**. In addition, the decision-making process also involves public and social services professionals, local civic elites, interest group representatives, lobbyists (see below), or other actors.[68]

According to Veselý's interpretation of Knoepfel et al. (2007: 40), the following typology of actors has proven useful in policy analysis and policy design at the level of specific public programs:

- **end beneficiaries** facing some negative social conditions that are to be remedied;
- **target groups** – individuals and organizations whose behavior must be changed to solve the end beneficiaries' problems;
- **third-party groups** – actors who are affected by the policy indirectly, whether positively or negatively.

Politicians master the technology of power. They are expected to skillfully and effectively advocate and assert the interests of their voters through the programs of the parties they represent, within the limits of applicable law. In this way, their political competition and cooperation with other politicians may also benefit the pursuit of *the public interest*.[69] Politicians have the most say in *agenda setting*. In addition to the skills of ordinary politicians, **statesmen and stateswomen** are also able to express "the challenges of our time" (which may or may not be in conformity with *the public interest*) and use their leadership qualities to persuade a critical number of actors and members of the general public.

Officials are expected to master the technicalities and procedures of preparing and passing decisions, as well as subsequent policy implementation (for example, in the process of preparing draft laws or budget proposals). In actuality, they actively engage in and influence those processes.

Experts typically possess in-depth knowledge of the nature of social problems and of the ways of solving them through policy instruments. While their public appearances are rare, they exert substantial influence on the final shape of policy solutions chosen,[70] whether by defining the policy options, by assessing their possible impacts or in the process of deciding between the options.[71]

---

68 Cf. Chapter A4.
69 The example of Members of Parliament in Chapter A2 shows that this is not always the case.
70 It is precisely at the stage of decision-making that policy analysts and think-tanks can put their expertise to use (and indeed, they have been doing so increasingly in recent years). Cf. Chapter A4.
71 Chapter A10 contains a more in-depth discussion of how to inquire about and understand public policy.

Whereas experts contribute available evidence to the decision-making process, politicians shape it by bringing in their priorities. Evidence can be solid or poor, while the goals of different politicians can be shared or extremely conflicting. All of this is ultimately reflected in the decision-making process.

Table A7.3 Decision-making situations

Relationship between level of consensus on knowledge and goals in decision-making		Goals	
		Conflicted	**Shared**
Nature of knowledge	**Conflicted or contested**	Ordinary incremental decision-making (Model 2 predominates)	Problem: Insufficient knowledge basis (Model 2 predominates)
	Consensual	Problem: Value conflict (Model 2 predominates)	Conditions for rational decision-making (Model 1 predominates)

Source: Hayes (2001), adapted.

From time to time, **citizens** attend elections to choose their political representatives. Those who do not find such participation satisfactory may get involved in civil society organizations, take part in public discourse, or use direct forms of engagement (see Table).

Table A7.4 Forms of democratic representation of interests

Type of democracy	**Instruments of interests' representation**
Representative democracy	Elections
Participative democracy	Advocacy NGOs
Corporative democracy	Tripartism
Direct democracy	Plebiscite, referendum, petition
Deliberative democracy	Public discourse, public hearing

Source: Author.

An overwhelming majority of decision-making situations are characterized by an inequality between actors. Some actors may become so privileged that decisions in a given area cannot even be taken without their consent.

An application of game theory to political behavior, the theory of veto players focuses on actors who are capable of preventing decisions from being taken. "Veto players are individual or collective actors whose agreement is necessary for a change of the status quo. From the definition follows that a change in the status quo requires a unanimous decision of all veto players" (Tsebelis 2002: 36). The more veto players there are in the game and the smaller their ideological differences, the higher the political stability and the less likely any decision is taken (Ibid: 40).

This theory helps us better understand situations where too many veto players interact, referred to by Scharpf (1988) as "joint decision traps." For example, it took eight years before EU member states agreed on the Union's current fundamental document, the Lisbon Treaty. Also, government coalitions find it difficult to reach some decisions. This is why many countries have instituted an electoral threshold for political parties to enter their representative assemblies.

It is almost impossible to overcome a conflict of ideas and satisfy all actors. Some decisions can only be taken as an **"overlapping consensus"** – a common ground approved by all main religious, philosophical or moral teachings that are passed from generation to generation in a given society (Rawls 1987, 1989). The goal is not to help one of the alternatives to prevail but to find a solution that ends all conflicts (Richardson, Kimber 1978). As noted by Kissinger (1957: 145), "...an international settlement which is accepted and not imposed will always appear somewhat unjust to any one of its components. Paradoxically, the generality of this dissatisfaction is a condition of stability."

The theory of multiple streams is another way of understanding the processes of decision-making in public policy.

EXAMPLE THEORY: MULTIPLE STREAMS [72]

This theory identifies a "problem stream" (What is going on?), a "policy stream" (What can we do about it?) and a "politics stream" (What can we get support for?) with "policy entrepreneurs" trying to find "windows of opportunity" to make links between the streams and so make policy change possible (Colebatch 1998, Novotný 2013).

The **problem stream** corresponds with the process of identifying social problems and related public policy problems, as described in the previous chapter.

The **politics stream** refers to the framework of political discourse in which public policies are formulated. It mainly involves political parties or coalitions that compete with

---

72   J. Kingdon and N. Zahariadis are the main authors who developed this theory.

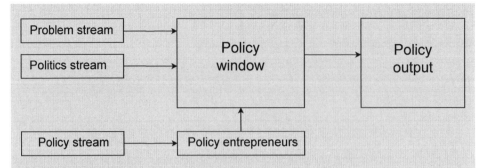

Figure A7.1 The theory of multiple streams
Source: Zahariadis (2007: 71), adapted by Novotný (2013) and the author.

one another for a chance to govern and thus directly shape the process of policy deci-sion-making. The different political parties build on certain ideological beliefs that make them more open to certain ideas. A role in this stream is also played by the evolving climate of public opinion, including any support or opposition expressed by interest groups. The exchange of office holders, with politicians and administrators coming and going, is also relevant (Zahariadis 2007: 69).

The **policy stream** is similar to what I referred to above as policy subsystems. The theory distinguishes between two parts of this stream: ideas and actors' networks. Ideas are formulated in actors' networks (Weir 1992: 207). Ideas are methods to shape the situation with given knowledge of the causes and effects; which ones will eventually prevail depends on their availability, technical feasibility, and value acceptability. An actors' network is characterized by its institutional configuration and level of integration.

The theory assumes that while the three streams are interrelated and together form the complex of policy making, they are basically independent of one another and each governed by its own rules. The relations between them are critically shaped by windows of opportunity and policy entrepreneurs.

The **policy windows of opportunity** open up at instances of confluence of all three streams. They are usually not available for a long time. Some may be predictable (e.g., the annual budgeting process) but most of them are unpredictable (e.g., when a corruption scandal or an earthquake breaks out). They provide a chance to make policy decisions during constellations when all three streams are inclined positively.

Whereas windows of opportunity open when structural circumstances are favorable for bringing the streams together, the actual success of such endeavor depends on the actions of **policy entrepreneurs,** who strive to connect the three streams and "are willing to invest … time, energy, reputation, money" to promote a policy change in antic-ipation of desirable effects (Kingdon 1995: 179). Successful policy entrepreneurs tend to have better access to centers of power (decision makers), can avail themselves of better resources, and are even willing to use manipulation to attain their goal – to make a connec-tion between the three streams (Zahariadis 2007: 74 and 77–78).

WHO IS AFFECTED BY DECISIONS?

All policy decisions change people's living conditions. Their impacts are differentiated, and public policy rarely manages to help many and harm no one. Therefore, before politicians decide which changes to support, they take more than just public benefits into consideration: "Given the fact that public policies have increasingly been used for political and ideological purposes rather than to find the best solution to a collective problem, policy analysts are well advised to study carefully the design elements and analyze them not simply in terms of their rationality, but also in terms of who gets what, who wins and who loses, whose image is emboldened and who is denigrated, and what are the messages being sent to the target populations and the broader public" (Schneider 2013: 227).

Compared to the actors directly involved in policy decision-making, those who cannot or do not want to take part in that decision-making find it more difficult to assert their interests.

EXAMPLES:

Children, single mothers, people with mental illness, animals, and plants.

This is especially apparent where the criterion of sustainability of life is brought forward – when one has to respect even the interests of generations yet unborn. Such cases give extra relevance to the cognitive preconditions of strategic decision-making in the perspective of years and decades, not months.

STRATEGIC DECISION-MAKING

The study of possible futures, along with systematic analytical and **foresighting activities,** are the preconditions of strategic decision-making. A report by the Club of Rome (Dror 2003) emphasizes how necessary such an approach is in the process of preparing global-level policy decisions, whereas Potůček et al. (2009) discuss the capacities of strategic governance in the Czech Republic.

EXAMPLE: HOW TO DECIDE STRATEGICALLY

In order to decide with due regard to the longer-run consequences of our decisions, one starts by defining social and policy problems, and proceeds to:
- analyze and anticipate relevant internal and external factors;

- discuss and define long-term objectives;
- discuss and define the means to attain them;
- agree on the responsibilities of participating actors;
- formulate policy options and choose one based on defined criteria; and
- plan the steps towards implementing the policy option (an implementation schedule).

Of course, those of us already born are, too, concerned with strategic decision-making insofar as it affects our lives in the following decades – especially when it comes to our health, education or pension provision.

The second stage of the public policy cycle (policy decision-making) is followed by the third stage – policy implementation. The next chapter deals with it in more detail.

REVIEW QUESTIONS

Explain why even the best-prepared public policy may fail in the end.

Explain the relationship between imperfect knowledge and disjointed incremental decision-making.

Outline the argument that the model of society governed by reason cannot be fully implemented because it is based on unrealistic assumptions.

What is a policy subsystem? Define its role in the decision-making process.

What are the typical contents of a policy proposal and why?

Characterize the major types of decision makers and their roles.

What are the typical democratic institutions of interest representation?

Present the theory of veto players by applying it to at least two examples.

Structure the theory of multiple streams, including the links between its elements.

What is strategic decision-making, why is it necessary, and at what stages is it practiced?

SOURCES

Axelrod, R. M. 1984. *The Evolution of Cooperation.* New York: Basic Books.

Axelrod, R. M. 1997. *The Complexity of Cooperation: Agent-based Model of Competition and Collaboration.* Princeton: Princeton University Press.

Becker, G. 1996. *Accounting for tastes.* Cambridge: Harvard University Press.

Colebatch, H. K. 1998. *Policy.* Minneapolis: University of Minnesota Press.

Drhová, Z., A. Veselý. 2007. "Identifikace variant řešení veřejně politických problémů" [Identifying alternative solutions to policy problems, in Czech]. Pp. 253–272 in *Analýza a tvorba veřejných politik. Přístupy, metody a praxe* [Policy Analysis and Design:

Approaches, Methods and Practices, in Czech], edited by A. Veselý, M. Nekola. Prague: Sociologické nakladatelství (SLON).

Dror, Y. 1969. "The Prediction of Political Feasibility." *Futures* 1 (June): 282–8.

Dror, Y. 2003. *Capacity to Govern*. London: Frank Cass.

Etzioni, A. 1967. "Mixed-Scanning: a 'Third' Approach to Decision-Making." *Public Administration Review* 27 (5): 385–392.

Fukuyama, F. 1995. *Trust: The Social Virtues and the Creation of Prosperity*. New York: Free Press.

Fukuyama, F. 1992. *The End of History and the Last Man*. New York: Free Press.

Fukuyama, F. 2004. *State-Building, Governance and World order in the 21st Century*. Ithaca: Cornell University Press.

Hayes, M. T. 2001. *The Limits of Policy Change: Incrementalism, World View, and the Rule of Law*. Washington: Georgetown University Press.

Howlett, M. 2002. "Do Networks Matter? Linking Policy Network Structure to Policy Outcomes: Evidence From Four Canadian Policy Sectors, 1990–2000." *Canadian Journal of Political Science* 35 (2): 235–67.

Howlett, M., M. Ramesh. 1995. *Studying Public Policy: Policy Cycles and Policy Subsystems*. Oxford: Oxford University Press.

Kingdon, J. 1984 (1995). *Agendas, Alternatives, and Public Policies*. Boston: Little, Brown.

Kissinger, H. A. 1957. A World Restored: *Metternich, Castlereagh and the Problems of Peace*, 1812–22. London: Weidenfeld and Nicolson.

Knoepfel, P., C. Larrue, F. Valone, M. Hill. 2007. *Public Policy Analysis*. Bristol: Policy Press.

Lindblom, C. E. 1977. *Politics and Markets*. New York: Basic Books.

Majone, G. 1975. "On the Notion of Political Feasibility." *European Journal of Political Research* 3 (September): 259–74.

Majone, G. 1989. *Evidence, Argument, and Persuasion in the Policy Process*. New Haven, CT: Yale University Press.

Malíková, L. 2003. *Verejná politika. Aktéri a procesy* [Public Policy: Actors and Processes, in Slovak]. Bratislava: Univerzita Komenského.

Marsh, D., R. A. W. Rhodes (eds.). 1992. *Policy Networks in British Government*. Oxford: Claredon Press.

Novotný, V. 2013. *Teorie veřejně politického procesu (výčet a výklad)* [Theories of Public Policy Process: Enumeration and Interpretation, in Czech]. Prague. Unpublished manuscript.

Potůček, M. et al. 2009. *Strategic Governance and the Czech Republic*. Prague: Karolinum.

Rawls, J. 1987. The Idea of an Overlapping Consensus." *Oxford Journal of Legal Studies* 7 (1): 1–25.

Rawls, J. 1989. "The Domain of the Political and Overlapping Consensus." *New York University Law Review* 64: 233–55.

Richardson, J., R. H. Kimber. 1978. "Lobbying, Administrative Reform and Policy Styles: The Case of Land Drainage." *Political Studies* 26 (1): 47–64.

Scharpf, F. W. 1988. "The Joint Decision Trap: Lessons from German Federalism and European Integration." *Public Administration* 66 (2): 239–78.

Schneider, A. 2013. "Policy Design and Transfer." Pp. 217–228 in *Routledge Handbook of Public Policy*, edited by J. E. Araral, S. Fritzen, M. Howlett, M. Ramesh, Xun Wu. New York: Routledge.

Tsebelis, G. 2002. *Veto Players: How Political Institutions Work*. Princeton: Princeton University Press.

Vickers, G. 1965. *The Art of Judgement*. London: Chapman and Hall.

Weir, M. 1992. "Ideas and the Politics of Bounded Innovation." Pp. 188–211 in *Structuring Politics*, edited by S. Steinmo, K. Thelen, F. Longstreth, F. Cambridge: Cambridge University Press.

Zahariadis, N. 2007. "The Multiple Streams Framework: Structure, Limitations, Prospects." Pp. 65–92 in *Theories of the Policy Process*, edited by P. Sabatier. 2nd ed. Boulder: Westview Press.

Zahariadis, N., Ch. S. Allen. 1995. "Ideas, Networks and Policy Streams: Privatization in Britain and Germany." *Policy Studies Review* 14 (1/2): 71–98.

Recommended sources for the theory of veto players:

Andrews, J. T., G. R. Montinola. 2004. "Veto Players and the Rule of Law in Emerging Democracies." *Comparative Political Studies* 37 (1): 55–87.

Scharpf, F. W. 1988. "The Joint Decision Trap: Lessons from German Federalism and European Integration." *Public Administration* 66: 239–78.

Tsebelis, G. 2000. "Veto Players and Institutional Analysis." *Governance* 13 (4): 441–474.

Tsebelis, G. 2002. *Veto Players: How Political Institutions Work*. Princeton: Princeton University Press.

Recommended sources for the theory of multiple streams:

Colebatch, H. K. 1998. *Policy*. Minneapolis: University of Minnesota Press.

Kingdon, J. 1984 (1995). *Agendas, Alternatives, and Public Policies*. Boston: Little, Brown.

Zahariadis, N. 1999. "Ambiguity, Time, and Multiple Streams." Pp. 73–93 in *Theories of the Policy Process*, edited by P. Sabatier. Boulder: Westview Press.

Zahariadis, N. 2003. *Ambiguity and Choice in Public Policy: Political Manipulation in Democratic Societies*. Washington: Georgetown University Press.

Zahariadis, N. 2007. "The Multiple Streams Framework: Structure, Limitations, Prospects." Pp. 65–92 in *Theories of the Policy Process*, edited by P. Sabatier. 2nd ed. Boulder: Westview Press.

/**A8**/
Policy Implementation

> *"It is hard enough to design public policies and programs that look good on paper. It is harder still to formulate them in words and slogans that resonate pleasingly in the ears of political leaders and the constituencies to which they are responsible. And it is excruciatingly hard to implement them in a way that pleases anyone at all, including the supposed beneficiaries or clients."*
> *Bardach (1977: 3)*

In public policy, implementation covers all that is related, in one way or another, to the realization of a policy or program – all that arises out of the previous stages of the policy process, from problem delimitation and recognition to decision-making (including the choice of the means and instruments of bringing the policy to life). Systematic study of policy implementation was pioneered by Pressman and Wildavsky (1984).

THEORETICAL MODELS OF IMPLEMENTATION

Scholarly literature provides us with four main theoretical models of implementation: the authoritative model, the participative model, the model of advocacy coalitions, and the cultural change model.

The **authoritative model** emphasizes a top-down flow of signals and information in a hierarchical structure. It applies instruments such as directive management, planning, inspection and audit, hierarchy, and authority. Government is the principal regulator.

The model relies on the assumption that a decision maker defines a task and an implementer subsequently carries it out in its entirety; yet this is rarely the case. Institutional economics and its **principal-agent theory** explains why: the agent of implementation (here a bureaucratic apparatus or individual officials) is supposed to pursue the interests of the principal (here politicians), yet a problem arises whenever there is a conflict of interest between principal and agent. It is not the principal but the agent who has resources such as time, information and skills. The principal cannot fully check the agent's compliance with his/her orders and interests. In such cases, according to this theory, the agent will deviate from the pursuit of the principal's interests, instead pursuing his value orientation and/or maximizing his own benefit, appropriating some of the utilities of the goods for which the principal made him responsible (Mlčoch 1996, Dowding 2011).[73]

Another way of looking at the authoritative model is to study the behavior of end implementers at sites of interaction between service providers and citizens (**street-level bureaucracy,** Lipsky 1980). The discretion that service providers enjoy in their direct contact with users is high, and their interests, attitudes, and responsibilities are among the key determinants of how a policy is ultimately implemented – no matter how "those on top" meant it or designed it.

The **participative model** of implementation emphasizes a bottom-up flow of signals and information, drawing attention to indirect implementation instruments such as spontaneity, coordination, learning, adaptation, negotiation, cooperation, and trust. It leans more towards the concept of participatory democracy. Nevertheless, this model, too, assumes cooperative relations between actors at different levels of governance.[74]

The **model of advocacy coalitions** postulates a plurality of policy implementation actors who not only communicate, negotiate and compromise with one another, but also share a set of values and strive to fulfill shared goals (Sabatier 1986). It was in this context that Bardach (1977: 250) coined the term **implementation coalitions.** In this model (also called Advocacy Coalition

---

73 The principal-agent theory will be outlined at the end of this chapter in more detail.
74 Cf. Chapter A3.

Framework, ACF), signals and information flow in both directions, yet the model emphasizes how actors form diverse coalitions to facilitate policy formulation and further their interests.

The **continuous learning process model** (sometimes referred to as "cultural change model") assumes that policy implementers gradually optimize the structure of goals and implementation methods in order to reach the best solutions (often through trial and error, specific experimenting or on-the-go learning) (Malinowski 1960, Browne, Wildavsky 1984). Implementation is viewed as an evolutionary process insofar as goals are continuously redefined, instruments modified, and one works with a number of goals and instruments inherited from the past (Pressman, Wildavsky 1984). This model integrates implementation as a stage of the policy cycle. Generally speaking, it operates at the level of a cultural-historical analysis of the processes of policy implementation.

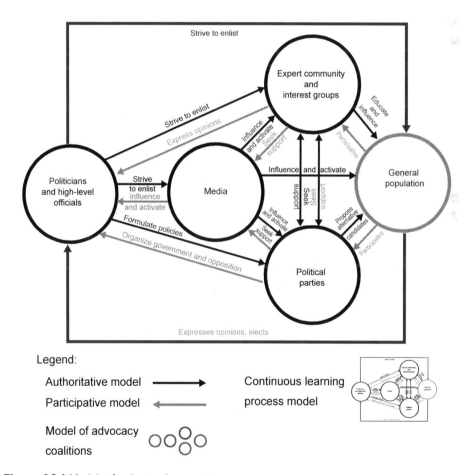

Figure A8.1 Models of policy implementation
Source: Author.

CRITICAL FACTORS OF IMPLEMENTATION

The process of policy implementation not only depends on the adequacy of the actual content of a policy design, but is also determined by the following critical factors:

1. **Competences of the implementer** who coordinates and facilitates the implementation process: Top-level politicians entrust implementation to individuals whom they trust – mostly bureaucrats.[75] Implementers should be recruited among actors who are committed to the intended policy and willing to sacrifice time, energy and resources for successful implementation (Weimer and Vining 2005: 278). An implementer's attitudes may have a strong positive influence on the attitudes of the general public (and more specifically the target groups). Bardach (1977: 273–278) characterizes the role of "fixers" who facilitate any communication between actors needed for successful policy implementation. They can serve as the implementer's "ears and eyes," supplying him/her with sufficient information about developments in the field.

2. **Degree of shared values among stakeholders**: in order to tell how likely a policy is to successfully attain its goals, one needs to understand the motivational and political background of not only implementers but all other stakeholders as well. The odds are better when their values are in concert, and worse when there are value contradictions. Therefore, an implementer should have sufficient information from the previous stages of the policy process to estimate how those affected by the policy might react.[76] Pressman and Wildavsky (1984) showed that even slight differences between actors' perspectives, priorities and time horizons may cause delay, distortion or even outright failure of implementation.[77]

3. **Coordination between the necessary elements of policy implementation**: Bardach (1977) understands implementation as putting together all the important pieces of an implementation "machine" (people and their qualifications, financial, material, and immaterial resources). The more numerous such elements and actors there are, the higher the risk of implementation difficulties. A poor choice of instruments may cause policy failure as well. Thus, the implementation process can also be viewed as an exercise in **effective collective action**. It is precisely its growing complexity that makes implementation more difficult.

---

75 See also the section on principal-agent theory below.
76 This is why it is both proven and recommended practice to involve relevant stakeholders as early as in the previous stages of the policy process, and especially policy formulation and decision-making.
77 Cf. Chapter A2.

Bardach (1977: 36) and Sabatier & Mazmanian (1980) discuss the conditions of effective implementation. The conclusions from both sources can be generalized into the following list of determinants of implementation success:

- Ensure steady political support, political legitimacy and backing by strong interest groups.
- Resist attempts by policy opponents to influence or destroy the implementation process.
- Set a legally binding structure for the implementation process, assign administrative responsibilities, and nominate loyal and competent implementers. As Peters (1981: 56) notes: "bureaucracy and administration are an increasingly significant – if not the most significant – feature of modern policy-making."[78]
- Allocate sufficient resources (institutional, intellectual, social and financial capital, human potential).
- Coordinate the implementation process effectively, overcome difficulties as they arise.
- Ensure stable political and social-economic conditions during the entire implementation process.

IMPLEMENTATION PROCESS

After making the choices that specifically shape the public policy, one proceeds in four stages:

1. **An implementer gets appointed**, responsible for bringing the policy to life. He/she is also responsible for mitigating any conflicts of interest that might arise, facilitating agreements between stakeholders, and assessing compliance with policy goals. Along with their decision to appoint an implementer, policy makers also typically set up an implementation structure such as a specialized administrative unit (Hjern and Porter 1981).
2. **An implementation project is drafted**. Implementation is a typical task which can make good use of **project management**. Under the project, one selects a regulator or a combination of different regulators (the market, government administration, the civic sector) that is adequate to the policy task at hand[79] – and picks specific implementation instruments.[80] For example, a **roadmap** can be drawn, setting strategic goals, key elements and necessary resources (including budgetary allocations). In order to minimize the risk of implementation failure, Bardach (1977:

---

78   The theory of bureaucracy will be outlined at the end of this chapter.
79   Cf. Chapter A3.
80   Cf. Chapter A5.

269) suggests **scenario writing** by different teams established for the purposes of analysis, evaluation and administration and cooperating with the lead implementer. Furthermore, the implementer should verify feasibility and minimize potential risks. More specifically, it is necessary to estimate the **political feasibility** of the preferred procedure with respect to different particular interests affected by the policy design, whether the timing is right (**opportunity window**) and how the public opinion might respond.[81]

Before formulating a policy recommendation, the implementer should make sure it is practicable and politically feasible, minimizing potential risks.

EXAMPLE: ADOPTION OF THE ACT ON REGISTERED PARTNERSHIP

The criminalization of homosexual behavior in Czechoslovakia was abolished in 1961. It was not until 1990 that homosexuality came to be treated equally to heterosexuality by the country's penal law. For the first time in Czech history, same-sex couples were allowed to enter into civil unions by Act No. 115/2006 Coll., on Registered Partnership. Majority support for the law by citizens and politicians was only possible thanks to a large enough shift in societal values.

---

3. **Implementation actors make choices and realize the policy.** The lead implementer makes decisions within his/her responsibility, while entrusting the management and realization of specific steps to other actors responsible.
4. **The implementation process is monitored and evaluated continuously, and problems are solved as they arise.**[82]

A given implementation process may differ according to the following factors:
- whether one implements an existing policy (based on an established logic of institutional workings and individual behaviors – using Lindblom's incremental approach) or an important innovation or fundamental reform that implicates substantial change to social life and in turn to the conditions for satisfying the interests of individuals and institutions (using Dror's rationalist model)[83];
- whether the process is continuous or discontinuous. In the latter case, it is important how the different actions are timed – when each of them starts and how they are linked to one another. A well-timed program launch

---

81 Cf. Chapter A7.
82 The task of assessing how implementation proceeds falls within the stage of policy evaluation – see Chapter A9 for more.
83 Cf. Chapter A7.

depends on access to sound information about the subjective and objective conditions of implementation.

When new public policies are about to be introduced, it is useful to discuss them in advance at a broader forum of politicians, experts and citizens. One might also benefit from piloting the policy in a limited temporal and spatial frame – so that the policy design can be modified early and unnecessary damage can be avoided.

EXAMPLE: BAD POLITICAL AND ADMINISTRATIVE PRACTICE – INTRODUCING THE S-CARD FOR CZECH WELFARE RECIPIENTS

S-Card was an identification card combined with electronic vouchers for social welfare benefits which were transferred to beneficiaries from a special bank account. The S-Card was also supposed to replace existing special IDs for people with disabilities. The project was pushed through by Czech Minister of Labor and Social Affairs Jaromír Drábek and one of the then coalition parties, TOP09, despite resistance from people with disabilities, left-wing opposition and the country's Ombudsman. Based on ministerial decrees and a contract of the Ministry of Labor and Social Affairs with Česká spořitelna bank, the latter started issuing the S-Card in July 2012. The cards were expected to reach all members of the target group, replacing other documents, by the end of 2013. In March 2013, another coalition party, the ODS, agreed to shut down the project. Following a legislative initiative by a group of senators from the opposition Social Democratic Party, the Chamber of Deputies approved Act No. 306/2013 Coll., abolishing the S-Card taking effect from October 2013. Social welfare continued to be channelled through the S-Card until April 2014. Pushed through against resistance from users and other stakeholders, the untested project consumed large amounts of money from the state budget, as well as the time and nerves of more than two hundred thousand welfare recipients, who were forced to acquire an S-Card only to see it discontinued soon again.

IMPLEMENTATION DIFFICULTIES

People who are responsible for implementing a policy in practice often tend to overestimate the (political, legislative, administrative or economic) decision itself. **Experience tells us that the pathway from a decision to actual realization is often thorny or outright impossible to walk.** We are faced with numerous, often unexpected complications, and what is more, it often changes our idea of what desirable goals are, and in turn how necessary we think different policies are. This is what literature refers to as **implementation deficit**. It is defined as the gap between the resources actually spent implementing a policy and the resources required for the effective realization of its goals; or shortly, as a gap between the original intentions and the realities of policy failure. Implementation deficits often arise out of the belief that implementation is easy – that once formulated and adopted, policies will somehow automatically become reality.

In this respect, Bardach (1977: 69) asks the following four questions:
- What are the competences and motivations of the actors that are about to get involved in implementation?
- How is the potentially affected public going to be addressed by the policy?
- Who is going to intervene in the implementation process?
- How can we make up for the delay that almost always arises during implementation?

Policies are rarely realized in line with their authors' original intentions because implementers are faced with a number of **fundamental difficulties of policy implementation in contemporary societies:**
- Difficult foresight: public policy has a limited means of preparing for the future.
- Risk of unintended consequences of measures taken: implementation can be discredited or undermined by negative effects on an area or interest where they were not anticipated.

EXAMPLE:

Although motivated by good intentions, the American prohibition of alcohol sales and consumption in the 1920s led to an enormous growth in crime. As a result, the policy had to be abolished without ever attaining its goals (the 18th and the 21st Amendments to the US Constitution).

- A growing complexity of societal relations, among other things, makes it difficult to influence the "fluid" environment we live in.
- No policy is realized in isolation. It coexists with dozens or hundreds of other policies. This situation is sometimes illustrated on a parallelogram of policies and actors' powers, with the typical conflicts, synergies, and unintended consequences of uncoordinated parallel implementation.
- Societal development can be modified, but hardly controlled (Ringen 1987). A policy analyst who accepts such a position is faced with the challenge of delimiting the field in which there is at least a limited chance of influencing autochthonous societal developments. This challenge arises as early as in the stage of policy formulation, and becomes even more urgent during implementation.

- There is a high level of inertia of people's and institutions' value orientations and behaviors (the value orientations of organizations are cemented by their members' stake in their survival).
- The problem of policy simulation: policy actors sometimes find it useful to pretend that a policy is to be implemented, offering it their symbolic support even if their actual interests and deeds are different.

EXAMPLE:

In the 1980s, the Czechoslovak government pretended it identified with a World Health Organization program entitled, "Health for All by the Year 2000." While the country's health prevention effort was falling behind, health indicators were becoming critical and entirely different policy priorities were being pursued, the Ministry of Health supplied WHO's European office in Copenhagen with reports that presented all the parameters of the national program with *couleur de rose*.

As mentioned above, a large share of responsibility for policy implementation rests upon the shoulders of bureaucratic apparatuses. Therefore, I find it beneficial to introduce a theory that helps us better understand the role of bureaucracy in this process. Subsequently I will discuss the relations between politicians and public administrators, which need to be grasped as a key precondition of successful policy implementation.

EXAMPLE THEORY: BUREAUCRACY

The theory of German sociologist and economist Max Weber is a classical, still frequently cited contribution to explaining the role and behavior of bureaucracy (and has been met with renewed appreciation in recent years). Weber assumed that bureaucracy is entrusted with "legitimate governance through 'rational' administration of the state on the basis of a defined set of impersonal rules" (Ochrana, Půček 2011: 30). Government was to serve citizens in compliance with applicable laws and perform its functions through an apparatus of trained professionals.

The classic Weberian model of bureaucracy **exhibits the following characteristics**:
- Impersonal exercise of authority.
- Formalized rules of decision-making.
- Hierarchy of authority and responsibility is defined and followed.
- Appointment of bureaucrats based on competence and performance.
- Clear, pre-defined rules of staff remuneration.
- No single bureaucrat has a personal interest in the assets managed by him/her.
- Exercise of official responsibility subject to discipline and strict monitoring.

Critics pointed to a number of differences between the realities of bureaucratic public administration and this ideal-typical model:

Michels studied the processes of the oligarchization of bureaucratic apparatuses.

Homans and Wilenski brought attention to the fact that bureaucrats apply not only their administrative competences, but also managerial competences and others related to their growing specialization.

Merton studied the unintended consequences of the behavior of bureaucratic apparatuses. The older and more established an office, the more it tends to replace ends with means.

Mills noticed that bureaucracy often pursues its own interests.

Blau focused on formal and informal relations in organizations, arguing that the latter are often more important in practice.

Waldo (one of the leading authors of **New Public Administration**) questioned the boundary between administration and politics. Public administration cannot be fully devoid of political values.

Aucoin, Pollitt and Walsh (founding fathers of **New Public Management**) emphasized that "the economic approach to managing public administration treats public administration as a system of production transforming limited (rare) resources into public services in demand" (Ochrana, Půček 2011: 34). The primary means to that end are to adopt management methods from the business sector, make more room for choice and competition, adopt a client orientation, decentralize, and improve regulatory quality. Government is supposed to make decisions but entrust their implementation to others, under the motto, "Steer but do not row."[84]

Pollitt and Bouckaert (2004) reviewed the critique of New Public Management and initiated a "learned return to traditions" by formulating the concept of a **Neo-Weberian state**, combining Weber's classic approach with novel elements.

Classic (Weberian) elements:

Government is the principal implementer of solutions to the new problems of globalization, technologic and demographic change, and environmental threats.

The role of representative democracy is reaffirmed.

The rule of law and administrative regulations serve as guardians of equality before the law and the legality of the actions of government authorities.

The role of public administration is reaffirmed, with its special status, culture and conditions.

---

84 Refer to Jenei, Hoós & Vass (2003) for a more extensive discussion on New Public Management.

New (neo-) elements

Orientation has shifted from mere knowledge of the law and application of internal bureaucratic rules to the professional management of the satisfaction of people's needs and wants. Instruments of representative democracy are complemented (but not replaced) by instruments of deliberative (consultative), participative and direct democracy.

Modernization of public funding – emphasis has shifted from mere correct application of budgetary rules to the fulfillment of defined goals.

EXAMPLE THEORY: PRINCIPAL-AGENT THEORY
(AS EXEMPLIFIED ON POLITICO-ADMINISTRATIVE RELATIONS)[85]

In order to better understand the position of politicians and public administrators in the implementation process, one should take into consideration not only the possibility of difficulties in the principal-agent relationship (see above) but also the following problematic aspects of politico-administrative relations:

The politicization of public administration: in contrast to the expectations of the founding fathers of public administration theory, Woodrow Wilson and Max Weber, it is apparent that many bureaucrats, not only those in the top ranks, are not and cannot be fully separated from the political dimension of implementation. As shown by Peters and Pierre (2004), political parties possess considerable influence in almost all systems for the selection of public officials.

The past couple of decades have seen an expanding role in other implementation actors – advisors (specialists, experts) – due to the increasing complexity and specialization of the tasks of public administration. Advisors may become civil servants at the level of central government or various ministries; or they may influence the implementation process externally. In any case, they constitute another type of actor involved in politico-administrative relations.

There is constant change in the general context of policy implementation in the governance process, with its increasingly multi-level nature, growing involvement of other stakeholders (for instance, through actors' networks), and engagement of additional actors from the business and civic sectors.[86]

Politicians and administrators may closely collaborate, but they may as well oppose one another, pursuing competing values and interests. Their relations oscillate anywhere between these two poles[87] (Peters 1998).

---

85 For a more in-depth discussion of politico-administrative relations, especially in the context of central-level public administration reforms in Central and Eastern Europe, see Connaughton, Sootla, Peters (2008).
86 Cf. Chapter A3.
87 The theme of politico-administrative relations has been also frequently elaborated outside the realm of science; among others, by the BBC's acclaimed TV sitcom, *Yes Minister* (1980–84), followed by *Yes, Prime Minister* (1986–88).

As we know, the study of the policy implementation process can never fully disregard the stages of policy formulation and decision-making.[88] Perhaps this would be possible in the study of dictatorships, but not democratic societies. Therefore, many have critiqued the effort to draw an analytical boundary between implementation and the rest of policy making (Sabatier 1999, Weimer and Vining 2005), including authors who originally pioneered specialized analysis of this stage of the policy process. Considering these limitations, however, it certainly benefits our knowledge to view this stage as separate from both the previous and the subsequent stages of the policy process.

Implementation as the third stage of the public policy cycle is followed by the fourth stage – policy evaluation. The next chapter deals with it in more detail.

REVIEW QUESTIONS

Delimit a specific policy problem. Define the regulators and instruments suitable for the implementation of a corresponding policy. Justify your choice.
Why and how do implementation deficits arise, and how can they be controlled?
Which theoretical model of implementation is best suited for a cultural-historical analysis of an implementation process? Justify your choice.
What are the different things a policy implementer should take into consideration?
What are the main conditions of effective implementation?
Name some skills that facilitate the implementation process.
In politico-administrative relations, who is typically the principal and who is the agent? Exemplify.
Why do unintended consequences arise in the course of policy implementation?
What kinds of implementation difficulties do you consider the most important?
Outline the evolution of the theory of bureaucracy from Max Weber to the Neo-Weberian State.

SOURCES

Bardach, E. 1977. *The Implementation Game. What Happens After a Bill Becomes a Law.* Cambridge, MA: MIT Press.

Browne, A., A. Wildavsky. 1984. "Implementation as Exploration." Pp. 232–256 in *Implementation: How great expectations in Washington are dashed in Oakland*, by J. L. Pressman, A. Wildavsky. Berkeley, Los Angeles, London: University of California Press.

---

88 Cf. Chapter A7.

Connaughton, B., G. Sootla, G. Peters (eds.). 2008. *Politico-Administrative Relations at the Center. Actors, Structures and Processes Supporting the Core Executive.* Bratislava: NISPAcee Press.

Dowding, K. 2011. "Rational Choice Theory." Pp. 36–50 in *The SAGE Handbook of Governance*, edited by M. Bevir. London: Sage Publications.

Hjern, B., D. O. Porter. 1981. "Implementation Structures: A New Unit of Administrative Analysis." *Organization Studies* 2 (3): 211–227.

Jenei, G, J. Hoós, L. Vass. 2003. "Public Policy Institutions: The State and Bureaucracy." Pp. 105–119 in *Public Policy in Central and Eastern Europe. Theories, Methods, Practices*, by Potůček, M., L. T. Leloup, G. Jenei, L. Varadi. Bratislava: NISPAcee.

Lipsky, M. 1980. *Street-Level Bureaucracy.* New York: Russell Sage.

Malinowski, B. 1960. *A Scientific Theory of Culture and Other Essays.* New York: Oxford University Press.

Mlčoch, L. 1996. *Institucionální ekonomie* [Institutional Economics, in Czech]. Prague: Karolinum.

Ochrana, F., M. Půček. 2011. *Efektivní zavádění a řízení změn ve veřejné správě – Smart Administration* [Effective Implementation and Management of Changes in Public Administration: Smart Administration, in Czech]. Prague: Wolters Kluwer.

Peters, B. G. 1981. "The Problem of Bureaucratic Government." *Journal of Politics.* 43 (1): 56.

Peters, B. G. 1998. *Managing Horizontal Government. The Politics of Coordination.* Canadian Center for Management Development.

Peters, B. G., J. Pierre (eds.) 2004. *Politicization of the Civil Service in Comparative Perspective: the Quest for Control.* London: Routledge.

Pollitt, Ch., G. Bouckaert. 2004. *Public Management Reform: A Comparative Analysis.* Oxford: Oxford University Press.

Pressman, J. L., A. Wildavsky. 1984. *Implementation: How great expectations in Washington are dashed in Oakland.* Berkeley: University of California Press.

Ringen, St. 1987. *The Possibility of Politics.* Oxford: Claredon Press.

Sabatier, P. A. 1986. "Top-Down and Bottom-Up Approaches to Implementation Research: a Critical Analysis and Suggested Synthesis." *Journal of Public Policy* 6 (1): 21–48.

Sabatier, P. A. 1999. *Theories of the Policy Process.* Boulder: Westview Press.

Sabatier, P. A., D. Mazmanian. 1980. "A Framework of Analysis." *Political Studies Journal* 8 (4): 538–560.

Weimer, D. L., A. R. Vining. 2005. *Policy Analysis: Concepts and Practice.* 4th ed. Upper Saddle River (NJ): Prentice-Hall.

Recommended sources for the principal-agent theory:
Connaughton, B., G. Sootla, G. Peters (eds.). 2008. *Politico-Administrative Relations at the Center. Actors, Structures and Processes Supporting the Core Executive.* Bratislava: NISPAcee Press.

Cook, K. S. (ed.). 2001. *Trust in Society: Series on Trust, vol. 2*. New York: Russell Sage Foundation.

Dowding, K. 2011. "Rational Choice Theory." Pp. 36–50 in *The SAGE Handbook of Governance*, edited by M. Bevir. London: Sage Publications.

Furubotn, E. G., R. Richter. 1997. *Institutions and Economic Theory: The Contribution of the New Institutional Economics. Economics, Cognition and Society Series*. Ann Arbor: University of Michigan Press.

Laffont, J. J., D. Martimort. 2002. *The Theory of Incentives: The Principal-Agent Model*. Princeton: Princeton University Press.

Mirrlees, J. A. 1974. "Notes on Welfare Economics, Information and Uncertainty." Chapter 9 in *Essays on Economic Behavior under Uncertainty*, edited by M. Balch, D. McFadden; S. WU. Amsterdam: North Holland.

Ross, A. 1973. "The Economic Theory of Agency: The Principal's Problems." *American Economic Review* 63 (5): 134–139.

Recommended sources for the theory of bureaucracy:

Downs, G. W. 1976. *Bureaucracy, Innovation, and Public Policy*. University of Michigan.

Goodsell, C. T. 1983. *The Case for Bureaucracy: A Public Administration Polemic*. Chatham: Chatham House.

Jacques, E. 1993. *General Theory Of Bureaucracy*. Gregg Revivals.

Jenei, G, J. Hoós, L. Vass. 2003. "Public Administration and Public Management: Approaches and Reforms." Pp. 123-142 in *Public Policy in Central and Eastern Europe. Theories, Methods, Practices,* by Potůček, M., L. T. Leloup, G. Jenei, L. Varadi. Bratislava: NISPAcee.

Lane, J.-E. 1993. *The Public Sector – Concepts, Models and Approaches*. London: Sage.

Peters, B. G. 1988. *Comparing Public Bureaucracies: Problems of Theory and Method*. University of Alabama Press.

Pollitt, C., G. Bouckaert. 2004. *Public Management Reform: A Comparative Analysis*. Oxford: Oxford University Press.

Potůček, M. 2008. "The Concept of Neo-Weberian State confronted by the Multidimensional Concept of Governance." The *NISPAcee Journal of Public Administration and Policy*. Special Issue: A Distinctive European Model? The Neo-Weberian State. 1 (2): 83–94.

Wood, B. D., R. W. Waterman. 1994. *Bureaucratic Dynamics: The Role of Bureaucracy in a Democracy*. Westview Press.

/**A9**/

Policy Evaluation

> *"Evaluation in the ultimate stage of the policy process plays a role as fundamental as problem structuring in the beginning of that process. (...) every public policy should be monitored and evaluated in the course of its implementation so that decisions can be taken to continue, adjust or discontinue the policy."*
> *Nekola (2007a: 338)*

Evaluation accompanies all walks of life. Whether knowingly or unwittingly, one evaluates all the time – in everyday situations ("The movie was nothing special," "I can still make it across the intersection"), under more important circumstances ("Is this life insurance policy worth the price?", "I am never traveling with this agency again") or with regard to life's most fundamental decisions ("What did I study this field for?", "Who the heck did I marry?").

Arguably, public policy is just like that. In one way or another, evaluation takes place throughout the policy process. Evaluation is based on values.[89] It is reflected in the choice of instruments.[90] It affects problem delimitation and recognition.[91] It plays an important role in the choice between policy options.[92] It cannot be avoided when assessing the critical factors of implementation, monitoring its course[93] and ultimately evaluating finalized programs ex post.

There is the obvious question of whether it is reasonable and adequate to devote a special chapter to policy evaluation. One can answer in the affirmative because there is a number of specific aspects to evaluation as such, just like there is a range of specialized evaluation methods (Greenberg 2003).

Policy evaluation uses specific procedures, criteria and methods to determine which public policy (or part thereof) to pick from a range of policy options and why. For existing public policies, evaluation strives to find out to what extent their planned goals were accomplished (external effectiveness), how many resources were spent and how effectively – compared to the goals accomplished (internal effectiveness), what kind of unexpected problems or complications arose in the implementation process – and thus also whether the policy design was adequate, whether the implementation was managed well and whether they ought to be modified. Evaluation of ongoing public policies proceeds in similar ways.

A GENERAL FRAMEWORK FOR POLICY EVALUATION

William Dunn proposed a general framework that helps us better understand the process of policy evaluation.

This framework offers a distinction between policy inputs that enter the policy process and are transformed into policy outputs, short-term policy outcomes (not depicted in figure A9.1) and long-term policy impacts. The latter only emerge in the order of years or decades later (Nekola 2007a: 343). Policy outputs may consist of laws, public services, financial or material products. Policy outcomes include the change of actors' behaviors, attitudes or life situations. Referring to Dunn (2003), Nekola (2007a: 343) emphasizes that it is desirable "to delimit as exactly as possible the policy or program being assessed and to determine the relevant indicators for each of the constituent parts of the assessment".

---

89   Cf. Chapter A2.
90   Cf. Chapter A5.
91   Cf. Chapter A6.
92   Cf. Chapter A7.
93   Cf. Chapter A8.

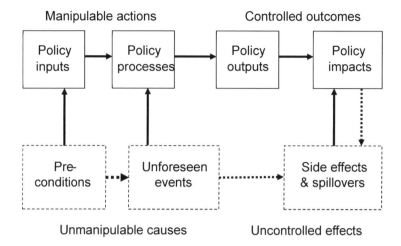

Figure A9.1 A general framework for policy evaluation (and monitoring)
Note: Continuous lines represent effects on manipulable actions and controlled outcomes. Dotted lines represent unforeseen events and side effects.
Source: Nekola (2007a), adapted from Dunn (2003: 286).

THE BASIS OF EVALUATION: CRITERIA, INDICATORS

Public policy can be viewed from many different angles. As a complex process of mutual influence it is characterized by defined goals, instruments intended for attaining them in the context of limited resources, and an institutional framework in which policy implementation takes place (and which is subject to change). Public policy depends on that framework as well as on the responsibilities and motivations of policy actors.[94] Before I can start discussing evaluation, I am going to specify the different parts of that process.

One proceeds by assigning to each part of the evaluation process certain **criteria as measures of evaluation** (Ochrana 2007: 292). They help us monitor and evaluate the development of a policy in a given time frame. There can be either qualitative or quantitative criteria. When one of the quantitative evaluation methods appears preferable (see below), one can transform qualitative criteria into quasi-quantitative ones (Ochrana 2007: 293) and apply those along with quantitative ones in order to reach comparable results using both qualitative and quantitative criteria. Nevertheless, one can rarely do with just a set of adequate quantitative criteria in policy evaluation – and quasi-quantitative criteria tends to be defined in highly arbitrary ways.[95]

94 See Chapters A4 and A6 for more details.
95 This is related to a more general issue of how we can combine qualitative and quantitative methods. In one of the most informative and methodologically refined studies in the field, Sirovátka et al. (2006) evaluated different instruments of active employment policy.

From another perspective, one distinguishes between criteria that are related to objective characteristics of interest (for example, whether or not an individual is employed) and ones that account for subjective states of target group members (such as a satisfaction or dissatisfaction with life, with politicians or with a public service).

EXAMPLE:

Evaluation of the social-economic condition of individual countries relies on indicators such as **Gross Domestic Product (GDP), unemployment rate** or the amount of **public debt**. However, rather than these indicators alone, it is their interpretation that determines politicians' decisions, and in turn government policies in a country. In order to fight unemployment, should we boost public investment even at the price of increasing public debt? Should we reduce government budget deficits even at the price of keeping high levels of or even increasing unemployment? Or should we start building our policies on other objective criteria that are covered by the **Human Development Index** (HDI) or even indices that encompass subjective indicators such as **Gross National Happiness** (GNH) or the OECD **Better Life Index**?[96]

Criteria are operationalized into indicators using available data (Nekola 2007a: 350). Data are obtained from statistics, other publicly available sources, or original research. Sets of indicators are increasingly popular in **evaluation at a general level** (e.g., organizations, administrative units or social structures) because they provide decision makers and managers with concentrated information for practice. Politicians are more inclined to reflect the results of such evaluations in their decisions, compared to other types of recommendations.

EXAMPLES: APPLYING SETS OF INDICATORS

State of the Future Index
Among other things, forecasting strives to evaluate the conditional futures of societies as a whole. Selected experts make an assessment based on identifying development trends, social problems and policy options, and may eventually identify such policies that might best contribute to increasing the National State of the Future Index (and thus improving

---

They concluded that "...the strength of qualitative methods lies in their complementarity to quantitative studies"; their weakness lies in a "difficult generalization to other individuals or groups" (Ibid.: 32). The researchers sought to solve that problem by combining both approaches and adopting a so-called mixed research design.

96   Cf. Chapter A2.

the condition of the country as a whole). Since the end of the 20th century, the Millennium Project has been elaborating on this approach (Glenn, Gordon, Florescu 2014).[97]

Governance indicators

The category of governance helps us grasp the increasing complexity of the human effort to govern public affairs. As we know, it covers a complex of interlinked processes and can be viewed from different perspectives.[98] In spite of that, analysts have been trying to propose and apply sets of indicators to measure that complex and compare how countries perform in governance overall. The results may help, for example, donors to better allocate international development aid, the EU to encourage under-performing member states to get in line with those governing themselves better, or firms to decide how to allocate their investment. Nekola (2009) published a critical review of different sets of governance indicators that have been practically tested worldwide. Among the better-known and more frequently cited sets of indicators are indices of competitiveness, democracy, corruption, business environment, etc. Bertelsmann Stiftung applies the sophistically developed "transformation index" every two years to assess the level of political management in developing countries (Transformation Index BTI 2016).

WHAT WE EVALUATE

Some possible objects of policy evaluation are listed in the following:
- **Specific policy areas** (for example, national-level family policy, foreign investment policy, local policy for the protection of persons and property).
- **Specific policy programs** (for example, a national government's policy statement or strategy to fight unemployment).
- **Application of specific instruments** (for example, a new tax or a new law).
- **Policy measures** (for example, building a road bypass or imposing a gambling ban).
- A specific quality of the **policy process** (for example, quality of governance, anti-corruption effectiveness).
- **Performance of administrative units** (for example, state, region, municipality, central government, ministry) in fulfilling a defined goal (quality of education, security provision, environmental protection).
- **Quality of service provision at the level of specific organizations** (for example, in health care, education, social services, regional public transportation or postal services).

---

97 For more on this project, including a set of fifteen global challenges mankind is facing, refer to http://www.millennium-project.org/millennium/challeng.html.
98 Compare Chapter A3 and Potůček et al. (2009).

WHEN WE EVALUATE

In one way or another, evaluation can be performed at every stage of the policy process. It forms a fundamental part of the decision-making stage, it occurs in the implementation stage, and it also plays a role in the subsequent assessment effort.

Table A9.1 Evaluation according to stages of the policy process

Policy process stage	Type of evaluation	Evaluation methods
Policy formulation, decision-making	Ex-ante evaluation	Ex-ante methods
Policy implementation	Interim/midterm evaluation	Interim methods
Policy evaluation	Ex-post evaluation	Ex-post methods

Source: Drhová, Ochrana (2011), adapted.

Thus, policy evaluation can be distinguished by the type of question it answers:

- Which of the policy options presented should be selected as best? (*ex-ante evaluation*)
- Is the policy proposed going to be truly beneficial and help attain the defined goals? (*ex-ante evaluation*)
- Why is a policy currently under implementation not producing the desired outcomes, why is it producing unintended consequences, or why does it require more resources than expected? Does it require improvements or modifications? If so, what kind? (*interim/midterm evaluation*)
- What were the outputs, outcomes or impacts of a public policy? In the course of its implementation, were the defined goals attained, did the implementation instruments prove useful, and what was the level of internal effectiveness? (*ex-post evaluation*)

EVALUATION METHODS

There is a range of evaluation methods available to public policy. In spite of recent progress in the field, the problem persists that every effort to provide the right answer to the evaluation question relies primarily on the gathering of all available evidence. That requires careful study and systematic collection of information and data. It is important to pay sufficient attention to preparing (and subsequently applying) a conceptual framework that helps us formulate conclusions about the results of the policy studied. Such an **evaluation design** should help us determine, by the end of the evaluation process, whether or to what extent the policy has actually produced a given set of effects and outcomes (Nekola 2007a: 361).

Of all disciplines, economics has the strongest tradition of policy evaluation. However, for the robustness of its quantitative methods of analysis, it pays the price of narrowing its perspective to those phenomena that can be quantified or quasi-quantified.

Economists have developed a range of **cost-output evaluation methods** (often collectively mis-titled as cost-benefit analysis). Ochrana (2007: 291–309) distinguishes between those using a single criterion and those applying multiple criteria.

Table A9.2 One-criterion cost-output methods

Method	Applications
Cost-minimization analysis – CMA	Cost measurement (e.g., total price of a project)
Cost-benefit analysis – CBA	Ratio between expenditure and output in monetary units
Cost-effectiveness analysis – CEA	Ratio between expenditure and output in kind
Cost-utility analysis – CUA	Ratio between expenditure and degree of goal fulfilment/satisfaction

Source: Ochrana (2007), adapted.

There are dozens of **methods of multi-criteria analysis**, including multi-goal analysis (Greenberg 2003: 213) or multiple-criteria decision analysis. Those are applied in situations when the individual criteria being considered are assigned different weights in line with their relative importance for defined goals. The criteria are defined and weighted by experts. The alternatives are ranked by summing up the weighted criteria.

Application of cost-output methods can clearly be traced back to Rational Choice Theory (RCT), which was highly acclaimed in the last third of the 20th century and found many uses in the political sciences; there were even some attempts to apply RCT in sociology.

EXAMPLE THEORY: RATIONAL CHOICE[99]

Rational Choice Theory dates back to Buchanan and Tullock (1962) and the Chicago school of economics. It postulates that the decisions of all (individual or aggregate) actors and institutions are, subject to a given institutional framework, a function of self-interest – of utility maximization.[100]

---

99 In public policy and economics, RCT is sometimes also referred to as public choice theory.
100 See Table A4.1.

Arguably, RCT builds on the model of *homo oeconomicus*. Individuals strive to maximize their individual utility while minimizing their costs: their actions can be explained by decisions based on cost-benefit comparison. If an actor's behavior is defined in this way and modeled in different institutional frameworks, one can assume (subject to certain conditions) that the market is the most effective regulator.[101] As opposed to the political system and government, the market operates without the inefficiencies incurred by the principal-agent relationship – primarily one between voters and politicians, and secondarily one between elected politicians and public officials.[102] In the 1970s, Garry Becker (1978) initiated an expansion of applied RCT outside the realm of economic behavior. Applying this theory, he tried to explain, among other social phenomena, the behavior of married couples, or the dynamics of social interactions.

STUDY TIP: Refer to **Chapter B3** for a case study which applies the theory of rational choice.

Nekola (2007b: 5) brings attention to some fundamental weaknesses of economic evaluation methods in policy practice, and especially the presence of ambiguous or non-legitimized policy goals, high volatility of public policies, limited evidence of policy outputs and impacts, and limited usefulness of results. This is why public policy applies a number of other evaluation methods as well.

Comparative analysis is one of the frequently used methods of policy evaluation. A specific application of this method is **benchmarking** (comparison of a policy with the best example). For example, in its programmatic activities, the European Commission cannot make decisions directly and merely recommends; it does so by presenting examples of good practice from different member states for the inspiration of others.

Greenberg (2003: 221) outlines the method of **process analysis** (sometimes called implementation analysis) for the purposes of comprehensive examination of who implements a policy/program, using what instruments, and in what environment. The method informs us about the technicalities of implementing policymakers' intentions in practice.

Nekola (2007a: 379) mentions **frame reflection** in policy evaluation. Proposed by Bovens et al. (2006), this approach complements the positivist, rationalist effort to evaluate policies "objectively", which builds on the assumption that knowledge is distorted by values, by an argumentative approach that strives to effectively moderate a necessarily value-laden discourse: "Reflective policy analysts may strive for a position as a systematic,

---

101 Cf. Chapter A3.
102 Cf. section on principal-agent theory in the previous chapter.

well-informed, thoughtful, and fair-minded provider of inputs to the political process of argumentation, debate, maneuvering, and blaming that characterizes controversial policy episodes" (Schön, Rein 1994). Nevertheless, it is clear that policy evaluators can never fully disengage from the values they hold dear.

Impact assessment is another frequently used approach in policy evaluation. It is applied mostly (albeit not exclusively) to the process of drafting or amending laws or policies, as ex-ante evaluation of their effectiveness. Based on the ways they are applied by OECD and EU bodies, Staroňová (2009) characterized impact assessment methods as follows:

- their goal is to evaluate a law, amendment or another policy instrument, or a policy as such, in the process of preparation, prior to actual implementation; that includes assessment of existing regulation;
- they consist of a coherent series of steps based on rational analysis and collection of pertinent evidence;
- they evaluate aspects of social, economic and environmental phenomena in systematic, prescribed and consistent ways;
- they focus on external phenomena as well.

Table A9.3 Impact assessment methods mandated in the European Union

Method	Acronym
Environmental Impact Assessment	EIA
Strategic Environmental Assessment	SEA
Regulatory Impact Assessment	RIA

Source: Drhová, Ochrana (2011: 224).

Staroňová (2014) evaluates the impact of applying EU-mandated impact assessment methodology in the political and administrative practice of the Czech and Slovak governments.

In addition to the methods above, the European Union has developed a range of other instruments that are not mandated by law but can help policymakers assess their intentions before any policies or measures are introduced in practice. They include, *inter alia,* sustainability impact assessment (SIA) of trade agreements, Commission-wide impact assessment (IA) of work programs, integrated impact assessment (IIA) with regard to local communities, life cycle assessment (LCA) of products, technology assessment (TA) with regard to the environment, or territorial impact assessment (TIA) of regional public policies.

DIFFICULTIES OF POLICY EVALUATION

A high level of caution is required in the evaluation process. Why?

The different stages of the policy process, actors' intentions or policy domains may overlap, feed back into or interfere (in conflicting or synergic ways) with one another. They are susceptible to a changing social, economic or political context.

EXAMPLE OF COMPLICATIONS IN PROGRAM EVALUATION WHERE IMPLEMENTATION WAS AFFECTED BY EXTERNAL FACTORS:[103]

After 1989, the highly enriched supply of food on the market and the liberalization of food prices changed the Czech population's eating habits: the consumption of unhealthy food decreased and the consumption of healthy food grew. This also applied to the selected districts in which a World Health Organization study of cardiovascular diseases, Countrywide Integrated Noncommunicable Diseases Intervention Program (CINDI), had been realized since the mid-1980s. One of the program's goals was to reduce the blood cholesterol levels in men at the age of economic activity. The reduction eventually occurred. However, the program's implementers themselves did not attribute the positive result to the program's effects, but rather to general social changes, and especially significant changes in people's food consumption behavior.

The typically long-term impacts of public policies are difficult to predict. For example, education policy impacts are reflected in an individual's competences. Former students utilize these competences throughout their working lives. Health-care outcomes may represent tens of additional (or lost) years of healthy lives for recovered patients. However, most policies are evaluated immediately after finalization, or at least in significantly shorter time frames.[104]

Since evaluation requires time and resources, decision makers can rarely afford it, and even when they can, the exercise tends to be insufficiently rigorous in its coverage and methods.

---

103 Even if we cannot control the external factors that intervene in the implementation of the program under evaluation, we are able to minimize the risk of evaluation failure by choosing an appropriate research design.

104 The only defense against short-sighted policy decisions is to consistently bolster provident ways of strategic governance (Potůček et al. 2009).

CAVEAT: A WARNING AND A CHALLENGE

Fiala and Schubert (2000: 84) warn us that "scientific evaluation of policy programs is a complicated and rarely successful exercise." Indeed, policy evaluation is one of the most demanding research tasks of all. It poses a challenge to a new generation of scholars who are motivated and able to assist politicians in raising the bar for policy practice and bringing public policies above the level offered thus far.

*   *   *

Although policy evaluation can be applied in all stages of the policy cycle, the simplest models assign it to the ultimate stage. Such ex-post evaluation may inform us that a social problem has been solved, a public interest has been satisfied and a policy has attained its goals. However, this is often not the case: evaluators conclude that the social problem has persisted and the policy has been partially or fully ineffective. In such a case, or whenever the nature of the social problem or the public interest pursued has changed, a new avenue opens up to modifying an existing policy and designing a new one—to initiating a new policy cycle. This is how the stage model of the policy cycle[105] reflects the fact that public policies are rarely able to solve a problem in its entirety, that several underlying assumptions may have changed by the time they are implemented, and therefore, that it is time for the policy to undergo an update or a radical overhaul, or even to shut down an unsuccessful policy and start working on a new solution.

REVIEW QUESTIONS

What are the differences between policy outputs, impacts and outcomes? Give examples.

Can Gross Domestic Product serve as a measure of internal effectiveness of government policies? Justify your answer.

What kind of difficulties or barriers might a policy analyst face in the process of evaluation?

Name some cost-output methods. How do they differ from one another?

What are the basic postulates of Rational Choice Theory? What does RCT have in common with cost-output methods?

Explain why policy evaluation cannot rely exclusively on quantitative methods.

What is the purpose of a "process analysis" of policy making? Which stage of the policy cycle does it typically cover and why?

What are some of the motives for applying impact assessment methods in policy practice?

---

105 Cf. Chapter A6.

Give examples of quantitative subjective, qualitative subjective, quantitative objective, and qualitative objective indicators in education policy.
What are the different objects of policy evaluation?

SOURCES

Becker, G. S. 1978. *The Economic Approach to Human Behavior.* Chicago: University of Chicago Press.

Bovens et al. 2006. "The Politics of Policy Evaluation." Pp. 319–335 in *Oxford Handbook of Public Policy*, edited by M. Moran, M. Rein, R. E. Goodin. Oxford: Oxford University Press.

Buchanan, J. M., G. Tullock. 1962. *The Calculus of Consent.* Ann Arbor: Michigan University Press.

Drhová, Z., F. Ochrana. 2011. "Úvod k metodám pro hodnocení dopadů" [Introduction to Impact Evaluation Methods, in Czech]. Pp. 222–226 in M. Nekola, H. Geissler, M. Mouralová (eds.). *Současné metodologické otázky veřejné politiky* [Contemporary Methodological Issues of Public Policy, in Czech]. Prague: Karolinum.

Dunn, W. N. 2004. *Public Policy Analysis: An Introduction.* 3rd ed. New Jersey: Pearson Prentice Hall.

Fiala, P., K. Schubert. 2000. *Moderní analýza politiky* [Modern Policy Analysis, in Czech]. Brno: Barrister & Principal.

Glenn, J., T. J. Gordon, E. Florescu. 2014. 2013–14 State of the Future. Washington: The Millennium Project.

Greenberg, D. 2003. "Evaluation of Public Programs." Pp. 203–228 in Potůček, M., L. T. Leloup, G. Jenei, L. Varadi. *Public Policy in Central and Eastern Europe. Theories, Methods, Practices.* Bratislava: NISPAcee.

Nekola, M. 2007a. "Monitoring a evaluace realizovaných politik" [Monitoring and Evaluation of Implemented Policies, in Czech]. Pp. 337–382 in A. Veselý, M. Nekola (eds.). *Analýza a tvorba veřejných politik: přístupy, metody a praxe* [Public policy analysis and making: approaches, methods, and practice, in Czech]. Prague: Sociologické nakladatelství.

Nekola, M. 2007b. "Rozdílné přístupy k hodnocení veřejných programů – ekonomická evaluace a její alternativy" [Different Approaches to Public Programs Evaluations: Economic Evaluation and Its Alternatives, in Czech]. Pp. 37–48 in F. Ochrana (ed.). *Theoretical and practical aspects of public finance.* Prague: Vysoká škola ekonomická.

Nekola, M. 2009. "Analyzing and Evaluating Major World Approaches to the Construction and Utilization of Governance Indicators." Pp. 28–63 in M. Potůček et al. 2009. *Strategic Governance and the Czech Republic.* Prague: Karolinum.

Ochrana, F. 2007. "Zhodnocení variantních politik" [Evaluation of Alternative Policies, in Czech]. Pp. 291–309 in A. Veselý, M. Nekola (eds.). *Analýza a tvorba veřejných politik: přístupy, metody a praxe* [Policy analysis and design: approaches, methods, and practice, in Czech]. Prague: Sociologické nakladatelství.

Potůček, M. et al. 2009. *Strategic Governance and the Czech Republic.* Prague: Karolinum.

Schön, D., M. Rein. 1994. *Frame Reflection.* New York: Basic Books.

Sirovátka, T., V. Kulhavý, M. Horáková, M. Rákoczyová. 2006. *"Hodnocení efektivity programů aktivní politiky zaměstnanosti"* [Evaluation of the Effectiveness of Active Employment Policy Programs, in Czech]. Prague: Výzkumný ústav práce a sociálních věcí.

Staroňová, K. 2009. *Hodnotenie vplyvov v teórii a praxi Slovenska a Európskej Únie* [Impact Assessment in Theory and Practice of Slovakia and the European Union, in Slovak]. Prešov: Adin.

Staroňová, K. 2014. "Institutionalization of regulatory impact assessment in the Czech Republic and Slovakia: do reforms bring RIA closer to be a decision-making tool?" Pp. 197–203 in *Current Trends in Public Sector Research.* Brno: Masaryk University.

Transformation Index BTI 2016. Gütersloh: Verlag Bertelsmann Stiftung 2016.

Recommended sources for the theory of rational (public) choice:

Becker, G. S. 1978. *The Economic Approach to Human Behavior.* Chicago: University of Chicago Press.

Becker, G. S. 1996. *Accounting for Tastes.* Cambridge: Harvard University Press.

Buchanan, J. M., G. Tullock. 1962. *The Calculus of Consent.* Ann Arbor: Michigan University Press.

Buchanan, J. M., R. D. Tollison (eds.). 1972. *The Theory of Public Choice I.* Ann Arbor MI: University of Michigan Press.

Buchanan, J. M., R. D. Tollison (eds.). 1984. *The Theory of Public Choice II.* Ann Arbor MI: University of Michigan Press.

Samuelson, P., W. D. Nordhaus. 2010. *Economics.* 19th ed. Boston: McGraw-Hill Irwin.

Schneider, F. (ed.). 2004. *The Encyclopedia of Public Choice.* New York: Kluwer Academic Publishers.

Simon, H. A. 1955. "A Behavioral Model of Rational Choice." *The Quarterly Journal of Economics* 69 (1): 99–118.

/**A10**/
How to Understand Public Policy

"However, when one turns to act within the world, rather than merely study it, one must deal with the world-as-it-is, with its complexity, and must concern oneself with all the major relevant factors, conditions, and constraints. Here, encompassing paradigms are more effective than very parsimonious but highly focused ones."
Amitai Etzioni (1988)

If the reader has made it through the book to this point, and if he or she is new to public policy, then the abundance of concepts, approaches and linkages must be perplexing. Certainly, the reader is not alone in this state of mind, as researchers themselves are often equally perplexed. Schlager (1997: 14) uses the following words to describe the landscape of scientific study of public policies: "Mountain islands of theoretical structure, intermingled with, and occasionally attached together by foothills of shared methods and concepts, and empirical work, all of which is surrounded by oceans of descriptive work not attached to any mountain of theory." No wonder that every student who is working on a thesis in the field of public policy struggles to find out "how it's done."

Many politicians have no idea what public policy as a discipline is about, yet somehow find their way through policy making in practice. What helps them? For example, the experience that it takes less effort and energy to insist on what people are used to, rather than strive for change. Or that the key to getting support for a policy intent lies in shared ideas, in prospects of personal or institutional benefits, or simply in actors' aversion to risk. Or that the higher number of actors have a say, the more difficult it is to find a compromise.

Table A10.1 Examples of links between the practical experience of politicians and theoretical knowledge

Practical political experience	Corresponding theory
Miles' Law: where you stand depends on where you sit.	Organizational behavior theory
Policy programs create constituencies, which in turn do everything they can to keep them running.	Path dependence theory
Framing issues to resonate with predominant cultural values may change public perceptions of the issues positively.	Framing theory, frame analysis
People's fear of loss is a more powerful motive than their anticipation of comparable gain.	Prospect theory

Source: Weimer (2008: 492), adapted.

This can hardly be too surprising. In any case, theories represent generalized past experience. Yet are they applicable under any circumstances? And how to reconcile values that interfere with the process of policy inquiry, affecting the different steps we take, expected outcomes and our recommendations?

I am going to start by outlining some of the difficulties of a scientific examination of policies. As long as one respects these obstacles, one can avoid the danger of overestimating the power of scientific inquiry in practice. Then I will outline a few guidelines for the examination process in general and for various cognitive tasks in particular. I will focus on the role of conceptual frameworks and then review the public policy theories elaborated in this book as well as other related theories. I will conclude by formulating a recommended structure for a scholarly study.

DIFFICULTIES OF A SCIENTIFIC EXAMINATION OF POLICIES

Application of any scientific discipline depends on a valid knowledge of the more general contexts, conditions, instruments, and dilemmas of scientific inquiry. Here, I can only recommend Ochrana's concise monographs on methodology of science (2012) and social sciences (2015). The author deals with all important issues and dilemmas of contemporary philosophy, methodology, and logic of scientific inquiry. Of special relevance to social science in general and public policy in particular are his analyses of the differences between the social and natural sciences, of individualist versus collectivist notions of society, of normative versus non-normative perspectives on problems studied, of approaches to defining terms and deductively and inductively formed theories, or of narration as a way of interpreting social events examined.

Let me now reiterate that public policy as social practice is viewed as a process of intentional interventions in the social environment. The problem is that the environment is shaped by different actors with competing goals, that researchers as well as these actors have limited knowledge of the environment, and that social phenomena are more-or-less difficult to predict and influence. Therefore, we are faced with all kinds of obstacles on our way to scholarship.

Table A10.2 Difficulties of the scientific examination of public policies

Difficulties	Examples
Unclear determination of phenomena.	Was the global financial downturn of the early 21st century caused by private banks' speculation, insufficient government regulation thereof, or the very architecture of global financial markets?
Embeddedness of a given policy in other social processes, including other policies implemented.	A decision to increase the value-added tax (VAT) rate will improve government revenue but, at the same time, also increase public sector expenditures for goods and services.
Dynamic of change vs. cognitive stereotypes.	Neglecting the role of electronic media and online social networks in the study of political processes.
The long-term effects of policies are unforeseeable and ambiguous.	How to anticipate the consequences of a current pension reform for decades ahead?
Contextualization limited by knowledge deficits (blank spots).	A health care reform along the motto, "privatization is a universal remedy for the healthcare system."

Uncontrolled value-, interest- and discipline-based biases in the processes of inquiry, decisionmaking and policy implementation.	An economic competitiveness strategy applied as a key strategic guideline for the country.
Risk of inadequate generalizations from particular theories.	Rational Choice Theory applied to explain actors' social behavior.
Risk of staking everything on a single method.	"In the absence of indicators, there is nothing we can say about the problem," a positivist argues.
Extensive time and other resources required for the inquiry process itself.	Politicians demand immediate recommendations at no cost, while researchers need enough time and money to guarantee their results.

Source: Author.

There is also the risk of uncritically adopting a simplistic view of the phenomenon studied.

EXAMPLE: COMMONSENSE VERSUS EXPERT POLICY ACCOUNTS OF THE DETERMINANTS OF PUBLIC HEALTH

Common sense:
The health of the general population improves with the quality of healthcare.
An expert policy account:
Public health depends on:
- genetic factors (an effect of 2–4%),
- quality of environment (up to 10%),
- structure and quality of healthcare (up to 30%),
- lifestyle: physical exercise, eating habits and quality of nutrition, prevalence of substance abuse and risk behavior (remaining percentage).
(Note: these expert estimates are not generally accepted by the expert community.)
A public policy conclusion:
Spending more on healthcare does not necessarily guarantee better public health. It is important to allocate these resources to promotion of healthy lifestyle, early detection (e.g., adequate screening programs), subsequent treatment and rehabilitation. Financial resources are spent ineffectively and wastefully if the healthcare system only intervenes following diagnosis. The ministry of health cannot be the only one responsible for better public health; cross-cutting programs of health promotion are required to penetrate the entire society.

GUIDELINES FOR THE EXAMINATION PROCESS

"Thinking is a struggle for order and at the same time for comprehensiveness. You must not stop thinking too soon—or you will fail to know all that you should; you cannot leave it to go on for ever, or you yourself will burst."

C. Wright Mills (1959)

In his splendid lecture, "On Intellectual Craftsmanship," one of the founding fathers of American critical sociology Mills (1959, Appendix) shared his idea of how to become an imaginative researcher. The following table summarizes his advice.

Table A10.3 Mill's intellectual craftsmanship

Do not inquire into what is already known. Start inquiry by a thorough review of existing knowledge.
Consider the value background of your own research activity.
Archive your knowledge, findings and ideas.
Think within context and strive for a comprehensive and coherent interpretation of the cognitive problem.
Compare, classify and sort by different criteria and combinations thereof; look for extremes and polar opposites.
Look for plausible theories (accounts, conceptual frameworks) for the cognitive problems, and build on them (cultivate hypotheses). Accept, reject, or adapt and develop explanations collected.
Be inspired by all life brings: newspapers, magazines, fiction, film, theater, conversations with friends and colleagues. Do not reject any sort of source, including correspondence, court cases or scandals.
Never separate inquiry from life. Take advantage of your own life experience.
Always look for the most simple and comprehensible explanation (Occam's razor).

Premature death ended Mills' skyrocketing career in 1962. Today, there is no doubt one should add to his advice that researchers should fully utilize the Internet's potential while remaining cautious about the validity of the information found online.

SOLVING A COGNITIVE TASK

Students who have defended their Master's theses or doctoral dissertations know that the final form of one's work is sometimes considerably different from the proposal originally submitted. One can never plan ahead for every step of one's solution to a cognitive task. Nevertheless, how one proceeds on the way to knowledge can be facilitated or even accelerated by an at least general understanding of the different steps one must take – even if those already taken often have to be critically reflected or reassessed.

Table A10.4 Recommended steps in solving a cognitive task in public policy

Formulate the question correctly – define the policy problem[106].
Formulate the policy problem's holistic contexts (preferably using a conceptual framework).
Search for and choose among theories that help you explain the policy problem defined.
Exclude expendable elements and relations; include missing ones.
Choose among models and methods; gather, analyze and interpret data and evidence about the defined problem.
Answer the question.
Define unsolved, open aspects of the cognitive task; if possible, recommend how to proceed solving it.

In the context of public policy, Veselý (2011: 47) highly appreciates Ostrom's distinction "between three layers of hierarchically arranged theoretical levels that range from the most general ones to the most concrete ones: frameworks, theories and models." Ostrom herself (1999: 40) characterizes them as follows:

Frameworks help us identify the necessary elements for a more systematic analysis, providing a list of possible variables and "a metatheoretical language that can be used to compare theories."

Theories "enable the analyst to specify which elements of the framework are particularly relevant to certain kinds of questions and to make general working assumptions about these elements. (...) Several theories are usually compatible with any framework."

Models "make precise assumptions about a limited set of parameters and variables."

CONCEPTUAL FRAMEWORKS[107]

Public policy is predestined, by its very nature, to solving cognitive tasks that arise at the boundary of several disciplines and that overlap with practice in a way that makes it necessary to study not only what is but also what might be – possible futures. To formulate a conceptual framework is perhaps one of the best ways to respect such holistic contexts of inquiry.

---

106 Cf. Chapter A6.
107 Sometimes also referred to as explanatory or conceptual schemes.

Ostrom (2005: 8–9) characterizes conceptual frameworks as "…a series of nested conceptual maps of the explanatory space that social scientists can use in trying to understand and explain the diversity of human patterns of behavior. (…) Our goal was to help integrate work undertaken by political scientists, economists, anthropologists, lawyers, sociologists, psychologists, and others interested in how institutions affect the incentives confronting individuals and their resultant behavior."[108]

Tondl (2005: 278) defines a conceptual framework as follows: "a system of concepts, usually an ordered system of sufficiently reliably interpretable and interrelated conceptual means which make it possible to express identified or potential states or situations related to a thematic or issue area in a comprehensible and sufficiently precise way, to explain these states and their possible predictions, or to express the procedures, methods or possibilities of their practical formation and application."

Practical application of conceptual frameworks can be exemplified in the study of the processes of cultivation and realization of human potential.

EXAMPLE: CONCEPTUAL FRAMEWORK: CULTIVATION AND REALIZATION OF HUMAN POTENTIAL IN THE PROCESS OF SOCIAL REPRODUCTION (POTŮČEK 1992, 2014)

By devoting themselves to certain activities or by creating or using various products and satisfying their needs, humans change their dispositions for performing these activities. Such changes in dispositions affect their "readiness" to perform activities (or to create or use products) or even shape the structure of their needs. As a consequence, they may even affect the activities themselves. This was the approach we took in the late 1980s when studying the status and role of so-called human development departments (education, health care, culture, sports, and social care) in the process of social reproduction. Human potential is a system of dispositions and inclinations of man to activity (and to the engagement in relationships), which develop human existential powers and society as well. Human potential is then a precondition of life activities (and relationships) of people by which individuals and social groups actualize themselves in society and change it. Both the development of human potential and the possibility of its realization depend on the degree of societal development. At the same time, however, human potential is a result of the life activities (and relationships) of people because these dispositions and inclinations can only grow out of active self-actualization. The "human-centered" nature of this approach was expressed in the thesis that people are the primary target, level of human development is the key criterion, and human potential is the fundamental source of social development. We proposed the following conceptual framework to reflect the different forms and positions of human potential in the process of societal reproduction:

---

108 The author was inspired by many years of experience developing and applying her Institutional Analysis and Development Framework (IADF), for which she was ultimately awarded the Nobel Prize.

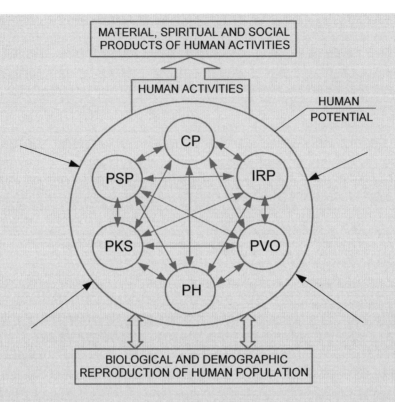

Figure A10.1 The forms of human potential and its internal and external links

Source: Author.

Legend:

The potential of health (PH) comprises physical and mental, genetically, behaviorally and socially determined fitness and resistance which gives rise to all other types of human potential.

The potential of knowledge and skills (PKS) is the command of such knowledge and skills that are essential for the realization of different human activities and relations, including a readiness to apply such knowledge and skills as necessary.

The potential of value orientation (PVO) is the inclination to devote oneself to only such life activities that are in line with one's internalized system of values. It is based on the ability to differentiate between the meanings of all aspects of individual life and its supra-individual context.

The potential of social participation (PSP) is the disposition to engage and actualize oneself in broader social relations while respecting the demands arising from participation in the functioning of social entities mediating such relations.

Individually integrative and regulative potential (IRP) is the ability to influence the course of one's life in order to cultivate and realize the entire human potential in an effective and balanced way.

Creative potential (CP) is the disposition to create new realities autonomously and the inclination to maximize its realization. Creativity is a function of life and the highest expression of humanity.

*The conceptual framework of cultivation and realization of human potential in the process
of societal reproduction* assumes close associations or even overlaps between the different
types of potential. Human development proceeds throughout ontogenesis and can be
divided into two stages. Stage 1 (typical of childhood and adolescence) cultivates one in
the processes of socialization and enculturation. At the same time, one begins to actively
participate in the process of social and individual reproduction and development. Stage
2 consists of the reproduction, re-creation and transformation of society and its natural
environment, and is mostly realized in adulthood. A research study which relied on this
conceptual framework analyzed the specific functions of the departments of education,
health care, culture and social care and of various institutions promoting sports.[109] The
study concluded that the empirically proved inhibitions of human potential in Czechoslovak society (such as life expectancy lagging considerably behind neighboring Western
European countries) lay not only in a deficient functioning of the individual departments
but also in the system as a whole. They rested in the political, economic and administrative model of socialism as it was realized in Czechoslovakia before 1989. I suspect that
such a generalization would have been difficult or even impossible without relying on the
conceptual framework of cultivation and realization of human potential in the process of
societal reproduction.

Furthermore, I should mention the risks related to the application of conceptual frameworks and some ways of tackling these risks:

There is a risk of *oversimplification*. The necessity to generalize may lead to
ignoring relevant entities or relations, resulting in a biased or harmfully narrowed cognitive scope. Here we must strive to prepare the knowledge base of
every research activity thoroughly, openly and critically.

We are also facing the risk of a *divergent perceptions of terms by different
(albeit collaborating) scientific disciplines.* For instance, misunderstandings
arise frequently between psychology, economics, and sociology with respect to
the term *need.* An adequate solution lies in a patient interdisciplinary debate,
which may lead to a consensus on an *ad hoc* working definition of terms.

*Correspondence is not guaranteed between users' ordinary language and the
conceptual apparatus* developed by researchers for the conceptual framework.
Therefore, public policy tends to engage users early in the process of inquiry,
namely while the given conceptual framework is being proposed and applied.
Users should be able to take an active part in that process or at least better
understand the framework.

---

109 At that time, these departments were collectively referred to as "human development
departments."

CHOICE OF THEORY (THEORIES)

Public policy (along with related disciplines) formulates a number of theories to account for different aspects of societal dynamics in relevant contexts. Obviously, there is no single all-embracing and all-illuminating theory. Orthodox attempts to apply such single theories are bound to produce more harm than good. Indeed, various theories may complement but also contradict one another. That, too, may facilitate the inquiry process because it forces us to search for a more consistent and more comprehensive approach. Formulating the kind of conceptual framework mentioned above should be instrumental for that purpose.

However, the ensemble of examples included can hardly exhaust the universe of applicable theories. It needs to be emphasized that each of the different areas in which public policy is applied (health care, education, migration, security...) depends on theories "borrowed" from respective collaborating disciplines (social medicine, pedagogy, demography, geopolitics...)

The kind of theory or combination of theories researchers eventually choose in order to solve a given cognitive task depends on their experience and level of comprehension of the policy processes at hand.

MODELING

When indicators can be assigned to the phenomena studied and there are theories that outline the relationships between them, one can choose to translate those theories into models. In their quantitative form, models are formal means of describing and contextualizing relationships defined by theories. This is how theories are linked with modeling methods in the social sciences (Ostrom 2005). Such linkages are established more easily and thus also more ordinarily in economics (e.g., econometric modeling) than in public policy, where this kind of quantification is rarely useful. Here it is timely to recall the words of antiquity's greatest philosopher, Aristotle: "...look for precision in each class of things just so far as the nature of the subject admits."

METHODS OF POLICY ANALYSIS AND POLICY MAKING

The main goal of this book is to provide a comprehensible set of instructions on how best to understand public policies. In other words, I do not primarily seek to describe the methods of policy analysis and policy making. Here I could refer to a number of existing publications offering a broad, insightful and comprehensive account of available methods of policy analysis and design as well as their strengths and weaknesses. These include, among others, the books of Bardach (2000), Dunn (2004), Mintrom (2011), Patton & Sawicki (1993) or Weimer & Vining (1999). For an overview of sociological methods used in policy analysis, refer to Purkrábek (2003).

Faced with an abundance of theories and methods, one is usually advised against staking everything on a single item. Similarly, it is not strategic for a researcher with a perfect command of a single method to apply that method in an uncritical, unreflected way, irrespective of the nature of the cognitive task at hand. Of course, experience plays an important role here as well.

CAVEAT: A WARNING AND A CHALLENGE

Children tend to be more curious and more creative than adults. They are not restrained by stereotypical, schematic approaches to life, by uncritical reliance on what is believed to be proven. As adults, we know very well that proven methods help steer us through life, but we are also committed to their boundaries. It is in this sense that everything that has been said in this book should be taken with caution. The information may be helpful, yet it may be blinding as well. "Since one can be trained only in what is already known, training sometimes incapacitates one from learning new ways" (Mills 1959). Do not incapacitate yourself by staking everything on one theory or method; do not fall for the charm of mainstream or trendy ideas. Find your own way!

APPENDIX: RECOMMENDED STRUCTURE OF A SCHOLARLY STUDY

1. Define the policy problem (how your study will help us better understand the social problem and the potentials for its solution by public policy)[110]
2. Review existing knowledge (using references to authors and sources)
3. Theoretical background (optionally: conceptual framework, hypotheses)
4. Characterize the methods applied (rationale, limitations, ways of application)
5. Procedure and results of investigation (can be further structured)
6. Conclusion (including critical appraisal of the results obtained and recommendations for future research)
7. Sources

Annexes (optional)

---

110 Cf. Chapter A6.

REVIEW QUESTIONS

When solving a cognitive task in public policy, how do we get to choose a theory (or a combination of theories)?

In public policy and beyond, how can we find the right answers to well-formulated questions?

What kind of difficulties should policy analysts and policy makers be prepared to face?

What are the fundamentals of intellectual work according to C. W. Mills?

What are the recommended steps in solving a cognitive exercise?

Define conceptual frameworks. What is their function?

What is the relationship between conceptual frameworks and theories?

Name two or perhaps three theories that provide complementary accounts of the policy process. Justify your choice.

What is the difference between models and theories? Do models have anything in common with methods?

SOURCES

Bardach, E. 2000. *A Practical Guide for Policy Analysis.* New York: Chatham House.

Dunn, W. N. 2004. *Public Policy Analysis: An Introduction.* 3rd ed. Upper Saddle River: Prentice Hall.

Etzioni, A. 1988. *The Moral Dimension: Towards a New Economics.* New York: The Free Press.

Mills, C. W. 1959. *The Sociological Imagination.* Oxford: Oxford University Press.

Mintrom, M. 2011. *Contemporary Policy Analysis.* Oxford: Oxford University Press.

Ochrana, F. 2012. *Methodology of Science.* Prague: Karolinum.

Ochrana, F. 2015. *Methodology of Social Sciences.* Prague: Karolinum.

Ostrom, E. 1999. "Institutional Rational Choice: An Assessment of the Institutional Analysis and Development Framework." Pp. 35–71 in *Theories of the Policy Process,* edited by P. A. Sabatier. Boulder: Westview Press.

Ostrom, E. 2005. *Understanding Institutional Diversity.* Princeton: Princeton University Press.

Patton, C. V., Sawicki, D. S. 1993. *Basic Methods of Policy Analysis and Planning.* Englewood Cliffs: Prentice Hall.

Potůček, M. 1992. "The Concept of Human Potential and Social Policy." *Acta Universitatis Carolinae Oeconomica,* 1: 51–67.

Potůček, M. 2014. "Konceptuální rámce v teorii a praxi veřejné politiky" [Conceptual Frameworks in the Theory and Practice of Public Policy, in Czech]. *Teorie vědy* XXXVI (1): 9–22.

Purkrábek, M. 2003. "The Application of Sociological Methods in Public Policy." Pp. 331–338 in *Public Policy in Central and Eastern Europe. Theories, Methods, Practices,* by M. Potůček, L. T. Leloup, G. Jenei, L. Varadi. Bratislava: NISPAcee.

Quattrone, G. A., Tversky, A. 1988. "Contrasting Rational and Psychological Analyses of Political Choice." *American Political Science Review* 82 (3): 719–736.

Schlager, E. 1997. "A Response to Kim Quaile Hill's." *Search of Policy Theory. Policy Currents* 7 (June): 14–5.

Tondl, L. 2005. "Sémiotické funkce konceptuálního rámce" [Semiotic Functions of a Conceptual Framework, in Czech]. *Organon F* 12 (3): 278.

Veselý, A. 2011. "Veřejněpolitický a 'klasický' sociálně-vědní výzkum: podobnosti a odlišnosti" [Public Policy Research and "Classical" Social Research: Similarities and Differences, in Czech]. Pp. in *Současné metodologické otázky veřejné politiky* [Contemporary Methodological Issues of Public Policy, in Czech], by M. Nekola, H. Geissler, M. Mouralová. Prague: Karolinum.

Weimer, D. L. 2008. "Theories of and in the Policy Process." *Policy Studies Journal* 36 (4): 489–495.

Weimer, D. L., A. R. Vining. 1999. Policy Analysis: Concepts and Practice. Upper Saddle River: Prentice Hall.

Literature – Part A

Anderson, J. E. 1975. *Public Policy Making*. New York: Praeger Publishers.

Abrahamson, P. 1995. "Welfare Pluralism: Towards a New Consensus for a European Social Policy." *Current Politics and Economics of Europe* 5 (1): 29–42.

Ashby, W. R. 1956. *Introduction to Cybernetics*. London: Chapman and Hall.

Axelrod, R. M. 1984. *The Evolution of Cooperation*. New York: Basic Books.

Axelrod, R. M. 1997. *The Complexity of Cooperation: Agent-based Model of Competition and Collaboration*. Princeton: Princeton University Press.

Bachrach, P., M. S. Baratz. 1970. *Power and Poverty*. New York: Oxford University Press.

Bardach, E. 1977. *The Implementation Game. What Happens After a Bill Becomes a Law*. Cambridge, MA: MIT Press.

Bardach, E. 2000. *A Practical Guide for Policy Analysis*. New York: Chatham House.

Barry, N. 1987. "Understanding the Market." Pp. 161–171 in *The State or the Market*, edited by M. Loney. London: SAGE Publications.

Bauman, Z. 1999. *In Search of Politics*. Cambridge: Polity Press.

Beblavý, M. et al. 2002. *Manuál pre tvorbu verejnej politiky* [Manual for Public Policy Making, in Slovak]. Bratislava: Inštitút pre dobre spravovanú spoločnosť.

Becker, G. 1996. *Accounting for Tastes*. Cambridge: Harvard University Press.

Becker, G. S. 1978. *The Economic Approach to Human Behavior*. Chicago: University of Chicago Press.

Berlin, I. 1958. *Two Concepts of Liberty*. Oxford: Clarendon Press.

Bertalanffy, von L. 1968. *General System Theory*. New York: George Braziller.

Bestuzhev-Lada, I. V. 1984. *Poiskovoe sotsiaľnoe prognozirovanie: perspektivnye problemy obshchestva: opyt sistematizatsii* [Exploratory social foresighting: future problems of society: systematization of experiences, in Russian]. Moskva: Nauka.

Birkland, T. 2005. *An Introduction to the Policy Process: Theories, Concepts, and Models of Public Policy-Making*. 2nd ed. Armonk: M. E. Sharpe.

Birkland, T. A. 2006. "Agenda Setting in Public Policy." Pp. 63–78 in *Handbook of Public Policy Analysis*, edited by F. Fischer, G. J. Miller, M. S. Sidney. New York: Taylor and Francis Group.

Bovaird, T. 2005. "Public Governance: Balancing Stakeholder Power in a Network Society." *International Review of Administrative Sciences* 71 (2): 217–228.

Bovens et al. 2006. "The Politics of Policy Evaluation." Pp. 319–335 in *Oxford Handbook of Public Policy*, edited by M. Moran, M. Rein, R. E. Goodin. Oxford: Oxford University Press.

Brown, B. 2003. "Ethics and Public Policymaking: An Incomplete Transition in Central and eastern Europe." Pp. 175–200 in *Public Policy in Central and Eastern Europe: Theories, Methods, Practices*, by M. Potůček, L. LeLoup, G. Jenei, L. Váradi. Bratislava: NISPAcee.

Browne, A., A. Wildavsky. 1984. "Implementation as Exploration." Pp. 232–256 in *Implementation: How great expectations in Washington are dashed in Oakland*, by J. L. Pressman, A. Wildavsky. Berkeley, Los Angeles, London: University of California Press.

Buchanan, J. M., G. Tullock. 1962. *The Calculus of Consent*. Ann Arbor: Michigan University Press.

Burns, T. R., T. M. Baumgartner, P. DeVille 1985. Man, Decisions, *Society: The Theory of Actor-system Dynamics for Social Scientists*. Milton Park: Gordon and Breach Science Publishers.

Burton, G., J. Jirák. 2001. *Úvod do studia médií* [Introduction to Media Studies, in Czech]. Brno: Barrister a Principal.

Cairney, P. 2011. *Understanding Public Policy: Theories and issues*. Palgrave Macmillan.

Campbell, J. L., O. K. Pedersen. 2007. "The Varieties of Capitalism and Hybrid Success: Denmark in the Global Economy." *Comparative Political Studies* 40 (3): 307–332. Retrieved May 24, 2016 (http://openarchive.cbs.dk/bitstream/handle/10398/7351/varieties_capitalism_hybrid_success_18.pdf?sequence=1).

Castells, M. 2000. "Materials for an Exploratory Theory of the Networked Society." British *Journal of Sociology* 51 (1): 5–24.

Císař, O. 2004. *Transnacionální politické sítě* [Transnational Policy Networks, in Czech]. Brno: Masarykova univerzita, Mezinárodní politologický ústav.

Cobb, R. W., C. D. Elder. 1983. *Participation in American Politics: The Dynamics of Agenda-Building*. Baltimore: Johns Hopkins University Press.

Cohen, B. C. 1963. *The Press and Foreign Policy. Princeton*. NJ: Princeton University Press.

Colebatch, H. K. 1998. *Policy*. Minneapolis: University of Minnesota Press.

Connaughton, B., G. Sootla, G. Peters (eds.). 2008. *Politico-Administrative Relations at the Center. Actors, Structures and Processes Supporting the Core Executive*. Bratislava: NISPAcee Press.

Council of Europe. 1950. *European Convention on Human Rights and Fundamental Freedoms*. Retrieved May 23, 2016 (http://www.echr.coe.int/Documents/Convention_ENG.pdf).

Curran, J. 2000. "Nový pohled na masová média a demokracii" [A New Perspective on Mass Media and Democracy, in Czech). Pp. 116–164 in *Politická komunikace a média*

[Political Communication and the Media, in Czech], by J. Jirák, B. Říchová. Prague: Univerzita Karlova.

Dearing, J. W., E. M. Rogers. 1996. *Agenda-Setting*. Thousand Oaks, London, New Delhi: SAGE Publications.

Dery, D. 1984. *Problem Definition in Policy Analysis*. Lawrence, KS: University Press of Kansas.

Dowding, K. 2011. "Rational Choice Theory." Pp. 36–50 in *The SAGE Handbook of Governance*, edited by M. Bevir. London: Sage Publications.

Drhová, Z., A. Veselý. 2007. "Identifikace variant řešení veřejně politických problémů" [Identifying alternative solutions to policy problems, in Czech]. Pp. 253–272 in *Analýza a tvorba veřejných politik. Přístupy, metody a praxe* [Policy Analysis and Design: Approaches, Methods and Practices, in Czech], edited by A. Veselý, M. Nekola. Prague: Sociologické nakladatelství (SLON).

Drhová, Z., F. Ochrana. 2011. "Úvod k metodám pro hodnocení dopadů" [Introduction to Impact Evaluation Methods, in Czech]. Pp. 222–226 in M. Nekola, H. Geissler, M. Mouralová (eds.). *Současné metodologické otázky veřejné politiky* [Contemporary Methodological Issues of Public Policy, in Czech]. Prague: Karolinum.

Dror, Y. 1968. *Policy Making Reexamined*. San Francisco: Chandler Publishing Company.

Dror, Y. 1969. "The Prediction of Political Feasibility." Futures 1 (June): 282–8.

Dror, Y. 1983. *Public Policy Re-examined*. New Brunswick and Oxford: Transaction Publishers.

Dror, Y. 2001. *The Capacity to Govern*. London: Frank Cass.

Dunleavy, P., B. O'Leary. 1987. *Theories of the State. The Politics of Liberal Democracy*. Basingstoke and New York: Macmillan.

Dunn, W. N. 1981. *Public Policy Analysis*. Englewood Cliffs, NJ: Prentice Hall.

Dunn, W. N. 1988. "Methods of the Second Type: Coping with the Wilderness of Conventional Policy Analysis." *Policy Studies Journal*. 7 (4): 720–737.

Dunn, W. N. 2004. *Public Policy Analysis: An Introduction*. 3rd ed. Upper Saddle River: Prentice Hall.

Dunn, W. N. 2012. *Public Policy Analysis*. 5th edition. Boston: Pearson.

Easton, D. 1953. *The Political System*. New York: Knopf.

Encyclopædia Britannica, Inc. 2014. "Lobbying." *Encyclopdia Britannica*. Retrieved May 24, 2016 (http://www.britannica.com/topic/lobbying).

Esping-Andersen, G. 1990. *The Three Worlds of Welfare Capitalism*. New Jersey: Princeton University Press, 1990.

Etzioni, A. 1967. "Mixed-Scanning: a 'Third' Approach to Decision-Making." *Public Administration Review* 27 (5): 385–392.

Etzioni, A. 1988. *The Moral Dimension: Towards a New Economics*. New York: The Free Press.

Fiala, P., K. Schubert. 2000. *Moderní analýza politiky* [Modern Policy Analysis, in Czech]. Brno: Barrister & Principal.

Fischer, J. L. 1969. *Pokus o nástin systému sociologie* [The Attempt to Outline the System of Sociology, in Czech]. Unpublished manuscript. Retrieved April 18, 2014 (http://www.insoma.cz/fischer.pdf).

Frič, P. 2002. "Bez korupce nejsou koláče" [No Corruption No Gain, in Czech]. Prague: *Lidové noviny*, 13. 7. 2002.

Frič, P. 2008. *Vůdcovství českých elit* [The Leadership of Czech Elites, in Czech]. Prague: Grada.

Frič, P. et al. 1999. *Korupce na český způsob* [Corruption in Czech Style, in Czech]. Prague: G plus G.

Frič, P., O. Angelovská, R. Goulli. 2009. *Revitalizace a konsolidace neziskového sektoru v ČR po roce 1989* [Revitalization and Consolidation of the Nonprofit Sector in the Czech Republic after 1989, in Czech]. Prague: Agnes.

Fukuyama, F. 1992. *The End of History and the Last Man.* New York: Free Press.

Fukuyama, F. 1995. *Trust: The Social Virtues and the Creation of Prosperity.* New York: Free Press.

Fukuyama, F. 2004. *State Building, Governance and World Order in the 21st Century.* Ithaca: Cornell University Press.

Gambetta, D. 1993. *The Sicilian Mafia. The Business of Private Protection.* Cambridge and London: Cambridge University Press.

Gibson, D. M., R. E. Goodin. 1999. "The Veil of Vagueness." Pp. 357–85 in *Organizing Political Institutions: Essays for Johan P. Olsen*, edited by M. Egeberg, P. Laegreid. Oslo: Scandinavian University Press.

Giddens, A. 1998. *The Third Way. The Renewal of Social Policy.* Cambridge: Polity Press.

Glenn, J., T. J. Gordon, E. Florescu. 2014. *2013-14 State of the Future.* Washington: The Millennium Project.

Gramsci, A. 1994. *Pre-Prison Writings.* Cambridge: Cambridge University Press.

Greenberg, D. 2003. "Evaluation of Public Programs." Pp. 203–228 in Potůček, M., L. T. Leloup, G. Jenei, L. Varadi. *Public Policy in Central and Eastern Europe. Theories, Methods, Practices.* Bratislava: NISPAcee.

Griffin, R. 1995. *Fascism.* Oxford: Oxford University Press.

Haas, P. M. 1992. "Epistemic Communities and International Policy Coordination." *International Organization* 46 (1): 1–35.

Hagen, L. 2004. "Informační kvalita a její měření" [Information Quality and its Measurement, in Czech]. Pp. 51–70 in *Analýza obsahu mediálních sdělení* [Analysing the content of media communication, in Czech], edited by W. Schulz, I. Reifová. Prague: Karolinum.

Hall, P. A., C. R. Taylor. 1996. "Political Science and the Three New Institutionalisms." *Political Studies*, XLIV: 936–957.

Hayek, F. 2006. *Constitution of Liberty.* London: Routledge.

Hayes, M. T. 2001. The *Limits of Policy Change: Incrementalism, World View, and the Rule of Law.* Washington: Georgetown University Press.

Heclo, H. 1978. "Issue Networks and the Executive Establishment." Pp. 88–124 in *The New American Political System*, edited by A. King. Washington, DC: American Enterprise Institute.

Heclo, H. 1995. "Networks and the Executive Establishment." Pp. 46–58 in *Public Policy. Essential Readings*, by S. Z. Theodoulou, M. A. Cahn. Englewood Cliffs, NJ: Prentice Hall.

Held, D., A. McGrew. 2002. *Governing Globalization. Power, Authority and Global Governance*. Cambridge: Polity.

Heywood, A. 2012. *Political Ideologies: An Introduction*. 5th ed. Basingstoke: Palgrave Macmillan.

Heywood, A. 2013. *Politics*. 4th edition. London: Palgrave Macmillan.

Hisschemöller, R., R. Hoppe. 2001. "Coping with Intractable Controversies: The Case for Problem Structuring in Policy Design and Analysis." *Policy Studies Review Annual* 12: 47–52.

Hix, S. 1999. *The Political System of the European Union*. New York: St. Martin Press.

Hjern, B., D. O. Porter. 1981. "Implementation Structures: A New Unit of Administrative Analysis." *Organization Studies* 2 (3): 211–227.

Högye, M. 2003. "Budgeting as a Political Process." Pp. 231–256 in *Public Policy in Central and Eastern Europe: Theories, Methods, Practices*, by Potůček, M., L. LeLoup, G. Jenei, L. Váradi. Bratislava: NISPAcee

Holländer, P. 1995. *Základy všeobecné státovědy* [Foundations of the General Theory of State, in Czech]. Prague: Všehrd.

Hoppe, R. 2002. "Cultures of Public Policy Problems." *Journal of Comparative Policy Analysis* 4 (3): 305–326.

Hoppe, R., A. Peterse. 1993. *Handling Frozen Fire*. Boulder, CO: Westview Press.

Howlett, M. 2002. "Do Networks Matter? Linking Policy Network Structure to Policy Outcomes: Evidence From Four Canadian Policy Sectors, 1990–2000." *Canadian Journal of Political Science* 35 (2): 235–67.

Howlett, M. 2014. From the "Old" to the "New" Policy Design: Design Thinking Beyond Markets and Collaborative Governance. *Policy Sciences*, 47(3), 187-207.

Howlett, M. 2016. *Matching Policy Tools & Their Targets: Beyond Nudges and Utility Maximization in Policy Design*. Paper presented to the ECPR conference in Pisa, Italy. Retrieved November 7, 2016 (https://ecpr.eu/Filestore/PaperProposal /7aa0ca4c-c689-4f0f-bad1-12286042cd0c.pdf).

Howlett, M., A. Perl and M. Ramesh, *Studying Public Policy*. 2009. Toronto: Oxford University Press.

Howlett, M., M. Ramesh. 1995. *Studying Public Policy: Policy Cycles and Policy Subsystems*. Oxford: Oxford University Press.

Human Development Report 2010. *The Real Wealth of Nations: Pathways to Human Development*. New York: Palgrave Macmillan.

Hupe, P. L., M. J. Hill. 2006. "The Three Action Levels of Governance: Re-Framing the Policy Process Beyond the Stages Model." Pp. 13–30 in B. G. Peters, J. Pierre. *Handbook of Public Policy*. London: SAGE Publications.

Hvížďala, K. 2000. *Média a moc* [Media and Power, in Czech]. Prague: Votobia.

Cheema, G. S., L. Maguire. 2001. *Governance for Human Development. Public Administration and Development* 21: 201–209. Retrieved June 24, 2016 (http://onlinelibrary.wiley .com/doi/10.1002/pad.178/pdf).

Immergut, E. M. 2005. "Paradigms of Change in Political Science: Historical-Institutionalism in Political Science and the Problem of Change." Pp. 237–259 in *Understanding Change:*

Models, Methodologies, and Metaphors, edited by A. Wimmer, R., Kössler. Basinngstoke: Palgrave.

Jakubowicz, K. 2011. *Nowa ekologia mediow. Konwergencja a metamorfoza* [New Media Ecology. Convergence and Metamorphosis, in Polish]. Warszawa: Wydawnictwo Poltext.

Jenei, G, J. Hoós, L. Vass. 2003. "Public Policy Institutions: The State and Bureaucracy." Pp. 105-119 in *Public Policy in Central and Eastern Europe. Theories, Methods, Practices*, by Potůček, M., L. T. Leloup, G. Jenei, L. Varadi. Bratislava: NISPAcee.

Jenkins, W. I. 1978. *Policy Analysis*. Oxford: Martin Robertson.

Jirák, J. 2001. "Medializace jako strašák politiky [Medialization as a Scarecrow of Politics, in Czech]. Pp. 203-209 in *Institucionalizace (ne)odpovědnosti: globální svět, evropská integrace a české zájmy I.* [Institutionalization of (Ir)responsibility: Global World, European Integration and Czech Interests I, in Czech], by J. Kabele, M. Mlčoch. Prague: Karolinum.

John, P. 2013. *Analyzing Public Policy*. Routledge 1998.

Jordan, A. G. 1981. "Iron Triangles, Woolly Corporatism and Elastic Nets." *Journal of Public Policy* 1 (1): 95–123.

Jordan, A. G., J. J. Richardson. 1987. *British Politics and The Policy Process – An Arena Approach*. London: Allen Unwin.

Kaul, I., I. Grunberg, M. A. Stern (eds.). 2009. *Global Public Goods*. Oxford: Oxford University Press.

Kenis, P., V. Schneider. 1991. "Policy Networks and Policy Analysis: Scrutinizing a New Analytical Toolbox." Pp. 25–59 in *Policy Networks: Empirical Evidence and Theoretical Considerations*, edited by B. Marin, R. Mayntz. Boulder, Frankfurt: Campus Verlag, Westview Press.

Kerbo, H. R., J. W. Coleman. 2006. "Social Problems." Pp. 362–369 in *21st Century Sociology: A Reference Handbook*, edited by C. D. Bryant, D. L. Peck. Vol. 1: Traditional and Core Areas. CA, London: SAGE Publications.

Kingdon, J. 1984 (1995). *Agendas, Alternatives, and Public Policies*. Boston: Little, Brown.

Kingdon, R. 1994. "The Genevan Consistory in the Time of Calvin," Pp. 21–24 in *Calvinism in Europe 1540-1620*, edited by A. Pettegree, A. Duke, G. Lewis. Cambridge: Cambridge University Press.

Kinkor, J. 1996. *Trh a stát: k čemu potřebujeme filozofii* [Market and State: What Philosophy Is For, in Czech]. Prague: Svoboda.

Kiss, J. (ed.). 1998. *Současná politická filosofie* [Contemporary Political Philosophy, in Czech]. Prague: Oikoymenh.

Kissinger, H. A. 1957. *A World Restored: Metternich, Castlereagh and the Problems of Peace, 1812-22*. London: Weidenfeld and Nicolson.

Knoepfel, P., C. Larrue, F. Valone, M. Hill. 2007. *Public Policy Analysis*. Bristol: Policy Press.

Kooiman, J. 2003. *Governing as Governance*. London: SAGE Publications.

Landry, M. 1995. "A Note of the Concept of 'Problem.'" *Organization Studies* 16 (2): 315-343.

Lane, J.-E. 1993. *The Public Sector. Concepts, Models and Approaches*. London: Sage.

Larson, C. U. 1994. *Persuasion*. 7th ed. Belmont, CA: Wadsworth.

Lasswell, H. 1936. *Politics: Who Gets What, When, How*. New York: Whittlesey House, McGraw-Hill.

Lasswell, H. D. 1956. *The Decision Process: Seven Categories of Functional Analysis*. College Park, MD: University of Maryland.

Lehmbruch, G. 1979. "Liberal Corporatism and Party Government." Pp. 147–184 in *Trends Towards Corporatist Intermediation*, edited by P. C. Schmitter, G. Lehmbruch. Beverly Hills/London: SAGE Publications.

Lindblom, C. E. 1968. *The Policy-Making Process*. Englewood Cliffs (NJ): Prentice-Hall.

Lindblom, C. E. 1977. *Politics and Markets*. New York: Basic Books.

Lindblom, C. E., E. J. Woodhouse. 1993. *The Policy-Making Process*. Englewood Cliffs (NJ): Prentice-Hall.

Lippman, W. 1955. *Essays in the Public Interest Philosophy*. Boston: Little, Brown and Co.

Lipsky, M. 1980. *Street-Level Bureaucracy*. New York: Russell Sage.

Lowi, T. J. 1972. "Four Systems of Policy, Politics, and Choice." *Public Administration Review* 33: 298–310.

Lupták, M., V. Prorok. 2011. *Politické ideologie a teorie od starověku po rok 1848* [Political Ideologies and Theories from Antiquity to 1848, in Czech]. Plzeň: Vydavatelství a nakladatelství Aleš Čeněk.

MacCrimmon, K. R., R. N. Taylor. 1976. "Decision Making and Problem Solving." Pp. 1397–1453 in *Handbook of Industrial and Organizational Psychology*, edited by M. D. Dunnette. Chicago: Rand-McNally.

Majone, G. 1975. "On the Notion of Political Feasibility." *European Journal of Political Research* 3 (September): 259–74.

Majone, G. 1989. *Evidence, Argument, and Persuasion in the Policy Process*. New Haven, CT: Yale University Press.

Majone, G. 2006. "Agenda Setting." Pp. 225–250 in *The Oxford Handbook of Public Policy*, edited by M. Moran, M. Rein, R. E. Goodin. Oxford: Oxford University Press.

Malíková, L. 2003. *Verejná politika. Aktéri a procesy* [Public Policy: Actors and Processes, in Slovak]. Bratislava: Univerzita Komenského.

Malinowski, B. 1960. *A Scientific Theory of Culture and Other Essays*. New York: Oxford University Press.

Mannheim, K. 1936. *Ideology and Utopia*. New York: Harvest Books.

Marks, G. 1993. "Structural Policy and Multilevel Governance." Pp. 402–403 in *The State of the European Community: The Maastricht Debates and Beyond*, edited by A. Cafruny, G. Rosenthal. 2nd ed. Harlow: Longman.

Marsh, D., R. A. W. Rhodes (eds.). 1992. *Policy Networks in British Government*. Oxford: Claredon Press.

Marshall, T. H. 1963. *Sociology at the Crossroads and Other Essays*. London: Heinemann.

Martenas, S. J. 1991. "Beyond Scandals & Statutes: Ethics in Public Administration." *University of Virginia News Letter* 67 (9): 1–8.

May, P. 1993. "Mandate Design and Implementation: Enhancing Implementation Efforts and Shaping Regulatory Styles." *Journal of Policy Analysis and Management* 12 (4): 634–63.

McCool, D. C. 1995. *Public Policy Theories, Models, and Concepts: An Anthology*. Englewood Cliffs, NJ: Prentice Hall.

McQuail, D. 2010. *Mass Communication Theory: An Introduction*. 6th edition. London: Sage.

Mills, C. W. 1959. *The Sociological Imagination*. Oxford: Oxford University Press.

Milward, H. B., K. G. Provan. 1999. *How networks are governed*. Unpublished paper.

Mintrom, M. 2011. *Contemporary policy analysis*. Oxford: Oxford University Press.

Mintrom, M., S. Vergari. 1996. "Advocacy Coalitions, Policy Entrepreneurs, and Policy Change." *Policy Studies Journal* 24: 420–35. doi: 10.1111/j.1541-0072.1996.tb01638.x.

Mlčoch, L. 1996. *Institucionální ekonomie* [Institutional Economics, in Czech]. Prague: Karolinum.

Musil, J. 1996. "Nový pohled na občanskou společnost" [A New Perspective on Civil Society, in Czech]. *Nová přítomnost* 2 (1): 31.

Myrdal, G. 1968. *Asian Drama: An Inquiry into the Poverty of Nations*. Harmondsworth: Pelican Books.

Nagel, S. 1994. *The Encyclopedia of Policy Studies*. New York: St. Martins.

Nakamura, R. 1987. "The Textbook Policy Process and Implementation Research." *Policy Studies Review* 7 (2): 142–154.

Nekola, M. 2007a. "Monitoring a evaluace realizovaných politik" [Monitoring and Evaluation of Implemented Policies, in Czech]. Pp. 337–382 in A. Veselý, M. Nekola (eds.). *Analýza a tvorba veřejných politik: přístupy, metody a praxe* [Public policy analysis and making: approaches, methods, and practice, in Czech]. Prague: Sociologické nakladatelství.

Nekola, M. 2007b. "Rozdílné přístupy k hodnocení veřejných programů – ekonomická evaluace a její alternativy" [Different Approaches to Public Programs Evaluations: Economic Evaluation and Its Alternatives, in Czech]. Pp. 37–48 in F. Ochrana (ed.). *Theoretical and practical aspects of public finance*. Prague: Vysoká škola ekonomická.

Nekola, M. 2009. "Analyzing and Evaluating Major World Approaches to the Construction and Utilization of Governance Indicators." Pp. 28–63 in M. Potůček et al. 2009. *Strategic Governance and the Czech Republic*. Prague: Karolinum.

Neuvonen, A. (ed.). 2005. *Hostages of the Horizon. The twin challenge of ignorance and indifference. Review on issues raised in the Club of Rome 2004 Annual Conference*. Helsinki: Finnish Association for the Club of Rome.

Novotný, V. 2012. *Vývoj českého studia veřejných politik v evropském kontextu* [Development of the Czech Study of Public Policies in European Context, in Czech]. Prague: Karolinum.

Novotný, V. 2013. *Teorie veřejně politického procesu (výčet a výklad)* [Theories of Public Policy Process: Enumeration and Interpretation, in Czech]. Prague. Unpublished manuscript.

Ochrana, F. 2005. *Veřejné rozpočty jako nástroj veřejné politiky a strategického vládnutí. Veřejná politika, veřejná volba, veřejný zájem* [Public Budgets as Instruments of Public Policy and Strategic Governance, in Czech]. Prague: CESES FSV UK. Retrieved May 24, 2016 (http://ceses.cuni.cz/CESES-20-version1-sesit05_06_ochrana.pdf).

Ochrana, F. 2007. "Zhodnocení variantních politik" [Evaluation of Alternative Policies, in Czech]. Pp. 291–309 in A. Veselý, M. Nekola (eds.). *Analýza a tvorba veřejných politik: přístupy, metody a praxe* [Policy analysis and design: approaches, methods, and practice, in Czech]. Prague: Sociologické nakladatelství.

Ochrana, F. 2012. *Methodology of Science.* Prague: Karolinum.

Ochrana, F. 2015. *Methodology of Social Sciences.* Prague: Karolinum.

Ochrana, F., M. Půček. 2011. *Efektivní zavádění a řízení změn ve veřejné správě – Smart Administration* [Effective Implementation and Management of Changes in Public Administration: Smart Administration, in Czech]. Prague: Wolters Kluwer.

Ostrom, E. 1999. "Institutional Rational Choice: An Assessment of the Institutional Analysis and Development Framework." Pp. 35–71 in *Theories of the Policy Process*, edited by P. A. Sabatier. Boulder: Westview Press.

Ostrom, E. 2005. *Understanding Institutional Diversity.* Princeton: Princeton University Press.

Ovseiko, P. 2002. *The Politics of Health Sector Reform in Eastern Europe: the Actor-Centered Institutionalist Framework for Analysis.* Budapest: Center for Policy Studies. IPF Working Paper No. 2002-01.

Patton, C. V., Sawicki, D. S. 1993. *Basic Methods of Policy Analysis and Planning.* Englewood Cliffs: Prentice Hall.

Peters, B. G. 1981. "The Problem of Bureaucratic Government." *Journal of Politics* 43 (1): 56.

Peters. B. G. 1992. "Government Reorganization: A Theoretical Analysis." *International Political Science Review* 13 (2): 199–218.

Peters, B. G. 1993. *American Public Policy.* Chatham: Chatham House.

Peters, B. G. 1998. *Managing Horizontal Government. The Politics of Coordination.* Canadian Center for Management Development.

Peters, B. G. 1999. *American Public Policy: Promise and Performance.* New York, London: Chatham House Publishers, Seven Bridges press, LLC.

Peters, B. G. 2015. *Advanced introduction to public policy.* Cheltenham, UK and Northampton, MA, USA: Edward Elgar Publishing.

Peters, B. G., J. Pierre (eds.) 2004. *Politicization of the Civil Service in Comparative Perspective: the Quest for Control.* London: Routledge.

Pierre, J., G. Peters. 2000. *Governance, Politics, and the State.* New York: St. Martin's Press.

Pierson, P. 1996. "The Path to European Integration: A Historical-Institutionalist Analysis." *Comparative Political Studies* 29 (2): 123–163.

Pierson, P. 2000. "Increasing Returns, Path Dependence, and the Study of Politics." *American Political Science Review* 94 (2): 251–267.

Polanyi, M. 1958. *Personal Knowledge. Towards a Post-Critical Philosophy.* London: Routledge.

Pollitt, Ch., G. Bouckaert. 2004. *Public Management Reform: A Comparative Analysis.* Oxford: Oxford University Press.

Potůček, M. 1992. "The Concept of Human Potential and Social Policy." *Acta Universitatis Carolinae Oeconomica* 1: 51–67.

Potůček, M. 1995. *Sociální politika* [Social Policy, in Czech]. Prague: Sociologické nakladatelství (SLON).

Potůček, M. 1999. *Not Only the Market. The Role of the Market, Government and Civic Sector in the Development of Postcommunist Societies.* Budapest: CEU Press.

Potůček, M. 2003. "Policy Coordination: Government, Markets, and the Civic Sector." Pp. 77–102 in *Public Policy in Central and Eastern Europe: Theories, Methods, Practices*, by Potůček, M., L. LeLoup, G. Jenei, L. Váradi. 2003. Bratislava: NISPAcee.

Potůček, M. 2007. "Czech Public Policy as a Scientific Discipline and Object of Research." *Central European Journal of Public Policy* 1 (1): 102–121.

Potůček, M. 2008. "The Concept of the Neo-Weberian State Confronted by the Multi-Dimensional Concept of Governance." *NISPAcee Journal of Public Administration and Public Policy* 1 (2): 83–94.

Potůček, M. 2009. *Will Global Public Policy Arise from Global Crisis?* Central European Journal of Public Policy. 3(2): 4–21.

Potůček, M. 2014. "Konceptuální rámce v teorii a praxi veřejné politiky" [Conceptual Frameworks in the Theory and Practice of Public Policy, in Czech]. *Teorie vědy XXXVI* (1): 9–22.

Potůček, M. et al. 2005 (new edition 2010). *Veřejná politika* [Public Policy, in Czech]. Prague: Sociologické nakladatelství (SLON).

Potůček, M. et al. 2009. *Strategic Governance and the Czech Republic.* Prague: Karolinum.

Potůček, M. et al. 2016. *Veřejná politika.* Prague: C. H. Beck.

Potůček, M., L. LeLoup, G. Jenei, L. Váradi. 2003. *Public Policy in Central and Eastern Europe: Theories, Methods, Practices.* Bratislava: NISPAcee.

Potůček, M., J. Musil, M. Mašková (eds.). 2008. *Strategické volby pro Českou republiku: teoretická východiska* [Strategic Choices for the Czech Republic: the Theoretical Foundations, in Czech]. Prague: Sociologické nakladatelství (SLON).

Potůček, M., L. Vass, P. Kotlas. 2005 (new edition 2010). "Veřejná politika jako proces" [Public Policy as a Process, in Czech]. Pp. 61–84 in *Veřejná politika* [Public Policy, in Czech], by M. Potůček et al. Prague: Sociologické nakladatelství (SLON).

Pressman, J. L., A. Wildavsky. 1984. *Implementation: How great expectations in Washington are dashed in Oakland.* Berkeley: University of California Press.

Publications Office of the European Union. 2012a. "Consolidated Version of the Treaty on European Union." *Official Journal of the European Union* C326/13, October 26. Retrieved February 2, 2016 (http://eur-lex.europa.eu/legal-content/EN/TXT/PDF/?uri=CELEX:12012M/TXT&from=EN).

Publications Office of the European Union. 2012b. "Consolidated Version of the Treaty on the Functioning of the European Union." *Official Journal of the European Union* C326/47, October 26. Retrieved February 2, 2016 (http://eur-lex.europa.eu/legal-content/EN/TXT/PDF/?uri=CELEX:12012E/TXT&from=EN).

Purkrábek, M. 2003. "The Application of Sociological Methods in Public Policy." Pp. 331–338 in *Public Policy in Central and Eastern Europe. Theories, Methods, Practices*, by M. Potůček, L. T. Leloup, G. Jenei, L. Varadi. Bratislava: NISPAcee.

Quattrone, G. A., Tversky, A. 1988. "Contrasting Rational and Psychological Analyses of Political Choice." *American Political Science Review* 82 (3): 719–736.

Rawls, J. 1987. "The Idea of an Overlapping Consensus." *Oxford Journal of Legal Studies* 7 (1): 1–25.

Rawls, J. 1989. "The Domain of the Political and Overlapping Consensus." *New York University Law Review* 64: 233–55.

Rhodes, R. A. W. 1997. *Understanding Governance: Policy Networks, Governance and Accountability*. Buckingham: Open University Press.

Richardson, J., R. H. Kimber. 1978. "Lobbying, Administrative Reform and Policy Styles: The Case of Land Drainage." *Political Studies* 26 (1): 47–64.

Ringen, St. 1987. *The Possibility of Politics*. Oxford: Clarendon Press.

Ripley, R., G. Franklin. 1981. Congress, the Bureaucracy and Public Policy. Homewood, II.: Dorsey Press.

Roebroek, J. M. 1992. *The Imprisoned State*. Tilburg: Tilburg University.

Rotberg, R. 2002. "The New Nature of Nation States Failure." *Washington Quarterly* 25 (3): 85–96.

Sabatier, P. A. 1986. "Top-Down and Bottom-Up Approaches to Implementation Research: a Critical Analysis and Suggested Synthesis." *Journal of Public Policy* 6 (1): 21–48.

Sabatier, P. A. 1995. "An Advocacy Coalition Framework of Policy Change and the Role of Policy-Oriented Learning Therein." Pp. 339–379 in *Public Policy Theories, Models, and Concepts: An Anthology*, edited by D. C. McCool. Englewood Cliffs, NJ: Prentice Hall.

Sabatier, P. A. 1999. *Theories of the Policy Process*. Boulder: Westview Press.

Sabatier, P. A., S. Hunter, S. McLaughlin. 1987. "The Devil Shift: Perceptions and Misperceptions of Opponents." *Western Political Quarterly* 40 (3): 51–73.

Sabatier, P. A., H. Jenkins-Smith. 1999. "The Advocacy Coalition Framework: An Assessment." Pp. 117–166 in *Theories of the Policy Process*, edited by P. A. Sabatier. Boulder, CO: Westview Press.

Sabatier, P. A., D. Mazmanian. 1980. "A Framework of Analysis." *Political Studies Journal* 8 (4): 538–560.

Salisbury, R. H., 1968. "The Analysis of Public Policy: A Search of Theories and Roles." Pp. 151–175 in *Political Science and Public Policy*, edited by A. Ranney. Chicago: Markham.

Samuelson, P., W. D. Nordhaus. 2010. *Economics*. 19th ed. Boston: McGraw-Hill Irwin.

Sartori, G. 1987. *The Theory of Democracy Revisited – Part One*. New Jersey: Chatham House Publishers.

Scharpf, F. W. 1988. "The Joint Decision Trap: Lessons from German Federalism and European Integration." *Public Administration* 66 (2): 239–78.

Scharpf, F. W. 1997. *Games Real Actors Play. Actor-Centered Institutionalism in Policy Research.* Boulder: Westview Press.

Scharpf, F. W. 2001. "Democratic Legitimacy under Conditions of Regulatory Competition: Why Europe Differs from the United States." Pp. 355–376 in *The Federal Vision: Legitimacy and Levels of Governance in the United States and the European Union*, edited by K. Nicolaidis, R. Howse. New York: Oxford University Press.

Schlager, E. 1997. "A Response to Kim Quaile Hill's." *Search of Policy Theory. Policy Currents* 7 (June): 14–5.

Schlager, E. 1999. "A Comparison of Frameworks, Theories, and Models of Policy Process." Pp. 233–260 in *Theories of the Policy Process*, edited by P. A. Sabatier. Boulder: Westview Press.

Schmidt, V. A. 2008. "Discursive Institutionalism: The Explanatory Power of Ideas and Discourse." *Annual Review of Political Science* 11: 303–326.

Schneider, A. 2013. "Policy Design and Transfer." Pp. 217–228 in *Routledge Handbook of Public Policy*, edited by J. E. Araral, S. Fritzen, M. Howlett, M. Ramesh, Xun Wu. New York: Routledge.

Schneider, V. 1992. "The Structure of Policy Networks." *European Journal of Political Research* 21 (1–2): 109–129.

Schön, D., M. Rein. 1994. *Frame Reflection.* New York: Basic Books.

Schulz, W. 2004. "Proces politické komunikace: vymezení problémů a kladení otázek" [Political Communication as a Process: Defining Problems and Asking Questions, in Czech]. Pp. 9–27 in *Analýza obsahu mediálních sdělení* [Analysing the content of media communication, in Czech], edited by W. Schulz, I. Reifová. Prague: Karolinum.

Schumpeter, J. 1939. *Business Cycles: A Theoretical, Historical and Statistical Analysis of the Capitalist Process.* New York: McGraw-Hill.

Schwarzmantel, J. 2008. *Ideology and Politics.* London: SAGE Publications.

Sirovátka, T., V. Kulhavý, M. Horáková, M. Rákoczyová. 2006. "Hodnocení efektivity programů aktivní politiky zaměstnanosti" [Evaluation of the Effectiveness of Active Employment Policy Programs, in Czech]. Prague: Výzkumný ústav práce a sociálních věcí.

Social Doctrine of the Czech Republic. 2002. Retrieved May 19, 2016 (http://martinpotucek.cz/index.php?option=com_rubberdoc&view=doc&id=503&format=raw).

Staniszkis, J. 2009. *O moci a bezmoci* [On Power and Powerlessness, in Czech]. Brno: Centrum pro studium demokracie.

Stankiewicz, W. J. 2006. *Hledání politické filosofie. Ideologie na sklonku dvacátého století* [Searching for Political Philosophy. Ideology in Late Twentieth Century, in Czech]. Brno: Centrum pro studium demokracie a kultury.

Staroňová, K. 2009. *Hodnotenie vplyvov v teórii a praxi Slovenska a Európskej Únie* [Impact Assessment in Theory and Practice of Slovakia and the European Union, in Slovak]. Prešov: Adin.

Staroňová, K. 2014. "Institutionalization of regulatory impact assessment in the Czech Republic and Slovakia: do reforms bring RIA closer to be a decision-making tool?" Pp. 197–203 in *Current Trends in Public Sector Research*. Brno: Masaryk University.

Stiglitz, J. E., A. Sen, and J.-P. Fitoussi. 2009. *Report by the Commission on the Measurement of Economic Performance and Social Progress*. Paris: Institut national de la statistique et des études économiques. Retrieved April 17, 2016 (http://www.stiglitz-sen-fitoussi.fr/documents/rapport_anglais.pdf).

Stoker, R. P. 1989. "A Regime Framework for Implementation Analysis." *Policy Studies Review* 9 (1): 29–49.

Streeck, W., P. C. Schmitter. 1985. *Private Interest Government. Beyond Market and State*. London: SAGE Publications.

Thelen, K. 2004. *How Institutions Evolve*. Cambridge: Cambridge University Press.

Theodoulou, S. Z. 1995. "Making Public Policy." Pp. 86–96 in Public Policy. *Essential Readings*, by S. Z. Theodoulou, M. A. Cahn. Englewood Cliffs, NJ: Prentice Hall.

Theodoulou, S. Z., M. A. Cahn. 1995. *Public Policy. Essential Readings*. Englewood Cliffs, NJ: Prentice Hall.

Thompson, J. B. 2013. *The Media and Modernity*. Cambridge: Polity.

Tilly, C. 1984. *Big Structures, Large Processes, and Huge Comparisons*. New York: Russel Sage Foundation Press.

Tondl, L. 2005. "Sémiotické funkce konceptuálního rámce" [Semiotic Functions of a Conceptual Framework, in Czech]. *Organon* F 12 (3): 278.

Transformation Index BTI 2016. Gütersloh: Verlag Bertelsmann Stiftung 2016.

Tsebelis, G. 2002. *Veto Players: How Political Institutions Work*. Princeton: Princeton University Press.

United Nations. 1948. *The Universal Declaration of Human Rights*. Retrieved May 23, 2016 (http://www.ohchr.org/EN/UDHR/Documents/UDHR_Translations/eng.pdf).

Uphoff, N. 1993. "Grassroots Organizations and NGOs in Rural Development: Opportunities with Diminishing States and Expanding Markets." *World Development* 21 (4): 607–622.

Vavroušek, J. 1993. "Závod s časem. Hledání lidských hodnot slučitelných s trvale udržitelným způsobem života" [Race Against Time. Searching for Human Values Compatible with a Sustainable Way of Life, in Czech]. *Literární noviny* IV (49), (9 Dec): 1, 3.

Veselý, A. 2007. Problem delimitation in public policy analysis. *Central European Journal of Public Policy*, 1(1), 80-100.

Veselý, A. 2010. *Vymezení a strukturace problému ve veřejné politice* [Problem Delimitation and Structuring in Public Policy, in Czech]. Prague: Karolinum.

Veselý, A. 2011. "Veřejněpolitický a 'klasický' sociálně-vědní výzkum: podobnosti a odlišnosti" [Public Policy Research and "Classical" Social Research: Similarities and Differences, in Czech]. In *Současné metodologické otázky veřejné politiky* [Contemporary Methodological Issues of Public Policy, in Czech], by M. Nekola, H. Geissler, M. Mouralová. Prague: Karolinum.

Veselý, A. 2014. *Vymezení veřejně politických problémů. Učební text k veřejné politice* [Delimitation of Public Policy Issues. Lecture Notes on Public Policy, in Czech]. Prague: Univerzita Karlova. Unpublished manuscript.

Veselý, A., Z. Drhová, M. Nachtmannová. 2005. *Veřejná politika a proces její tvorby. Co je "policy" a jak vzniká* [Public Policy and the Policy Process. What Is Policy and How It Arises, in Czech]. Studie CESES, vol. 8. Prague: CESES FSV UK.

Veselý, A., M. Nekola (eds.). 2007. *Analýza a tvorba veřejných politik: přístupy, metody a praxe* [Policy Analysis and Design: Approaches, Methods and Practices, in Czech]. Prague: Sociologické nakladatelství (SLON).

Veselý, A., M. Nekola, E. Hejzlarová (eds.). 2016. *Policy Analysis in the Czech Republic.* Bristol: Policy Press.

Vickers, G. 1965. *The Art of Judgement.* London: Chapman and Hall.

Weigle, M. A., J. Butterfield. 1993. "Civil Society in Reforming Communist Regimes." *Comparative Politics* 25 (2): 1–23.

Weimer, D. L. 2008. "Theories of and in the Policy Process." *Policy Studies Journal* 36 (4): 489–495.

Weimer, D. L., A. R. Vining. 1992. *Policy Analysis: Concepts and Practice.* 2nd ed. Englewood Cliffs, NJ: Prentice Hall.

Weimer, D. L., A. R. Vining. 1999. *Policy Analysis: Concepts and Practice.* Upper Saddle River: Prentice Hall.

Weimer, D. L., A. R. Vining. 2005. *Policy Analysis: Concepts and Practice.* 4th ed. Upper Saddle River (NJ): Prentice-Hall.

Weir, M. 1992. "Ideas and the Politics of Bounded Innovation." Pp. 188–211 in *Structuring Politics*, edited by S. Steinmo, K. Thelen, F. Longstreth, F. Cambridge: Cambridge University Press.

Weiss, C. H. 1983. "Ideology, Interests and Information." Pp. 213–245 in *Ethics, the Social Sciences, and Policy Analysis*, edited by D. Callahan, B. Jennings. New York: Plenum Press.

Wildavsky A. 1974. *The Politics of the Budgetary Process.* Boston: Little, Brown & Co.

Wildavsky, A. 1979. *Speaking Truth to Power: The Art and Craft of Policy Analysis.* Boston: Little, Brown and Co.

Winkler, J. 2007. *Teorie rozhodování a dynamika sociální politiky* [Theory of Decision Making and the Dynamics of Social Policy, in Czech]. Brno: Masarykova univerzita.

Zahariadis, N. 2007. "The Multiple Streams Framework: Structure, Limitations, Prospects." Pp. 65–92 in *Theories of the Policy Process*, edited by P. Sabatier. 2nd ed. Boulder: Westview Press.

Zahariadis, N., Ch. S. Allen. 1995. "Ideas, Networks and Policy Streams: Privatization in Britain and Germany." *Policy Studies Review* 14 (1/2): 71–98.

Zürn, M., S. Liebfried. 2005. "Reconfiguring the national constellation." *European Review* 13 (1): 1–36.

Journals and Internet Sources

JOURNALS

PUBLIC POLICY

Central European Journal of Public Policy (CEJPP): http://cejpp.eu/
Journal of European Public Policy: http://www.tandfonline.com/toc/rjpp20/current
Journal of European Social Policy: http://esp.sagepub.com/
Journal of Public Policy: http://journals.cambridge.org/action/displayJournal?jid=PUP
Policy and Society: http://www.journals.elsevier.com/policy-and-society
Public Policy and Administration: http://ppa.sagepub.com/

POLICY ANALYSIS

European Policy Analysis: http://www.ipsonet.org/publications/open-access/epa
Evaluation: http://evi.sagepub.com/
Journal of Comparative Policy Analysis: Research and Practice: http://www.tandfonline
.com/toc/fcpa20/current
Journal of Policy Analysis and Management: http://www.appam.org/publications
/jpam/
Review of Policy Research: http://www.ipsonet.org/publications/journals/review-of
-policy-research/

GOVERNANCE, PUBLIC ADMINISTRATION

Gouvernement et action publique: http://www.cairn-int.info/about_this_journal.php?ID
_REVUE=E_GAP

Governance: http://onlinelibrary.wiley.com/journal/10.1111/(ISSN)1468-0491
International Review of Administrative Sciences: http://ras.sagepub.com/
Lex localis - Journal of local self-government: http://journal.lex-localis.press
NISPAcee Journal of Public Administration and Policy: http://www.nispa.org/journal
.php
Public Administration: http://onlinelibrary.wiley.com/journal/10.1111/(ISSN)1467-9299
Public Management Review: http://www.tandfonline.com/loi/rpxm20

POLITICAL SCIENCE

Critical Policy Studies: http://www.tandf.co.uk/journals/rcps
Policy and Politics: http://www.ingentaconnect.com/content/tpp/pap;jsessionid
=68u3luqoo56n6.victoria
Policy Sciences: http://link.springer.com/journal/11077
Policy Studies Journal: http://www.ipsonet.org/publications/journals/policy
-studies-journal
Politiques et Management Public: http://pmp.revuesonline.com/accueil.jsp

INTERNET SOURCES

The Almanac of Policy Issues: http://www.policyalmanac.org/directory/General
-Organizations.shtml
The European Union: http://www.europa.eu/
The European Union Policy Agendas Project: http://www.policyagendas.eu/
The International Conference on Public Policy: http://www.icpublicpolicy.org/
The Network of Institutes and Schools of Public Administration in Central and Eastern
Europe (NISPAcee): http://www.nispa.sk/
The Organization for Economic Co-operation and Development: http://www.oecd.org/
The Policy Design Lab: http://policy-design.org/
The Public Policy Exchange, Great Britain: http://www.publicpolicyexchange.co.uk/
The Comparative Agendas Project http://www.comparativeagendas.net/
The Institute for Public Policy Research, Great Britain: http://www.ippr.org/
The World Bank: http://www.worldbank.org/

English-Czech Glossary of Public Policy Terms

governance	vládnutí
government	vláda
policy analysis	analýza politiky
policy design	tvorba politiky
policy evaluation	hodnocení politik
policy issues	veřejně politická témata
policy networks	veřejně politické sítě
policy research	veřejně politický výzkum
political science	politologie, politické vědy
politics	politický proces střetávání a vyrovnávání zájmů
polity	obecná idea a strukturálně-funkční rámec politického procesu; "volba společnosti"
public affairs	veřejné záležitosti
public interests	veřejné zájmy
public policy (policy, policy science, policy studies)	veřejná politika
public tasks	veřejné úlohy

List of Tables – Part A

List of Figures – Part A

PART B

Introduction to Part B

In this part of the textbook we present several case studies documenting the ways one can apply selected theories in analyzing the history of the Czech pension system reform after 1989.

Why did we choose precisely the Czech pension system and a series of more-or-less successful attempts to reform it? It is a complex system, and a range of social and economic contexts have to be considered when its analyses or reforms are drafted. It is determined not only by past, and current, but also future demographic development; in one way or another, it concerns all citizens of the country. It is marked by a relatively high degree of path dependence and thus may resist attempts to change.[111] And in turn, decisions once adopted may influence the course of the system and, consequently, people's behavior for many decades. Decision-making about the pension system is shaped not only by the evidence and conclusions of experts but also by political ideologies, as well as by a diverse range of people's and institutions' interests. And despite the national specifics of its pension system, the Czech Republic faces challenges similar to many other countries – an opportunity for comparative analysis and for drawing lessons from abroad.

Students with a preference for narratives and vivid accounts of events will start their encounter with public policy by looking at this part of the textbook. To make the following chapters as reader-friendly as possible, we chose the case study format. In each study we analyzed a selected area or event in the history of the Czech pension system. To better explain the process, we sorted

---

111 For a broader insight into the modern history of the Czech Republic, refer to Ash, T. G. 1990. *The Magic Lantern: The Revolution of '89 Witnessed in Warsaw, Budapest, Berlin and Prague.* New York: Random House, or Shepherd, R. H. E. 2000. *Czechoslovakia. The Velvet Revolution and Beyond.* New York: Palgrave.

through a wide range of public policy theories and picked those that we found most useful with regard to the case at hand.

In order to better understand the complex ways old-age provision is secured through pension systems, this part starts with a brief retrospective account in Chapter **B1, Historical Overview of Pension Systems in the World and in the Czech Republic. Case Study B2** analyzes many repeated attempts to utilize expertise in policy decision-making with respect to the Czech pension system, demonstrating that the cooperation between experts and politicians has never been easy. **Case Study B3** examines the responses by the Czech government and parliament to a ruling of the Constitutional Court which considered applicable provisions of the Act on Social Insurance as unlawful discrimination against those groups of participants who contributed the most in the course of their economically active careers. **Case Study B4** discusses an attempt to structurally reform the pension system as a whole by establishing a new element – a fully funded, private, so-called second pillar that absorbed a part of mandatory social insurance premiums from the pay-as-you-go public first pillar. In all three case studies we apply selected public policy theories while referring to the respective passages of **Part A** in this textbook. For a basic outline of theories and applications presented in this book, see the table "**Overview of public policy theories**" in the beginning of this book. Finally, Chapter **B5 on Pensions Basics** makes an important contribution to our understanding of pension systems by outlining their key parameters and instruments and by discussing possible approaches to pension reforms around the world.

November 2017
prof. Dr. Martin Potůček, Ph.D.
Mgr. Veronika Rudolfová, Ph.D.

Terminology of the Pillars in the Czech Pension System

Pillar	Characteristic	Availability
First	Mandatory, public, defined benefit (DB), pay-as-you-go (PAYG)	1948 +
Second	Voluntary, private, defined-contribution (DC), fully-funded (FF) pension savings co-funded from individual contributions reallocated from the first (public) pillar	2013–2015
Third	Voluntary, private, defined-contribution (DC), fully-funded (FF) pension insurance with a state contribution	1994–2012
	Voluntary, private, defined-contribution (DC), fully-funded (FF) pension savings with a state contribution	2013 +

Source: Authors.

/B1/

Historical Overview of Pension Systems in the World and in the Czech Republic

HISTORICAL OVERVIEW OF PENSION SYSTEMS IN THE WORLD

Ancient Greeks used amphorae to deposit their future pension resources in the form of quality olive oil, which was in demand as a commodity and could be stored over extensive periods of time.

    Rome's first emperor Augustus was afraid of rebellion by veteran troops. In order to secure them for "retirement age," he introduced one of the first pension schemes in human history – the military treasury. Edward Gibbon states that the growth of pension entitlements over the years, and especially the inability of the Roman government to pay, was one of the main reasons of the eventual collapse of the Roman Empire.

In the **medieval period,** the "economic security" of serfs (who comprised the majority of society) was provided only as long as they were able to work. Then, it was primarily up to families to take care of their elderly and incapacitated members. Rulers also instituted care for their soldiers and administrative officials; sometimes noblemen helped their subjects and the church took care of the poor and the ill. Specialized organizations developed with the aim to provide a certain degree of economic security to their working members and their families. The **medieval institution of "the guild"** was one of these types of organizations. Community-based "friendly societies" were on the rise in the 17th, 18th and especially 19th centuries. The work of **Thomas Paine** introduced a new concept of pension security. In his 1795 article entitled, *Agrarian Justice*, the revolutionary, philosopher, and radical (and the author of *Common Sense*) was the first (or one of the first) to conceptualize a universal pension scheme for all citizens (Paine 2004). Arguing passionately that "poverty is not God's will," he proposed to establish a "National Fund" and to make every man and woman, upon reaching the age of 21 years, eligible to receive a grant (not a mere charity but an entitlement) sufficient so "they could buy a cow, and implements to cultivate a few acres of land."

In the wake of the **industrial revolution**, people's style of living and working went through dramatic changes and the issue of social security became even more urgent. A milestone for social security in continental Europe was reached in the year 1881 when Chancellor **Otto von Bismarck** proposed, via a letter by Emperor William I to the German Parliament, to establish a mandatory and universal scheme of accident and sickness insurance for workers. Bismarck's concept later became synonymous of one of the basic models of social insurance and was successfully implemented in most European and many non-European countries.

The development of social security systems, especially in Anglo-Saxon countries, was importantly shaped by Sir **William Henry Beveridge**, who presented to British Government a revolutionary concept of social system entitled, "Social Insurance and Allied Services" (Beveridge 1942). According to his recommendations, the government would take responsibility for social security and set "freedom from poverty" as the main goal of the system. Beveridge insisted that the new system should provide flat-rate benefits to all, independently of their prior income and without means testing.

Both these concepts are currently reflected in the basic distinction between two models of social security – Bismarckian insurance schemes (with benefits based on the level of earnings) and Beveridgean flat-rate schemes (with universal benefits).

The **Great Depression** of the 1930s was another milestone in the development of social security. In 1935, Franklin Delano Roosevelt (in office 1933–1945 as the 32nd President of the United States) institutionalized old-age security by establishing a system of social insurance, the first of its kind in the US, based on employee and employer contributions into a pension fund. The retirement age was set at 65 years, whereas 57 years was the mean life expectancy of an American at that time.

The realm of pension systems saw an expansion after WWII. Among other things, the criteria of eligibility were loosened, the retirement age lowered and additional pre-retirement options introduced (Arza, Johnson 2005). Pension schemes became more and more complex during that expansion. The original purpose of eliminating and preventing poverty was replaced by the more ambitious goal to provide an adequate level of income replacement during retirement. Pension schemes grew into one of the most important – and most costly – parts of public and social policy.

HISTORICAL OVERVIEW OF THE PENSION SYSTEM IN THE TERRITORY OF TODAY'S CZECH REPUBLIC

AUSTRIA-HUNGARY (UNTIL 1918)

Civil servants were the first group of citizens to which the state budget of Austria-Hungary granted coverage upon reaching retirement age. Interestingly, disability was referred to as "premature coming of age" and civil servants who had to retire from service prematurely due to their health condition were eligible for what is known today as early retirement. At the end of the 19th century, new laws were adopted – the Act on Workers' Accident Insurance (1888), the Act on Workers' Sickness Insurance (1888), and subsequently also the Mining Sector Community Funds Act (1889). Insurance coverage for administrative staff was provided by major farmers, followed by large industrial plants; subsequently, administrative workers' unions mobilized under the flag of mandatory pension insurance. The first public and mandatory insurance scheme for private administrative officials was adopted in 1907. This measure legalized and unified private pension schemes, transforming them into institutions of public law (Tomeš 1996, Rákosník, Tomeš 2012).

INTERWAR CZECHOSLOVAKIA (1918–1938)

Independent Czechoslovakia started writing the history of its pension policy with the Act on Insurance of Employees in the Event of Illness, Disability and Old Age (passed 1924). Effective from 1926, the law introduced pension insurance for workers and other employees not covered by other laws. Until then, workers were only insured against disability. The proposal was perceived as highly controversial at the time. In the preceding parliamentary debate, a concern was voiced, among others, that the law would "(...) result in an accumulation of assets (...) that [would] remain idle and, on the other hand, the act [would] negatively affect enterprise by increasing production costs considerably" (Mimra 1936, as cited in Rákosník, Tomeš 2012: 250). A 1928 amendment to the law lowered the rate of insurance premiums.

Under Nazi occupation (1939–1945), the parliament was dissolved in the Protectorate of Bohemia and Moravia and only government decrees were issued, especially with regard to the indexation of pensions and to rates.

CZECHOSLOVAKIA (1945–1989)

Czechoslovakia was not left out of the trend of pension scheme expansion in post-war Europe. Effective as of 1 October 1948, the Act on National Insurance introduced coverage mandated by law – *ipso jure* – and what was then a modern comprehensive concept of a social security system. Pension insurance premiums were set at 10% of the assessment base for employees (occupational accident premiums at 1%). Employers were expected to pay the premiums. Self-employed persons paid, for both themselves and their collaborating family members, the entire amount of pension insurance premium excluding the accident surcharge. The Central National Insurance Company became the country's only insurance provider. The system implemented a mix of Beveridgean and Bismarckian elements. "Whereas Beveridge intended to provide an actual subsistence minimum, the Czechoslovak system was much more generous" (Rákosník, Tomeš 2012: 139). The benefits were calculated from two parts (the same construction continues to be applied to present day). The first part complied with Sir Beveridge's goal of providing a flat-rate benefit, while the other part reflected the level of earnings and thus came more closely to Bismarck's concept.

The Communist Party of Czechoslovakia seized power in the coup d'état of 1948 and started writing a completely different chapter of the history of social systems. The Act on Social Security (passed 1956) dramatically transformed the concept of pension insurance. Inspired by Soviet models, the reform sought to fully eliminate the insurance principle from pension security and instead to rely on the government budget. The retirement age was set at 60 years for men and 55 years for women. The level of equivalence was further weakened in 1964. As a new element, a variable retirement age for women was set at 53–57 years, depending on the number of children raised. By levying a tax on pensions in excess of CZK 700 a month, the law violated the principle that vested rights cannot be taken away. Some deformations from 1964 and the following years were eliminated in 1975. The merit principle was strengthened by abolishing the special pension tax and raising the relative and absolute maximum levels of pensions. The Act on Social Security (1988) was applicable to pension security, social services, and sickness insurance. In the area of pensions, it primarily addressed the growing gap between wages and pensions, an excessively flat distribution of pensions, and increasing differences between pensions granted to different age cohorts.

CZECHOSLOVAKIA (1990–1992)

When the democratic form of governance was reinstituted in December 1989, the primary task was to adapt the existing system of social security to changing political, economic and social conditions. The first strategic document in the field of pensions was entitled, **Scenario of Social Reform**. Tabled in the Federal Assembly in September 1990, it built on the traditions of interwar and post-war Czechoslovakia and introduced a mix of classic Bismarckian social insurance with elements of Beveridgean social assistance. An in-built corporatist element, one of the Scenario's priorities was to establish a Pension Insurance Fund as an independent corporation governed by public law (and /or additional social funds).

However, the government never met either the declared goal of separating the pension system from the government budget and establishing a system of funds, or that of separating social security administration from government administration.

THE CZECH REPUBLIC

1993–1998

At the end of 1992, Czechoslovakia split into the Czech Republic and Slovakia. In the following time period, Czech social policy came to be shaped by the liberal welfare state model. The Act on Social security premium and contribution to state employment policy, effective as of January 1, 1993, introduced the social security premiums as a special levy separated from the tax system. They consisted of retirement insurance premiums, sickness insurance premiums, and contributions to state employment policy. While this was still in line with the original Czechoslovak concept of pension reform, a separation of pensions from the state budget was never implemented. Subsequently, two legislative proposals were adopted that were key to the Czech pension system as we know it today. First, the State-contributory Supplementary Pension Insurance Act became effective on March 21, 1994. Whereas the federal concept was based on the collective or occupational principle (that had become widespread in advanced capitalist countries, especially after WWII), the private funded pillar was based on the principle of individual contracts between citizens and insurance companies; the direct participation of employers was not foreseen. The participants received contributions from the state (as mentioned in the title of the law). Supplementary pension insurance in the Czech Republic was not supported by tax credits. Nevertheless, since 1999 participants have become eligible for a tax credit of CZK 12,000 annually as long as they have saved at least CZK 1,500 monthly. Employers that contributed to their employees' supplementary pension insurance were eligible for a tax credit of up to 3% of their social insurance assessment base.

A new law on pension insurance was drafted by the Ministry of Labor and Social Affairs in 1995. It was still, to some extent, inspired by the federal concept of social system reform. The raising of the retirement age became the central point of conflict between government coalition parties. While the Civic Democratic Party (ODS) and the Civic Democratic Alliance (ODA) supported the proposal, the Christian Democrats were against it. The law was eventually passed thanks to the votes of opposition parties. The retirement age started gradually increasing by two months per year, from the original 60 to 62 years (for men born in the years 1936–1947) and by four months per year for women, from a lower original age to the target age of 57–61 years, depending on the number of children raised.

The Act on Pension Insurance (1995) meant another milestone in Czech pension policy, establishing a pension system governed by public law and providing universal coverage, with some exceptions for military personnel and self-employed persons. It was designed as a pay-as-you-go, defined-benefit and mandatory scheme for all economically active individuals. The pensions consisted of two parts, namely the basic assessment (a fixed amount for all types of pensions irrespective of length of insurance or amount of earnings) and the percentage assessment (based on the amount of earnings). Effective as of January 1, 1996, the new law replaced the existing Act on Social Security.

In the year 1994, the World Bank (WB) made an impressive entry into the arena of pension reforms with its publication entitled, *Averting the Old Age Crisis: Policies to Protect the Old and Promote Growth* (1994). In an arena previously dominated by the International Labor Organization (ILO), the book boosted the WB to the forefront and remained the bible of radical pension reformists for many years to come. Since the WB concept was primarily acknowledged by the political right, it comes as a curiosity that the international institution had a rather weak influence in the Czech Republic under the rule of strong right-wing governments. In its own documents, the Bank referred to relations with the country as non-standard. Above all, the Czech Republic found itself in a highly specific situation, compared to most other post-communist countries, enjoying very low levels of public debt, unemployment and inflation and a stable rate of economic growth. After a short period of economic stabilization, the country chose not to take any loans from international creditors.

As another characteristic trait, Czech governments at that time frowned upon "foreign models" and preferred taking a specifically "Czech way." According to general opinion, the country's expert community had enough knowledge to do without foreign money or consultants. This distanced attitude was probably one of the reasons why the WB's "new pension orthodoxy" was met with little support among Czech politicians. "Pension reforms had been discussed as early as 1993 and several scenarios were constructed, but the Government decided not to engage the World Bank at that time" (World Bank 2006: 22). In other worlds, one of the most important global actors then did not play an important role in the Czech Republic.

In 1995 and the following years, a group of young economists (Schneider, Kočišová and Kreidl) came out in response to the WB's new concept and to pension reforms under preparation in neighboring Hungary and Poland. In their analyses, they proposed establishing a mandatory fully funded pillar. Their work certainly initiated and improved the quality of scholarly debate about possible pension reform scenarios. Nonetheless, without any immediate political outcome.

In the years 1996–1997, the rate of social security premiums was discounted from 27.2% to 26% and the conditions for early retirement were loosened. This was a restriction on the pension system's revenue side and simultaneous expansion on the expenditure side. The likely motive was to support the Czech economy *vis-à-vis* signs of external imbalance. Eventually, economic reality (a restrictive monetary policy of the Czech National Bank and an "overheating" of the Czech economy) forced the Czech government to make corrections to its economic policy, namely to reduce government expenditure. Among other things, the pension system was affected by the elimination of the recent discount. Effective from December 2, 1997, the following amendments were introduced:

- cutting down the crediting of most non-contributory insurance periods,
- restricting the conditions for a mandatory indexing of pensions,
- repealing a gradual reduction of age of eligibility for early retirement.

In the years 1997–1998, the WB once again offered assistance in the area of pension reform, this time under a program aimed at reforming capital markets. Czech authorities rejected the assistance, referring to the existence of mixed experience from neighboring countries and the availability of their own internal expertise in the area of social security. The main achievement of the WB was raising public awareness of the issue of pension reform and its implications for fiscal stability and public budgets, and thus also bringing it to the top of the political agenda.

1998–2006

After snap parliamentary elections, a minority government formed by the Czech Social Democratic Party (ČSSD) postponed the introduction of a funded pillar. Instead, the option of collective pension security was taken back onto the agenda when the government proposed to establish workplace pension schemes. Once again a plan re-emerged to separate the funding and administration of pension insurance from the state.

Based on its strategic document of 2001, the government intended to proceed with pension reform by establishing an NDC scheme within the pension system's first pillar and separating the system of pension and sickness insurance from the state budget, both organizationally and financially (to make the NDC scheme operational, it was necessary to found a Social Insurance Company as a corporation governed by public law and managing people's individual accounts within the scheme). At the same time, the government planned to build a new pension pillar on an occupational basis (occupational pension insurance). However, in the autumn of 2001, both bills were rejected by the Chamber of Deputies.

Between the elections of 2002 and 2006, several coalition governments were formed, all dominated by the ČSSD. In 2004, at the initiative of Prime Minister Vladimír Špidla, an expert platform was established to assess pension reform in the Czech Republic. The platform was later named by its Coordinator and came to be known as **Bezděk Commission I**; it was joined by political parties represented at that time in the Chamber of Deputies. Its Executive Team was responsible for so-called expert tasks, i.e., for assessing different pension reform scenarios proposed by political representatives.[112]

The Final Report of the Executive Team of Bezděk Commission I outlined the so-called baseline (zero) option in order to present the cost of "political inactivity." The desired effect was achieved and political parties represented in the Chamber of Deputies agreed on the necessity of a pension reform. Following the Final Report, a draft Agreement of Political Parties on Further Procedure of the Pension Reform was formulated. However, the parties failed to sign the agreement before the elections of 2006, mainly as they disagreed whether it was necessary to raise the retirement age above 65 years.

2006–2010

The following four years were marked by two ODS-led governments (and one caretaker government) that strived to win support for paradigmatic pension reform. Expert advisory bodies were established.

In 2007, political parties represented in the Chamber of Deputies formed a political working group on pension reform with a view to achieving the broadest possible political consensus on the different stages of pension reform. The parties involved agreed that none of them would strive to legislate

---

112 This was the first of the five advisory bodies formed to assist the consecutive governments with the design of a pension reform. Cf. Chapter B2.

mandatory pension savings. The group's members assessed the wording of a proposed amendment to Act on Pension Insurance, which was designed as the first stage of a parametric pension reform. Once again, they disagreed on provisions raising the retirement age and gradually extending the insurance period required for entitlement to old age pension from 25 to 30 years (excluding the non-contributory insurance periods credited) and to 35 years (including those periods). The amendment was passed by the least possible majority of MPs and became effective on January 1, 2009. On one hand, the parliamentary opposition and labor unions formulated negative positions on these restrictive changes. On the other hand, the parametric changes legislated effectively and improved the financial balance of national pension insurance in the longer term.

The so-called Expert Advisory Forum was established in 2010. Once again chaired by Mr. Vladimír Bezděk, it was also referred to as **Bezděk Commission II**. Its mission was to update the results of **Bezděk Commission I**. In general terms, it agreed on the necessity of pension reform, but failed to reach consensus on any specific concept.

The pension reform concepts debated largely reflected the WB's new recommendations to focus on parametric changes in state pillars and strengthen the role of private pillars. For more on how the WB updated its recommendations, see Wodsak and Koch (2010).

2010–2013

A ruling of the Constitutional Court of 23 March 2010 (effective as of 30 September 2011) repealed as unconstitutional the provision of Section 15 of the Act on Pension Insurance on the reduction of the personal assessment base. According to the Court's reasoning, the construction of pension benefits "establishes marked disproportionality between the level of contributions to the insurance system, income levels, and the level of allocated pension benefits for some insured persons, whereby it violates Art. 1 and Art. 3 par. 1 of the Charter [of Fundamental Rights and Freedoms]" (Ústavní soud 2010). The ODS-led coalition government was thus placed under urgent pressure to change the parameters of the pension system's first PAYG pillar in a way to strengthen the role of merit in the pension formula. An amendment to the Act on Pension Insurance (2011) responded by improving the formula for the highest contribution decile, at the expense of the vast majority of participants whose contributions were higher than minimal. By the same token, it instituted a continuous and unlimited rise of the retirement age.[113]

In July 2011 the government agreed with the strongest opposition party, the ČSSD, to form an expert working group with three issues on the agenda:

---

113 Cf. chapter B3.

"pre-pensions," provisions on retirement age, and guarantees to individual participants in a transformed pillar of State-Contributory Supplementary Pension Insurance. The design of what would become the second pillar was not tabled at all because the positions of the government and the opposition were clearly irreconcilable. As a result, the group formulated specific provisions on "pre-pensions" that would provide an additional source of income to third-pillar members until reaching standard retirement age.

The National Economic Council of the Government (NERV)[114] resumed its work at that time. In its economic advisory role, the government body participated in discussions of concepts for a Czech pension reform. However, its expert recommendations were only partially reflected in the final design of the legislative changes. In the years 2011–2012, the Czech legislature adopted the Act on Pension Savings (2011) and the Act on Retirement Savings Premiums (2012). Effective as of January 1, 2013, these laws instituted important changes in the Czech pension system. A new second pillar was established when participants were allowed an opt-out, taking three percent of their earnings away from their pension insurance premiums. The second pillar was designed as a fully funded, defined-contribution scheme. The participants had to top up their 3% opt-out with an additional two percent of their earnings. The total amount of 5% of earnings was transferred to a private pension fund of the participant's choice.

The establishment of the second pillar was closely associated with the operation of the first pillar, i.e., the public pension insurance scheme. Those who opted out contributed only 25% instead of 28% of their assessment base, i.e., three percentage points less than those who chose to rely exclusively on the public scheme. At the same time, their total contribution to both pillars grew to 30% of the assessment base.

After more than a decade of debates, involvement of the expert community, and preparation of a number of studies and evaluations, the Czech Republic legislated a pension reform that was rejected both by many experts and by three-quarters of the general public. The reform did not rely on a consensus across the political spectrum, a necessary condition of stability of such a ground-breaking measure. Instead, the government outnumbered the opposition by a close margin, adopting the law against the will of the strongest oppositional party, ČSSD, which moreover had pledged to abolish the law in case it won the following elections. Ultimately, the President of the Republic attempted to veto the pension reform precisely due to the absence of a broad political consensus, seen as essential for the stability of this kind of fundamental, long-term measures.

---

114 This advisory body was formed under Prime Minister Topolánek in 2009 with the primary mission to propose measures for mitigating the impacts of the global financial crisis. The experts were commissioned to find measures to support economic growth and at the same time to analyze the potential harmful effects of the financial crisis on the Czech Republic.

The reform was adopted as a compromise between parties of an unstable government coalition, and as such was also presented inconsistently to the general public. The reluctant attitudes of the general public translated into a low level of participation in the second pillar (albeit there are undoubtedly other reasons why so few Czech citizens joined). The paradigmatic reform of the Czech Republic's pension system became effective on January 1, 2013.[115]

2014–2017

After snap elections in the autumn of 2013, a coalition government was formed by the ČSSD, KDU-ČSL, and ANO in 2014. The government's pension policy goals were formulated in its Policy Statement. One of its first decisions was to abolish the just recently established subsystem of pension savings (so-called second pillar).

It also founded **the Expert Committee on Pension Reform**[116]. The Committee consisted of the following permanent members:

- delegates of all political parties represented in the Chamber of Deputies of the Parliament of the Czech Republic,
- experts (sociologists, economists and demographers) nominated by those parties,
- delegates of social partners (trade unions and employers).

Various interest groups and professional associations nominated a number of associate members. The meetings were regularly attended by representatives of the government administration and public institutions. The main political task of the Expert Committee was to form a basis for reaching a broad consensus on a further course of the pension reform. The following key parameters were identified for each pension reform proposal:

- to guarantee a decent living for pensioners,
- to strengthen the merit principle,
- to reconcile transfers between family and society,
- to make the pension system sustainable.

One of the Committee's goals was to advise the government on a suitable way to abolish pension savings (the second pillar of the Czech pension system). This was accomplished when the Act on the Termination of the Pension Savings Scheme was adopted in December 2015 and became effective in January 2016. Thus, the second pillar operated for just three years (2013–2015) and attracted altogether less than 85 thousand participants.

---

115 Cf. Chapter B4.
116 For more details, see http://www.duchodova-komise.cz/?page_id=1248.

SOURCES

Arza C., P. Johnson. 2005. "The development of public pensions from 1889 to the 1990s." in *Oxford Handbook of Pensions and Retirement Income*, edited by G. Clark, A. Munnell, M. Orszag. Oxford: Oxford University Press.

Beveridge, W. 1942. *Social insurance and allied services. Report by Sir William Beveridge*. London: HMSO.

Mimra, S. 1936. *Systém nemocenského, invalidního a starobního pojištění dělníků.* [System of workers' sickness, disability and old age insurance, in Czech]. Prague: Čs. ústředí nemocenských pojišťoven.

Paine, T. 2004. *Common Sense [with] Agrarian Justice*. London: Penguin.

Rákosník, J., I. Tomeš et al. 2012. *Sociální stát v Československu.* [Welfare State in Czechoslovakia, in Czech]. Prague: Auditorium.

Tomeš, I. 1996. *Sociální politika. Teorie a mezinárodní zkušenost* [Social Policy. Theory and International Experience, in Czech]. Prague: SOCIOKLUB.

Ústavní soud ČR. 2010. *Nález Ústavního soudu Pl. ÚS 8/07* [Ruling of the Constitutional Court, in Czech]. Retrieved June 14, 2016 (http://www.usoud.cz/en/decisions/20100323 -pl-us-807-right-to-adequate-material-security-1).

Wodsak V., M. Koch. 2010. "From three to five: The World Bank's pension policy norm." Pp. 48-69 in *Owning Development*, edited by S. Park, A. Vetterlein. Cambridge: Cambridge University Press.

World Bank. 1994. Averting the old age crisis: policies to protect the old and promote growth. Washington, D.C.: Oxford University Press. Retrieved June 2, 2016 (http://documents.worldbank.org/curated/en/973571468174557899/Averting-the -old-age-crisis-policies-to-protect-the-old-and-promote-growth).World Bank. 2006. *Hodnocení spolupráce České republiky a Světové banky 1998–2005* [Evaluation of Collaboration, the Czech Republic and the World Bank 1998–2005, in Czech]. Retrieved July 8, 2016 (http://siteresources.worldbank.org/INTCZECH/Resources/evaluation -Czech-partnership-cz.pdf).

RECOMMENDED SOURCES

Baroni, E. 2007. *Pension Systems and Pension Reform in an Aging Society: An Introduction to the Debate*. Working Paper 2007:6. Stockholm: Institute for Future Studies.

Barr, N., P. Diamond. 2008. *Reforming pensions: principles and policy directions*. Oxford: Oxford University Press.

Barr, N., P. Diamond. 2009. "Reforming pensions: principles, analytical errors and policy directions." *International Social Security Review* 62 (2): 5–29.

Blake, D. 2006. *Pension Economics*. West Sussex: John Wiley & Sons.

Clark, G., A. Munnell, M. Orszag (eds.) 2006. *Oxford Handbook of Pensions and Retirement Income*. Oxford: Oxford University Press.

Green Paper. 2010. *Towards adequate, sustainable and safe European pension systems.* SEC (2010) 830. Brussels: European Commission,

Hinrichs, K., 2000. Elephants on the Move: Patterns of Public Pension Reform in OECD. *European Review* 8: 353–378.

Holzmann, R., R. Hinz. 2005. *Old-Age Income Support in the 21st Century.* Washington, D.C.: World Bank.

Iglesias, A. 2003. *Strengthening of the Private Voluntary Pension Scheme in the Czech Republic.* Unpublished manuscript.

Lasagabaster E., R. Rocha. P. Wiesse. 2002. *Czech Pension system: Challenges and Reform Options.* Washington, D.C.: World Bank.

Orszag, P. R., J. E. Stiglitz. 2001. "Rethinking Pension Reform: Ten Myths about Social Security Systems." Pp. 17–56 in *New Ideas about Old Age Security: Toward Sustainable Pension Systems in the Twenty-First Century,* edited by R. Holzmann, J. E. Stiglitz. Washington, D.C.: World Bank.

Pierson, P. 1994. *Dismantling the Welfare State? Reagan, Thatcher, and the Politics of Retrenchment.* Cambridge, New York: Cambridge University Press.

Schludi, M. 2005. *The Reform of Bismarckian Pension Systems: A Comparison of Pension Politics in Austria, France, Germany, Italy and Sweden.* Amsterdam: Amsterdam University Press.

Weaver, K. 2003. *The Politics of Public Pension Reform.* Retrieved July 8, 2016 (http://ssrn.com/abstract=1136874).

Wheeler, P. M., J. R. Kearney. 1996. "Income Protection for the Aged in the 21st Century: A Framework to Help Inform the Debate." *Social Security Bulletin* 59 (2): 3–19.

Legislation

Act No. 589/1992 Coll., on social security and state employment policy premiums.
Act No. 42/1994 Coll. – State-contributory Supplementary Pension Insurance Act.
Act No. 155/1995 Coll., on pensions insurance.

/B2/

The Role of Politicians and Experts in the Preparation of Czech Pension Reform[117]

Although pension systems are among the most stable elements of social systems, even they evolve. In recent decades, dozens of countries have joined in by enacting minor adjustments or significant reforms. What has happened in the Czech Republic in this respect after 1989? The country went through a transition from a centrally planned to a market economy and from an authoritarian political regime to a democracy. It gradually integrated into the structures of the European and global economy, and with this it underwent turmoil as well as the financial crisis at the end of the first decade of the third millennium. To politicians, it was clear that the pension system had to be

---

117 This is an updated version of a paper by Potůček and Rudolfová (2017).

reformed *vis-à-vis* both current and future challenges. In order to address the problems identified, they began collaborating with experts.

In this chapter, we analyze the spirit and content of this dialogue on Czech pension reform between 2004 and 2017, relying on discursive institutionalism theory and methods of frame analysis. In the center of our focus lies the institutional framework, the content of the communication between its key actors (politicians and experts), and the outputs of their collaboration. How did this collaboration take place? What institutional forms did it take? How did the proposals put forward reflect the ideological schemes of politicians, on the one hand, and scientific evidence, on the other? Which ideas of experts were ultimately reflected in the laws and political practice, and which ones were not – and why?

ANALYTICAL APPROACH

HYPOTHESES

The object of our investigation is the nature and content of the discourse regarding the Czech pension reform, its trends, and institutional configurations since 2004. The focus of our analytical attention will be this discourse by the key actors – politicians and experts.

As we do not deal with the evolution of the pension system as such, we do not intend to describe its changes in detail. In the text, we refer mostly to political concepts associated with the changes in its three pillars.[118]

Based on a preliminary study of the subject matter, we developed four hypotheses:

A. Participation of experts is necessary in proposing specific institutions as well as in conceiving pension reform policy.
B. Ideological and cognitive frames blended in the pension reform discourse.
C. Politicians have a final say on the reform changes.
D. The broader the ideological spectrum of the stakeholders, the more robust the proposed solution.

To analyze the process of discussions over the preparation and implementation of the individual steps of Czech pension reform, we chose the most suitable theory of discursive institutionalism in combination with the method of frame analysis.

---

118 Refer to the Table on Terminology of Pillars in the Czech Pension System in the beginning of Part B.

THE THEORY OF DISCURSIVE INSTITUTIONALISM

This theory explains the role of ideas and discourse in politics. At the same time, it offers a more dynamic approach to analyzing institutional change than other institutionalist theories.[119] Ideas are seen as a fundamental part of discourse. **There is a distinction between cognitive ideas and normative ideas. Discourse** is an interactive process of idea development. It **serves two functions: coordination between political actors, and communication between political actors and the public**. These functions exist in distinct formal institutional contexts: simple policies are dominated by the element of communication, whereas complex policies are primarily based on the element of coordination. Moreover, discursive institutionalism does not view institutions as structures shaped merely by external rules, but also as constructions that have been internalized by actors and that arise and exist dependently on actors' "background ideational abilities" in a given "meaningful context." Institutional continuity and change then, are explained by actors' "foreground discursive abilities" following the "logic of communication." Interests exist as subjective and immaterial ideas. Norms are dynamic intersubjective constructions, rather than static structures (Schmidt 2008).

Ideas occur at levels of polity, policy as well as politics. At polity, it is the most general idea of what kind of ideal society is desired. Specific measures at the level of policy are constituted by the formulation of specific proposals and programs. At the level of politics, there is an ongoing confrontation between actors, a political struggle which ultimately results in the approval or rejection of these measures.

We can apply this three-tier structure to pensions as follows:
1. Polity: A fundamental systemic change – for example, the decision to introduce a compulsory defined-contribution pension pillar;
2. Policy: Parametric change to the existing pension system – such as changing the threshold retirement age;
3. Politics: Clash of advocacy coalitions, politicians and political parties about the approval or rejection of specific legal norms.

STUDY TIP: Refer to Chapter A2 for more on values in public policy and **Chapter A5** on the Theory of discursive institutionalism.

---

119 Compare, for example, the theories of historical institutionalism in Chapter A2, actor-centered institutionalism in Chapter A4 and neo-pluralism *ibidem*.

METHOD OF FRAME ANALYSIS

One aspect that allows us to understand how discourses are constructed and made up is called "framing" (Stone 1997, Rein, Schön 1993). A frame can be seen as an "interpretive scheme" which shows us how to identify, perceive and name events and circumstances which accompany them (Schön, Rein 1994, Goffman 1974). Framing can be termed a process in which the high-lighting and naming of a (selected) aspect of the problem occurs, whereby attention (selective attention) subsequently increases. What logically fol-lows is a disregard for or insufficient perception of attributes which were not included in the "problem frame" and remained outside the spotlight – an imaginary picture frame of socio-political reality. In this way, actors (some knowingly, some unknowingly) "overlook" other aspects of the problem (Entman 1993).

By adequately "framing" the problem, we can, to some extent, predefine its social meaning, its essence and ultimately possible strategies for solving it (Rein, Schön 1993). It is assumed that frame analysis comprises:

1. naming the issue area;
2. identifying the competing frames within the issue area;
3. identifying the frame sponsors, such as civil servants or special interest groups, including their institutional positions and interests;
4. delimiting the forums in which they compete (Rein, Schön 1996, in Morávek 2011).

Thus applied, frame analysis becomes an appropriate tool for applying the theory of discursive institutionalism in an empirical analysis of this topic.

Discourse is connected with the processes of conversation and communica-tion. With regard to communication and type of discourse, framing is shaped by two types of interactions – articulation and amplification of the frame of choice (Benford, Snow 2000). Frame articulation "involves the connection and alignment of events and experiences so that they hang together in a relatively unified and compelling fashion" (Ibid.: 624). In this process, emphasis is placed on the urgency of the issue. Facts, experiences, trends, etc., can be interpreted in different (carefully selected) ways. Frame amplification is a process which "involves accenting and highlighting some issues, events, or beliefs as being more salient than others" (Ibid.). In this way, a political problem is declared and presented – selected tasks, events and beliefs are selectively highlighted to attract attention. It is often at this stage that the problem is connected to values, ideas, etc.

A problem frame includes a set of four elements: "Frames, then, **define problems** – determine what a causal agent is doing with what costs and ben-efits, usually measured in terms of common cultural values; **diagnose caus-es** – identify the forces creating the problem; **make moral judgments** – eval-uate causal agents and their effects; and, **suggest remedies** – offer and justify treatments for the problems and predict their likely effects" (Entman 1993: 52, emphasis in original). However, as Leweke (1999, in Morávek 2011) highlights, it is not necessary to identify all of the above elements in each frame.

A HISTORY OF INSTITUTIONS AND DISCOURSES

In the history of pension debates in the Czech Republic between 2004 and 2015 we find a few more-or-less formalized attempts to institutionalize a discourse. In this study, we will work with five such attempts. We will try to analyze them in terms of the type of discourse used in mapping out ideas (both normative and cognitive) and to evaluate their potential to bring about institutional change.

Table B2.1 Institutions of discourse regarding Czech pension reforms

Characteristic Institution	Time period	Political representation (normative ideas)	Expert representation (cognitive ideas)	Acceptance of proposals by political representatives
Executive team and Team of experts (Bezděk Commission I)	2004	All political parties represented in the Chamber of Deputies	Yes – economics, demography and law	No
Expert Advisory Forum - PES (Bezděk Commission II	2010	No	Yes, mainly economics, partially law	No
National Economic Council of the Government (NERV)	2011– 2012	No	Yes – economics	Partly
Expert Group: government and opposition party (EG)	2011– 2012	Representatives of the ruling coalition and the strongest opposition party (ČSSD)	Yes – economics, sociology and law	Partly
Expert Committee on Pension Reform (OK)	2014– 2017	All political parties represented in the Chamber of Deputies	Yes – sociology, demography, economics and law	Partly

Source: Authors.

THE EXECUTIVE TEAM AND TEAM OF EXPERTS
(BEZDĚK COMMISSION I)

The first attempt to create an institutional platform for the professional assessment of pension reform in the country occurred in 2004. Vladimír
Špidla, the prime minister then and chairman of the leading coalition party,
the Czech Social Democratic Party (ČSSD), suggested establishing a commission that would participate in the assessment of pension reform options put
forward by political parties' experts in order to broaden the range of actors
involved in the pension reform agenda.

The working group established came to be known as Bezděk Commission
I (named after its chairman). Each of the political parties serving at the time in
the Chamber of Deputies nominated two representatives. The group's primary
task was to agree on the basic parameters for an analysis of pension reform
scenarios proposed by the political parties. Professional work, i.e., assessment of scenarios, was carried out by its Executive Team, which consisted of
five economists from the Czech National Bank, the Ministry of Finance, and
the Ministry of Labor and Social Affairs, as well as one external consultant.
In addition, each party nominated alongside their two "political members"
two other experts to ensure high-quality work in both specifying the exercise and undertaking the final analysis. The preparation of documents for
decision-making on pension reform was delegated according to the wishes of
the parties represented, and subsequently the Czech government created the
conditions for the function of the group. The analysis carried out by the Executive Team of Bezděk Commission I resulted in a final report, which included
the so-called baseline (zero) option in order to present the cost of "political
inactivity." The desired effect was achieved and political parties represented
in the Chamber of Deputies agreed on the necessity of pension reform.

In the second half of 2005, following the Executive Team's conclusions,
a draft Agreement of Political Parties on further continuation of pension
reform was prepared. Negotiations were undertaken during the first half of
2006 and ended before the general election. Due to disagreement about raising the retirement age to 65 years, however, the draft was not signed in the
end. The draft envisaged establishing a special fund for pension reform, support for voluntary pension schemes as well as some parametric changes to
the public first pillar.

The framing of the issue of pension reform in the actions of Bezděk Commission I reflected on the "climate" of pension reform discussions in the international context. The World Bank had "reframed" the issue of old age security
in 1994, when it released the publication, "Averting the Old Age Crisis: Policies
to Protect the Old and Promote Growth" (World Bank 1994). This gave rise
to the frame of "financial unsustainability" of public pension systems. Bezděk Commission I widely accepted that frame. Within the final report of the

Executive Team, we find the main issues which the experts tried to resolve. These questions provide an opportunity to identify a "frame" with which the Commission approached the issue of pension reform. The diagnostic framing or defining "what the problem is" can be located in the central question which the Executive Team defined as follows: "How will long-term financial sustainability of the mandatory pension system be secured?" The definition of the problem affects, to some extent, the range of possible solutions. By delimiting the problem as one of financial imbalance, the set of possible solutions was logically narrowed down to funding measures. Attention was paid to the revenue and expenditure sides of the system. Other questions combined other elements of a frame foreseen in the theory, namely moral judgments and proposed solutions: "Can the financing of the mandatory pension system be diversified? And if so, how? What will income solidarity look like in the mandatory pension system?"

Raising public awareness of the topic of pension reform can be seen as one of the effects of this commission. It appealed to the menacing threat of increasing deficits, the system's unsustainability, the irreversibility of demographic trends and the ensuing threat to future pension entitlements. In the introduction to its final report, the Executive Team stated: "The current pension system is not sustainable over the long run, and this will cause the already high deficits to escalate significantly. It also maintains a high level and volume of income redistribution, which could be problematic from the standpoint of the labor market. The pension system needs to be radically reformed, and it is not just a question of adjusting the parameters" (MPSV 2005). Bezděk Commission I used language that clearly evoked the urgency of the problem and its exceptional importance for the functioning of society.

Figure B2.1 Ideas and discourse – Executive team and a team of experts (Bezděk Commission I)

> **Cognitive ideas** – macro-economic criteria and related projections, demographic criteria and related projections, assuming the World Bank's 1994 pension orthodoxy.
> **Normative ideas** – differentiated pension reform proposals of the political parties.
> **Communicative discourse** – by presenting its findings to the public, the Commission raised public awareness of pension policy. Due to the nature of this interest, its presentation was at the same time connected with persuasion about the necessity and urgency of pension reform.
> **Coordinative discourse** – decision-making on the basic parameters for the analysis of pension reform scenarios showed elements of a coordinative type of discourse. It was the first systematic attempt to debate the issue across the political spectrum.

Source: Authors.

EXPERT ADVISORY FORUM PES (BEZDĚK COMMISSION II)

The caretaker government of Jan Fischer established the Expert Advisory Forum (PES) in January 2010. Management of this team was again assigned to Mr. Vladimír Bezděk (hence the alternative name, Bezděk Commission II). PES was composed mainly of professionals from the financial sector, representatives of government administration, and one representative of the Czech-Moravian Confederation of Trade Unions (ČMKOS).

The Forum's mission was to update the projection of the development of the pension system and to recommend reforms to ensure its financial stability. The experts agreed on the need for pension reform. With regard to specific ideas about its parameters, however, no single consensus emerged. PES developed two concepts of possible pension reform:

1. The majority option envisaged 3 percentage points taken from the first pillar's mandatory contribution rate and channelled into individual retirement savings in the private second pillar of the pension system, which would be mandatory for all citizens under 40 years of age at the start of reform;
2. The minority option allowed for a significant increase of state budget subsidies to the (transformed) third pillar. The condition of individual eligibility for this subsidy (3 percentage points) would be to save at least the same amount (3% of wages). The decision to save/not to save would, however, remain fully voluntary.

Issue framing was influenced by the fact that PES was more-or-less "just" building and updating on the activity of Bezděk Commission I. Stability of the financial system was the key issue that remained. This framing was also reflected in the definition of the main task of PES, namely to formulate recommendations for the direction of adjustments to the pension system to ensure stability. The problem, therefore, was defined as financial instability of the pension system. This was eventually reflected in the proposed solution: "In the area of the creation of a savings pillar for pensions, the Expert Advisory Forum has agreed on the need to create such a pillar and to reform the area of pension insurance."

The final report contained "mobilization vocabulary" aimed primarily at the political representation, arguing: "It is also possible to state that the current pension system in the Czech Republic is not overly diversified and that it includes an extreme degree of solidarity which makes it risky in the long term both for the state and from the point of view of individuals. (...) It will not be possible to maintain the standard of living in old age without savings" (MPSV 2005).

PES experts also recommended avoiding voluntary opt-out due to the expected low interest of citizens in entering the second pillar: "The Expert Advisory Forum did not incline towards the 'optout' variant of pension reform,

especially due to the fact that a significant part of the population would probably never enter the second pillar. This would water down the fulfillment of
the goals of greater diversification and stronger contributory principle of the
pension system" (MPSV 2010). This recommendation was very prescient, as
attested by Czech citizens' extreme reluctance to enter the voluntary second
pillar in 2013.[120]

Figure B2.2 Ideas and discourse – Expert Advisory Forum PES (Bezděk Commission II)

> **Cognitive ideas –** macro-economic criteria and related projections, demographic crite-
> ria and related projections, assuming the World Bank's 1994 pension orthodoxy.
> **Normative ideas** – focus on increasing the degree of equivalence, narrowing the dis-
> course to the financial stability of the public pension system.
> **Communicative discourse** – weak, as PES operations leaned more toward the exec-
> utive side.
> **Coordinative discourse** – due to the nature of PES, which was a government advisory
> board, not a platform for a broad consensus on pension reform, the coordinative aspect
> of the discourse was limited to the activities of the expert group, whose main task was
> to update the projections of the pension system and to formulate recommendations for
> adjustments to secure the system and its stability. Coordinative discussions with polit-
> ical representatives were not a working priority for the group. "The Expert Advisory
> Forum also considers it important to emphasize the fact that the discovery of substantial
> socio-political agreement concerning its form and the subsequent stability of the chosen
> solution and its parameters over time is a key prerequisite for successful pension reform.
> This is a fundamental task for the representatives of the political parties and not for
> economists or experts."

Source: Authors.

NATIONAL ECONOMIC COUNCIL OF THE GOVERNMENT – NERV

Formed after the 2010 snap elections, the Petr Nečas government restored
the National Economic Council (NERV) as its advisory body. Amongst other
areas, the experts of NERV were logically involved in the preparation of key
government reforms, not excluding pensions. They followed up on the work of
the previous professional groups, especially the Bezděk Commissions I and II.
The proposed solution was again based on an argument about the financial
unsustainability of the Czech pension system. NERV promoted increasing the

---

120 Even if the government expected to achieve between half and one million applicants, the real
    record was 84 thousand.

degree of equivalence, especially through the introduction of a second pillar to the Czech pension system.

Issue framing was consistent with the approach of Bezděk Commission II. NERV openly declared that it was building on its work, and used its recommendations as a starting point. As a central diagnostic theme, we identified, once again, the financial unsustainability of the pension system. The proposed solution envisaged the introduction of a mandatory private second pillar to the Czech pension system: "NERV recommended that the pension reform:

1. Add a new compulsory private fully-funded pillar alongside the statutory public pillar;
2. Ensure fiscal sustainability;
3. Reduce intergenerational inequality;
4. Strengthen the degree of equivalence within the public pension pillar" (Bezděk et al. 2011).

The mobilization vocabulary was directed primarily at the executive branch. "There needs to be a political decision in the next few months if reforms are to be carried out during the current electoral period," said NERV, suggesting that the draft reform should begin in 2015. The urgency of the problem was presented to the public along with NERV's pension reform concept in order to stimulate debate about this problem.

The concept of paradigmatic pension reform was finally adopted by the government of Petr Nečas. But this version had been created as a compromise solution within the unstable ruling coalition and contained a wide range of concessions and deviations from NERV's proposed concept. Communication was eventually negatively influenced by differences of opinion between NERV members and the government coalition. Reception of the proposal was negative not only from the opposition but also among professional circles. NERV's pension reform recommendations were, in many aspects, ignored by the government, which prompted NERV to present in the media the differences from its original ideas, among other things. Government's presentation of pension reform to the public (communicative discourse) was also weakened by low support both within and outside the coalition. The opposition as well as social partners were able to lead the communicative discourse in a way that affected public opinion on the pension reform proposal. This opinion was possibly reflected in a lower willingness of citizens to join the newly created second pillar of the pension system.[121]

Thus, the pension reform concept designed by NERV was adopted by the political representation in a significantly modified form, from which some members of NERV eventually felt the need to distance themselves. They disagreed namely with the switch from compulsory to voluntary participation in the second pillar.

---

121 To learn more on actors' behavior, refer to Chapter B3 or to Potůček, Rudolfová (2015).

Figure B2.3 Ideas and discourse – National Economic Council (NERV)

Cognitive ideas – macro-economic criteria and related projections, demographic criteria and their related projections, assuming the World Bank's 1994 pension orthodoxy.
Normative ideas – focus on increasing the degree of equivalence, narrowing the discourse to financial stability of the public pension system.
Communicative discourse – limited. Presentation of the final pension reform strategy to the public.
Coordinative discourse – the absence of a coordinative discourse was surprising, as it could be expected given both the political context (proportional electoral system, the social partners, etc.) and the nature of the topic of pension reform as such (long-term effects, robust solution requires a broad consensus). Despite (or because of) the absence of a coordinative discourse the Government finally adopted the concept of paradigmatic pension reform without securing the support of the general public, NERV, the opposition or social partners.

Source: Authors.

EXPERT GROUP: GOVERNMENT AND OPPOSITION PARTY (EG)

In July 2011 a meeting was held between then Prime Minister Petr Nečas (Chairman of the ODS – Civic Democratic Party) and the head of the strongest opposition party, ČSSD, Bohuslav Sobotka. The politicians agreed to establish an Expert Group (EG) to deal with the proposed changes to the pension system in defined areas. The group had eight members – four civil servants from the government, two politicians and two specialists nominated by the Social Democrats – and met for a total of thirteen times (first in August 2011, last in May 2012). Its political assignment was limited to three themes:

- Preparation of specific "pre-pensions" that would allow Supplementary Pension Savings policyholders to retire before reaching retirement age by using their accumulated funds in the intervening period. In less than a year, the EG entered the design phase of the solution.
- Setting of the retirement age. Here, the EG contributed to the preparation of an empirical public opinion survey on this issue.
- Defining guarantees to Supplementary Pension Savings policyholders. Here, the EG prepared a project to simulate the implications of the guarantee measure; however, it did not find an institution or a professional willing to carry out such a project.

The work of this group was governed by a very specific framing. The EG was given three politically designated topics to address. The framing of the problem eliminated a hot controversial topic, government preparation of the second pillar, as views of the government and the Social Democrats regarding this part of the pension reform were diametrically divergent, and thus incompatible.

The EG's main outcome was its proposal of specific "pre-pensions" that would allow Supplementary Pension Savings policyholders (the so-called third pillar of the Czech pension system) to retire before reaching retirement age by using their savings in the intervening period. In less than a year, the EG started designing the solution, which, after being discussed in other bodies (tripartite meeting), was green-lighted for preparation. The relevant Act No. 403/2012 Coll. came into force on January 1, 2013.

The EG's language was professional and, given the nature of its work, was targeted at the politicians of the governing coalition. The urgency of the problems was not communicated to the public. And while work on specific "pre-pensions" progressed to designing a solution, work on the remaining topics two did not go beyond the preparatory phase of diagnosing the causes, which was due to a lack of resources (time, financial, and organizational).

Figure B2.4 Ideas and discourse – Expert Group: government and opposition party (EG)

Normative ideas – not expressed explicitly. The political tasks of the EG were narrowed down to finding pragmatic solutions in the first pillar of the pension system (setting the retirement age) and in the transformed third pillar (introduction of the new institute of pre-pensions and proposal for a guaranteed scheme). The actual composition of the EG was designed so that it would be able to get results out of the proposed substantive solutions despite the participants' different normative ideas.

Cognitive ideas – the EG studied different countries' pension systems comparatively (determination of retirement age). The work of the EG was hampered by a fundamental lack of analytical information on which it could base its recommendations.

Coordinative discourse – fundamentally prevailed. Officials representing the coalition government coordinated the preparation of policy and administrative decisions with opposition politicians and experts. They ensured policy coordination with officials in the political parties represented in the government; opposition politicians were represented in the negotiations directly. In the first half of its work schedule, the EG collided with slow response by representatives of the executive branch; the situation did improve significantly when the proposals were discussed and approved by the EG on the grounds of tripartism. Strong coordinative discourse showed that the adopted solution (in this case pre-pensions) may be more robust in terms of implementation and support in future.

Communicative discourse – non-existent. The expert group worked intensively for nine months, but it primarily partnered with the politicians of the government coalition who had access to the preparation of legal norms.

Representation of institutions in discourse – preparation and implementation of a sustainable pension reform is not possible without a broader social consensus.

The EG managed to find the form in which it could coordinate the preparation of pension reform with representatives of competing political parties and ideologies: through explicit delimitation of issues on the agenda, and through a formalized procedural agreement by cooperation between the parties involved. Both experiences were applied in the work of the Expert Committee on Pension Reform, established about two-and-half years later.

Source: Authors.

THE EXPERT COMMITTEE ON PENSION REFORM (OK)[122]

The Expert Committee on Pension Reform was formed after the elections in 2013 on the basis of the coalition agreement and the policy statement of the new center-left government. It met for the first time in May 2014. The Committee consisted of permanent members, which included delegates of all political parties represented in the Chamber of Deputies of the Czech Parliament, experts nominated by these parties, and delegates of the social partners. Associate members included representatives of associations and professional organizations. Meetings were regularly attended by civil servants and representatives of interest groups. The main political task for the operation of OK was to find a broad consensus about the continuation of the pension reform. Key criteria for its work was defined as follows:

1. *ability of the system to ensure a decent life for pensioners,*
2. *increasing the degree of equivalence;*
3. *settlement of transfers between family and society;*
4. *sustainability of the pension system.*

The Expert Committee on Pension Reform had *"to assess the status and developmental trends of the Czech pension system in terms of demography, sociology and economics and to prepare proposals for such a follow-up in the pension reform that will stabilize the pension system in the long run, be acceptable across the political spectrum, and shall be adopted also by the public"* (Mandate of the Expert Committee 2015). One of its explicitly stated goals was also to find a suitable way of eliminating the voluntary private second pillar from the Czech pension system.

The OK was established to develop expertise in finding a consensus on pension reform. Already in its opening statement, it attempted to reframe the issue by expanding its scope. In its presentation of the subject matter, it abandoned a clear emphasis on financial balance within the system and brought quality of life of seniors into focus. "The Expert Committee shall propose, assess and subsequently recommend changes to the pension system, which shall ensure adequate and dignified pensions,

122 http://www.duchodova-komise.cz/?page_id=1248.

strengthening of the principle of merit, settlement of transfer between the family and society…".

This reframing also changed the spectrum of areas addressed and solutions proposed. New attention was paid, among other things, to pension system transfers between citizens, families and the state, or to strengthening the motivation of people for creating long-term retirement savings through the third pillar (the voluntary Supplementary Pension Savings). One part of the discourse remained with traditional topics such as indexation of pensions and definition of retirement age. Thanks to the wider frame of problems addressed, new alternative solutions to "standard" questions surfaced. The reframing can be illustrated in the way of previously asked questions, such as: "to increase retirement age – yes/no, how much?", which had provoked sharp disagreements and transformed into the following question: "How can we successfully set the retirement age taking into account changes in life expectancy?"[123]

After three years and six months of activity (May 2014 – October 2017), OK proposed ten reform proposals to the government, and developed other themes and concepts relevant for the continuation of the Czech pension reform.

Figure B2.5 Main proposals of the Expert Committee on Pension Reform

---

Proposals approved by the Government and reflected in accepted acts:

First pillar:
- The regularly applied revision system of setting of the pension age limit.
- The stipulation of the minimum adjustment of percentage indexation of pensions according to general consumer price index (living costs). In case that this index is of the lower value than consumer price index (living costs) of pensioner households then to stipulate the minimum adjustment of the percentage assessment of pensions applying consumer price index of pensioner households.
- The determination of the minimum indexation of average old-age pension represents the amount by which the basic assessment of pension will increase and the amount by which the percentage assessment of pension will increase, at the amount of the sum of given growth of consumer prices and one half of the growth of real wage.

Second pillar:
- The method of smooth abolishment of the system of pension saving.

Third pillar:
- Extension of the exemption from income tax to pension payments for a period of at least 10 years.
- Reduction of the minimum age for the participation from 18 to 0 years.

---

123 This change is, to some extent, determined by new international trends which include, among other things, automatic or semi-automatic changes to the retirement age.

- Increase in the limit for collective investment in standard funds from 35 to 40% (finally increased to 60%) and in special funds from 5 to 10% (finally increased to 20%) from the value of assets in the participation fund.
- Change in the obligation of the Czech National Bank to remove the permit due to non-fulfilment of existing legal requests for considering the supervision body when assessing individual situations of the participant fund.

Proposal which the Government passed to the Parliament for approval:
First pillar:
- Differentiation of rates of insurance payments for families with children.

Proposal approved by the Expert Committee, the negotiation interrupted at the level of MPSV ČR:
First pillar
- Sharing of the assessment bases of husband and wife for the exercise of pension entitlements.

Facilitation of permanent discussion about political borderlines of the continuation of the pension reform among the representatives of political parties and movements represented in the Chamber of Deputies.

Source: Expert Committee on Pension Reform (2017).

Figure B2.6 Ideas and discourse – Expert Committee on Pension Reform[124]

Normative ideas – explicitly expressed in four criteria: ensuring a decent life for pensioners, increasing the degree of equivalence, settlement of transfers between family and society, sustainability of the pension system.

Cognitive ideas – a significant expansion of the analytical basis of work, of the repertoire of social sciences applied.

Coordinative discourse – a wide spectrum of actors from legislature (delegates of all political parties represented in the Chamber of Deputies), executive (represented by the central level of government, especially the Ministry of Labor and Social Affairs and the Ministry of Finance), experts from various fields, social partners, representatives of associations and professional organizations.

Communicative discourse – great emphasis on cultivating communication, primarily through the website of the OK, which published not only all discussion and background materials, but also citizens' views, as well as further briefings, press conferences, and media appearances. The OK's emphasis on media communication with the public potentially had a positive impact on increasing public awareness of pension issues. At its plenary meetings, team meetings and professional events, the OK also naturally blended communicative and coordinative discourse.

Source: Authors.

---

124 http://www.duchodova-komise.cz/?page_id=1248.

Table B2.2 Institutions of discourse regarding Czech pension reforms

Characteristic institution	Time period	Cognitive ideas	Normative ideas	Acceptance of proposals by political representatives
Executive team and Team of experts (Bezděk Commission I)	2004	Macro-economic criteria and related projections, demographic criteria and related projections, assuming the World Bank's 1994 pension orthodoxy	Differentiated pension reform proposals of political parties	No
Expert Advisory Forum – PES (Bezděk Commission II)	2010	*ditto*	Increasing the degree of equivalence, financial stability of the public pension system	No
National Economic Council of the Government – NERV	2011–2012	*ditto*	*ditto*	Partly
Expert Group: government and opposition party (EG)	2011–2012	Comparison of pension systems from different countries	Not expressed explicitly	Partly
Expert Committee on Pension Reform (OK)	2014–2017	A significant expansion of the analytical basis of work, inviting sociologists, demographers and economists	Explicitly expressed by four criteria: ensuring a decent life for pensioners, increasing the degree of equivalence, settlement of transfers between family and society, sustainability of the pension system	Distinctly

Source: Authors.

CONCLUSIONS

Through a detailed analysis of the discourses in question, we have prepared the ground for a final test of the hypotheses formulated in the introduction.

A. PARTICIPATION OF EXPERTS IS NECESSARY IN PROPOSING SPECIFIC INSTITUTIONS AS WELL AS IN CONCEIVING PENSION REFORM POLICY

Pension policy was traditionally an area that required a greater extent of expertise than some other areas. Traditional partners (government, employer and worker representatives) possessed almost a monopoly in this arena for a long time, with exclusive access to most relevant information and data possessed by governmental entities (statistics, demographic data, data on pension schemes, etc.) Although a number of radical changes have become necessary, we have seen little change in the approach by professionals (data, design development methodology, etc.). Responsible, evidence-based decision-making requires the engagement of a range of fields of expertise and methodologies, including the use of extensive datasets. For politicians, it would be very difficult to cover all these skills from their own resources (though undoubtedly they have in their ranks specialists who deal with long-term issues and possess extensive knowledge). None of the discourses observed could have worked without their expertise; contrarily, expert opinion was the dominant element in all the issues discussed. Politicians were aware of this situation and that is why we can observe their efforts to establish and institutionalize the scientific component of pension reform discourse over time. We can, therefore, confirm the hypothesis.

B. IDEOLOGICAL AND COGNITIVE FRAMES BLENDED IN THE PENSION REFORM DISCOURSE

This hypothesis was clearly confirmed in the study. First, crystal-clear connections between the different reform concepts and ideologies of the left-right political spectrum were corroborated. Second, experts and politicians participated in side-by-side discussions on the preferred version of pension reform. Third, the participation of experts helped reach politically feasible solutions (as in the case of pre-pensions).

C. POLITICIANS HAVE A FINAL SAY ON THE REFORM CHANGES

This hypothesis was confirmed not only by the political rejection of the first recommendation of the Executive Team and the Team of Experts (Bezděk Commission I) in 2004, but also by the case of NERV recommendations later on. The majority of decision makers did not accept NERV's design of the second pillar. The political compromise proved to be unacceptable to the experts, further affecting the reform's communicative discourse. Expert advice was in most cases affected by the process of finding political continuity and consensus. Although politicians have the final say, their decisions may – to a lesser or greater extent, depending primarily on how public political discourse is moderated – reflect the opinions of experts. Even if pension reform was a highly political issue, in reality the decision makers applied neither purely technical nor apparently ideological concepts of pension reform.

D. THE BROADER THE IDEOLOGICAL SPECTRUM OF STAKEHOLDERS, THE MORE ROBUST THE PROPOSED SOLUTION

The connection of the pension reform concepts with the ideological foundations of political parties intensifies the rivalries among actors and complicates the search for a compromise. Finding a solution that has support across the political spectrum is very tricky in the case of pension schemes, where the effects of change are anticipated for decades ahead. The cases examined have shown a higher level of stability of solutions (albeit particular ones) which were adopted as part of discourses where actors from across the ideological spectrum were represented (e.g., the work of the Expert Group on the pre-pensions proposal, or eight proposals of the Expert Committee on Pension Reform which were incorporated in the new legislation), compared to solutions that could not rely on such support (paradigmatic reform, including the Second Pillar). Due to the long-term nature of pension reform and the relatively short time period in which the discourses are analyzed, we can only partially confirm the hypothesis.

It is obvious that the time period analyzed, though eventful, was not long enough to allow us to generalize beyond the development of a pension system discourse in one country at a given time. We believe, however, that our approach may inspire researchers to apply institutionalist theory and frame analysis with a view to better understanding the role of experts and policy makers in the design and implementation of changes in social systems. In this respect, it will be interesting to study, among other things, the continuation of the work of the Czech Expert Committee on Pension Reform.

SOURCES

Benford, R. D., D. A. Snow. 2000. "Framing Processes and Social Movements: An Overview and Assessment." *Annual Review of Sociology* 26: 611–639.

Bezděk, V., D. Münich, J. Procházka, J. Rusnok, P. Zahradník, M. Zámečník. 2011. 'Experti z NERVu: Důchodová reforma očima NERVu' [NERV Experts: The Pension Reform from NERV's Perspective, in Czech]. *Hospodářské noviny*, March 14. Retrieved June 2, 2016 (http://archiv.ihned.cz/c1-51131930-experti-z-nervu-duchodova-reforma -ocima-nervu).

Entman, R. M. 1993. "Framing: Toward clarification of a fractured paradigm." *Journal of Communication* 43 (4): 51–58.

Expert Committee on Pension Reform. 2015. *Final report on activities in 2014*. Prague: The Expert Committee on Pension Reform. Retrieved March 23, 2016 (http://www.duchodova-komise.cz/wp-content/uploads/2015/02/Final-report-CoE-2014.pdf).

Expert Committee on Pension Reform. 2016. *Final report on activities in 2015*. Prague: The Expert Committee on Pension Reform. Retrieved March 23, 2016 (http://www.duchodova-komise.cz/wp-content/uploads/2016/02/Final-report-ECPR-2015.pdf)

Expert Committee on Pension Reform. 2017. *Final report on activities in 2016*. Prague: The Expert Committee on Pension Reform. Retrieved September 18, 2017 (http://www.duchodova-komise.cz/wp-content/uploads/2017/02/Zpráva-o-činnosti-OK-za-rok-2016.pdf)

Goffman, E. 1974 (reprint 1986). *Frame Analysis*. New York: Harper and Row. Retrieved June 2, 2016 (https://nellalou.files.wordpress.com/2014/07/83646510-erving-goffman-frame-analysis-an-essay-on-the-organization-of-experience-1974.pdf).

Leweke, R. W. 1999. *News Frames and Policy: Frame-building in Mainstream News and Political Commentary Media, 1992–1997*. Unpublished dissertation. University of North Carolina at Chapel Hill.

Mandate of the Expert Committee on Pension Reform. 2015. Prague: MPSV. Retrieved June 6, 2016 (http://www.duchodova-komise.cz/wp-content/uploads/2015/02/Mandate-of-the-Expert-Committee.pdf).

Morávek, J. 2011. "Analýza rámců" [Frame Analysis, in Czech]. Pp. 105–135 in M. Nekola, H. Geissler, M. Mouralová (eds.). *Současné metodologické otázky veřejné politiky* [Contemporary Methodological Issues of Public Policy, in Czech]. Prague: Karolinum.

MPSV. 2005. *Final Report: Executive Team*. Prague: MPSV. Retrieved August 6, 2016 (www.mpsv.cz/files/clanky/3445/Final_report.pdf)

MPSV. 2010. *The Expert Advisory Forum's Final Report*. Prague: MPSV. Retrieved August 6, 2016 (http://www.mpsv.cz/files/clanky/8897/Final_Report_PES.pdf)

Potůček, M., V. Rudolfová. 2017. "The Role of Politicians and Experts in the Preparation of the Czech Pension Reform." In: Sánches-Cabeduzo, S. S., López Peláez, A. (eds.) *The Ailing Welfare State*. Navarra: Thomson Reuters Aranzadi, pp. 165–190.

Rein, M., D. Schön. 1993. "Reframing policy discourse." Pp. 145–166 in *Argumentative Turn in Policy Analysis and Planning*, edited by Fischer, F. London: Routledge.

Rein, M., D. Schön. 1996. "Frame-critical policy analysis and frame reflective policy practice." *Knowledge and Policy* 9 (1): 88–90.

Schmidt, V. A. 2008. "Discursive Institutionalism: The Explanatory Power of Ideas and Discourse." *Annual Review of Political Science* 11: 303–326.

Schön, D., M. Rein. 1994. *Frame Reflection: Toward the Resolution of Intractable Policy Controversies*. New York: Basic Books. Retrieved June 2, 2016 (http://www.colorado.edu/conflict/peace/example/Frame_refl_sum.htm).

Stone, D. A. 1997. *Policy paradox. The art of political decision making*. New York: Norton, W. W. & Company, Inc.

World Bank. 1994. *Averting the old age crisis : policies to protect the old and promote growth*. Washington, D.C.: Oxford University Press. Retrieved June 2, 2016 (http://documents.worldbank.org/curated/en/973571468174557899/Avering-the-old-age-crisis-policies-to-protect-the-old-and-promote-growth).

LEGISLATION

Act No. 403/2012 Coll., amending Act No. 427/2011 Coll. on supplementary pension savings.

Act No. 376/2015 Coll., on the termination of pension savings.

Act No. 203/2017 Coll., amending Act No. 155/1995 Coll., on pension insurance, as amended, and other related Acts.

Act No. 377/2015 Coll., amending certain Acts in relation to the adoption of the Act on termination of the pension savings system.

/B3/

Czech Pension Reform: How to Reconcile Equivalence with Fiscal Discipline[125]

---

125 This is an updated version of a paper written by Potůček and Rudolfová (2015).

With the emergence of an independent Czech Republic in January 1993, the Act on Social Security Premium and Contribution to the State Employment Policy (No. 589/1992 Coll.) came into force. Pension insurance premiums were introduced as special compulsory payments outside the scope of the tax system in order to emphasize the merit-based nature of the Czech pension system.

Subsequent years saw a number of parametric adjustments related to indexation, retirement age, periods for which premiums are paid by the state, and contributory periods. Although there were discussions on the need of a fundamental reform of the pension system in both the political arena and professional circles, there was a lack of lasting political consensus to adopt a so-called paradigmatic reform of the pension system.

Public pension expenditures in the Czech Republic oscilate between 8 and 10% of GDP. Prior to its reforms, the Czech pension system ranked among the most solidary systems in the OECD. Its Gini coefficient on a model income distribution had a value of 9.8% (the OECD average is 15,8%) (OECD 2013). With respect to the adequacy of pensions, the Czech Republic's system is comparable to other OECD countries. The following two tables show the pension replacement rates, according to OECD statistics (*ibid.*), for the country and for the OECD as a whole.

Table B3.1 Gross pension replacement rates by earnings

Level of earnings	Median	0.5 × mean	1 × mean	1.5 × mean
Czech Republic	59.9	85.2	52.2	41.2
OECD	57.9	71.0	54.4	48.4

Source: OECD (2013).

Table B3.2 Net pension replacement rates by earnings

Level of earnings	Median	0.5 × mean	1 × mean	1.5 × mean
Czech Republic	73.4	99.1	64.7	51.6
OECD	69.1	81.7	65.8	59.7

Source: OECD (2013).

On 13 April 2007, the Constitutional Court received a petition in which the Regional Court in Ostrava sought the annulment of the provisions of part of Section 15, second sentence, of Act No. 155/1995 Coll., on Pension Insurance that concerned **the setting of bend points for determining the amount of pensions depending on the previous earnings of the insured**. The petition was related to the case of JUDr. K. S., who, before the Regional Court in Ostrava, contested the amount of pension granted to him and pointed to the fact that the total amount of the pension granted accounts for only a small part of his income, which he does not consider to be adequate material security as guaranteed by the Charter of Fundamental Rights and Freedoms.

The plaintiff had worked as a judge; the average salary of this profession is several times higher than the average salary in the country. He was dissatisfied with the percentage assessment and although he agreed that it was determined in accordance with applicable law, he complained that it accounted for only 19% of his previous income, while the average replacement rate was about 44% of gross wage in 2004. He referred to Article 30 Paragraph 1 of the Charter of Fundamental Rights and Freedoms which, as a part of the Czech constitutional order, stipulates that "**citizens have the right to adequate material security in old age and during periods of work incapacity, as well as in the case of the loss of their provider**." According to the plaintiff, the income reduction for the purposes of calculating the percentage assessment of his pension disadvantages him and places him in an unequal position. He thus contested the provision of the Section 15 of the Act on Pension Insurance as unconstitutional, arguing that **it discriminates against insured persons with higher incomes**. He referred to the fact that even the name of the Act indicates that it involves insurance, i.e., a legal institution that has its settled content, while premiums should not be treated as taxes. **For insurance, there should be a clear and proportionate link between the contributions paid and the pension received.** There was an interesting argument against solidarity as a justification for setting the bend points and different treatment of different categories of insured persons. According to the petitioner, the principle of solidarity in itself does not give rise to certain rights and obligations. Solidarity, according to the petitioner, is ensured sufficiently in the fact that insurance premiums are consistently based on the level of pay.

The contested provision – Section 15 of Act No. 155/1995 Coll., on Pension Insurance – in the original wording as of 2009

The calculation base equals the personal assessment base (Section 16) provided it does not exceed CZK 10,500. If the personal assessment base exceeds CZK 10,500, the calculation base is determined as follows: the sum of CZK 10,500 is counted in full; the amount of the personal assessment base of over CZK 10,500 and up to CZK 27,000 is reduced to 30%; and any amount of the personal assessment base over CZK 27,000 is reduced to 10%.

The plaintiff thus **contested the degree of equivalence of the pension system**, i.e., the ratio between the pension benefits calculated and previous work-related income **as insufficient**.

THEORY AND METHODS

We offer a detailed analysis of the decision-making process with regard to two conflicting criteria of the pension reform: strengthening the equivalence of pensions compared to previous contributions, on the one hand, and keeping public pension expenditures under control, on the other. Such an analysis has to take into account the complex legal, political, and institutional environment of the Czech Republic at the beginning of the second decade of the 21st century.

In order to understand the policy process from filing the petition to the Constitutional Court, to adopting the amendment to the Act on Pension Insurance, to implementing it in practice, we proceed as follows. First, we apply the perspective of actor-centered institutionalism. We briefly characterize the main institutions and actors that were involved in that process. Then we try to identify the actor constellation and modes of interaction leading to the political decisions. We supplement this analysis by deconstructing the policy process into its individual stages. In the conclusion, we assess to what extent our analytical approach to the pension reform case proves to be useful.

From the nature of the case analyzed, it follows that we pay attention mainly to the legislative process which resulted in the amendment to the relevant legal norm. Within the scope of the adopted methods, analysis of documents (legal norms, court decisions, political programs, official publications) and political and administrative communications (including debates on legislative drafts at the levels of the government, the parliament and the president of the Czech Republic) dominate.

ACTOR-CENTERED INSTITUTIONALISM

The theory of actor-centered institutionalism by Renate Mayntz and Fritz Scharpf (Mayntz, Scharpf 1995; Scharpf 1997) assumes that the behavior of policy actors is significantly, though never entirely, determined by existing (either formalized or informal) institutions, which influence their perceptions, preferences and available resources. Such significant determination is also given by the power of actors' expectations that other actors will also act in accordance with these institutions. The theory further assumes that individuals interacting within formalized institutions are governed by their internal rules: "Rules and systems of rules in any historically given society not only organize and regulate social behavior but make it understandable – and in a limited conditional sense – predictable for those sharing in rule knowledge" (Burns, Baumgartner and Deville 1985: 256, quoted in Scharpf 1997: 40).

The theory works with two specific concepts. An **actor constellation** is a structure of actors involved, their strategic options and outcome preferences, and the outcomes associated with the combinations of those strategies and preferences. These processes may vary considerably and can be described as different **modes of interaction**. There are four different modes: unilateral action, negotiated agreement, majority choice, and hierarchical direction.

STUDY TIP: Refer to **Chapter A4** for more on the Theory of actor-centered institutionalism.

ACTORS' BEHAVIOR

Imported from economics, the normative assumption of rational choice theory is that the decision maker should choose the option that results in the highest utility (Jaeger et al. 2001). When the preferences of more than one actor are involved, the Pareto optimality criterion is used.

STUDY TIP: Refer to **Chapter A9** for more on the Theory of rational choice.

Actor-centered institutionalism avoids the extreme assumptions of neoclassical economics. In contrast to the *homo oeconomicus* model of individual behavior that assumes "rational choice" in terms of maximizing individual utilities, actor-centered institutionalism uses the term "bounded rationality" (Scharpf 1997). Actors do not seek to strictly maximize but rather satisfy their needs according to disposable information and their own cognitive capabilities. The concept of bounded rationality is related to what Scharpf terms "intentional actors" (1997, also cited in Korpi 2001).

A composite actor is defined by Scharpf (1997) as "an aggregate of individuals" that has "a capacity for intentional action at a level above the individuals involved" (Ibid.: 52), i.e., an organization. The problem of composite actors acting on behalf of or in the name of a group or organization (Scharpf 1997) is that their preferences are not only a sum of the members' self-interests, but also include shared norms and identities. The composite actor can be perceived as an actor per se or as an institutional structure. Therefore, on the one hand, rational choice theory is not always easy to apply. On the other hand, even what appears as irrational behavior (or Scharpf's bounded rationality) at first sight can be explained using rational choice theory (Rahmatian and Hiatt 1989). Actors may be misinformed (some of their factual beliefs are false), mistaken (some of their causal beliefs are false), or misguided (some of their evaluative beliefs are false) (Bots 2008).

THE THEORY OF THE POLICY CYCLE

Specifying the actors and institutions involved is usually only the first step towards a better understanding a given public policy. Neither can their modes of interaction reveal enough to fully comprehend the course of the entire process. The policy process occurs at multiple levels, the relationships of actors and institutions tend to change, and a given public policy depends on other policies together with external context. Therefore, it is necessary to resort to conceptual frameworks that attempt, even at the cost of simplification, to

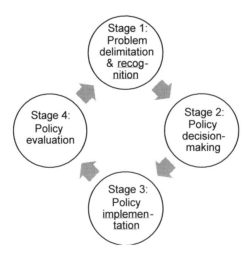

Figure B3.1 The phase model of the policy process
Source: Howlett and Ramesh (1995), adapted.

capture this variability in time. The phase model of the policy cycle is one of the oldest tools used for that purpose. In our discussion we restrict ourselves to a simple four-stage model, as depicted in Figure B3.1. In the following section, we will proceed to identifying key institutions and actors.

STUDY TIP: Refer to **Chapter A6** for more on the Theory of the policy cycle.

ANALYSIS – INSTITUTIONS AND ACTORS

INSTITUTIONS

The constitutional order of the Czech Republic is a set of constitutional acts and documents of constitutional relevance. It consists of the Constitution of the Czech Republic (1992), the Charter of Fundamental Rights and Freedoms (1992), and constitutional acts adopted pursuant to the Constitution.

The Constitutional Court is a judicial body protecting constitutionality pursuant to Section 83 of the Constitution of the Czech Republic. Its judgments are final and cannot be appealed. The Constitutional Court decides in situations when there is a breach of fundamental human rights and freedoms guaranteed by the constitution.

The Parliament of the Czech Republic is the bicameral national legislature. It consists of the Chamber of Deputies (200 members elected using a proportional representation system) and the Senate (81 senators elected using a majoritarian electoral system).

The President of the Czech Republic has minimal executive powers. S/he has the right to turn back an Act adopted by the Parliament of the Czech Republic. The so-called suspense veto does not apply to constitutional acts and acts subject to shortened debate under legislative emergency or state of war. The president must justify his/her veto. Pursuant to the procedural rules of the Chamber of Deputies, the President shall not sign an Act against which s/he has unsuccessfully used the right of veto.

ACTORS

THE PLAINTIFF

Citizen JUDr. K. S., former judge, challenged the degree of equivalence of the pension system as inadequate in terms of discrimination against insured persons with higher incomes (in violation of the Charter of Fundamental Rights and Freedoms).

THE GOVERNMENT OF THE CZECH REPUBLIC

A decision by the Constitutional Court was made public on 16 April 2010, in the run-up to early parliamentary elections in which the pension reform played the role of an important campaign issue. The elections to the Chamber of Deputies were held on 28–29 May 2010 and resulted in the formation of a right-center government coalition of the Civic Democratic Party (ODS), TOP 09 and "Public Affairs" (VV).[126] The preparation of a solution to which the Constitutional Court committed the executive power took place following the elections. It was a period of continuing global financial crisis in which the Czech Republic was affected by economic depression, as well as rising unemployment rates, and growing deficits of the state budget. The government reacted by declaring radical restriction of public expenditures its top priority.

THE MINISTRY OF LABOR AND SOCIAL AFFAIRS OF THE CZECH REPUBLIC (MPSV)

The MPSV prepared alternative proposals for a solution. It was the only actor to do so. Two solutions were basically unworkable; the so-called "zero variant" would abolish the principle of equivalence in the pension system and go completely against the spirit of the decision of the Constitutional Court; and the second variant, replacing the system of insurance by a system of social security, could not be accomplished under the given time constraint. The third option, the so-called "substantive solution", was elaborated in three variants. The potential impact on the pension account's balance became the main assessment criterion. With regard to the priority of fiscal discipline, the MPSV finally recommended the variant of structural adjustments only to the expenditure side of the pension account, without any additional demands for revenues.

THE RESEARCH INSTITUTE OF LABOR AND SOCIAL AFFAIRS (VÚPSV)

The Research Institute of Labor and Social Affairs (VÚPSV) provided analytical capacities for the MPSV. In the case of the so-called Minor Pension Reform, it published analyses on the decision of the Constitutional Court and the degree of equivalence of the pension system, including proposals of possible solutions (Holub 2010a, 2010b).

POLITICAL PARTIES

The coalition parties (Civic Democratic Party, TOP 09, Public Affairs), although presenting the legislative proposal as enforced by the decision of the Constitutional Court, had accentuated in their election programs, as well as in

---

126 See section on the decision-making phase below for more details.

the government policy statement, the fiscal unsustainability of the pension system and promoted, among other things, strengthening the degree of equivalence through compulsory savings in private pension funds.

The opposition parties, the Czech Social Democratic Party (ČSSD) and the Communist Party of Bohemia and Moravia (KSČM), criticized the decision of the Constitutional Court, primarily due to concerns about weakening the degree of solidarity and its position in the pension system. The Czech Social Democratic Party argued the decision was "not to be under the authority of the Constitutional Court." The Communist Party of Bohemia and Moravia argued the decision essentially abolished solidarity in the pension system.

SOCIAL PARTNERS[127]

The position and strength of social partners within a political system depends on the country's historical tradition and political culture. Traditionally, the strongest positions have been assumed by social partners (representatives of employees, employers and the government) in countries which perceive social partnership as crucial. Corporatist countries exhibit a high degree of institutionalization of social partners and a key role of social dialogue in the workings of the political system (e.g., Austria). In other countries, the relationship between social partners and the government has no impact on the functioning of the political system and social partners *de facto* do not participate on policy decision making. Social dialogue is not institutionalized and the partners do not have functionally formalized ways of influencing the decision making processes in these countries. They in turn use lobbying and various other methods to influence and appeal to the public. However, this situation is not typical among EU states and primarily concerns the UK and possibly also Greece.

In the Czech Republic, tripartism constitutes a firm, integral part of the political system, though the status of **the Council of Economic and Social Agreement (RHSD)** (as the institutional embodiment of tripartism) is not legally regulated, and the configuration of the governing coalition affects the position and power of social partners. The changes proposed under the so-called Minor Pension Reform were consulted within the Plenary Session of the Council.

The Czech-Moravian Confederation of Trade Unions (ČMKOS) was the strongest opponent of the decision of the Constitutional Court of all the social partners. In accordance with its fundamental values, it mainly perceived the strengthening of the degree of equivalence at the expense of solidarity as negative: "The proposed solution will, in the future, worsen the pension rights of 80% of citizens in favor of a higher income for the richest 10%" (ČMKOS 2011: 1). The Confederation presented at the Council of Economic and Social

---

127 More on corporatist democracy can be found in Chapter A3.

Agreement meeting its own, socially more sensitive design of the pension reform, which would not lead to a reduction of the newly calculated pensions.

The Confederation of Industry of the Czech Republic (SP ČR) concurred with the solution as proposed and submitted by the MPSV while adding that it would prefer a higher ceiling to the premiums. Instead of the level of three times the average wage, it suggested four times (that was, of course, an adjustment to the revenue side, while the government in its response to the decision of the Constitutional Court designed only modifications to the expenditure side).

CZECH SOCIAL SECURITY ADMINISTRATION (ČSSZ)

First and foremost, ČSSZ carried out an executive role with respect to the calculation and disbursement of pension entitlements, and its crucial concern was to ensure sufficient time to prepare the calculation and disbursement of pensions in accordance with the newly approved provisions. In addition, ČSSZ raised awareness about the changes brought by the so-called Minor Pension Reform. It published a leaflet, "Minor Pension Reform in Questions and Answers," in which changes associated with the new law were summarized in a comprehensive manner for the general public.

ACTOR CONSTELLATION

Shortly after the Constitutional Court's decision, an early election gave rise to a new right-center government. There was a significant consensus among the coalition parties on the pension reform issue, in particular on the need to strengthen the degree of equivalence in the Czech Republic's pension system.

The Expert Advisory Forum (PES) was established in 2010 with the main objective to analyze the current state of the pension system and suggest possible ways to reform it. As a possible solution to the situation, it proposed reducing the degree of solidarity in the state PAYG pillar, strengthening the degree of equivalence and monitoring its long-term fiscal sustainability.

The decision by the Constitutional Court, the outcomes of the parliamentary elections and the subsequently formed coalition government, and the rising professional discourse thus created favorable conditions for a rapid progress of preparation of changes to the pension formula to strengthen equivalence. Since none of the actors concerned questioned either the decision of the Constitutional Court itself or the need to implement it, the agenda of the day evolved around the manner in which that decision should be reflected within the wording of an amendment to the Act.

This seemingly technical question, however, had significant economic connotations. Increasing the degree of equivalence for higher

income categories within the pension formula would *ceteris paribus* **lead to higher demands on the state budget. This, however, was not in accordance with the right-center government's pledge to a fiscal stabilization of the pension system.** The task to propose the manner in which to combine within the pension system higher equivalence with fiscal stabilization eventually fell on the shoulders of the MPSV.

MODES OF INTERACTION

In the Czech Republic, single-party majority governments are not typical due to the proportional representation system. The institutional environment allows a government coalition to enforce its proposals in spite of possible disapproval by the second chamber of the Parliament (i.e., the Senate) or by the President of the Czech Republic, or even despite opposition from social partners. As a result, the governing elites do not necessarily have to seek a consensual style of policy making in a broader context.

As neither opposition parties nor the Czech-Moravian Confederation of Trade Unions liked the government's intention to strengthen the equivalence principle for higher income categories without increasing the burden on the state budget, it was obvious that the scope for a nation-wide consensus was narrowing. Despite debating the topic in the Council of Economic and Social Agreement, the social partners did not show any efforts to find compromise solutions and there were no broad discussions. The Constitutional Court claimed that reform had been "enforced" – under pressure of its deadline – so the government resorted to unilateral action and pushed through the amendment as its "proposed solution to the issue" against the opposition and without the consent of the Tripartite.

ANALYSIS – PHASES OF THE POLICY CYCLE

PHASE OF PROBLEM DELIMITATION AND RECOGNITION

In 2007, Prime Minister Mirek Topolánek formed a right-center coalition of the Civic Democratic Party (ODS), the Christian and Democratic Union – Czechoslovak People's Party (KDU-ČSL), and the Green Party (SZ). Pension reform was one of the key issues and tasks formulated in the government policy statement. One of the objectives of the so-called first stage of the pension reform was to strengthen individual responsibility and to implement parametric changes to the pension system towards strengthening the degree of equivalence and fiscal stabilization. This way, the criterial foundation of the government's political choices was clearly established.

Following the above-mentioned proposal, the Constitutional Court forwarded the petition to the individual parties of the proceeding. It requested responses to the petition from the Chamber of Deputies and the Senate of the Parliament of the Czech Republic, and also requested a written statement from the Ministry of Labor and Social Affairs.

The Chamber of Deputies responded in a statement that within the legislative process of adopting the Act on Pension Insurance, which governs the setting of bend points, no factual objection to the section in question had been raised. The act was adopted following a duly executed legislative process.

The Senate stated that as a chamber of the Parliament of the Czech Republic, it was not yet constituted at the time the act in question was adopted (the first elections to the Senate were held in the fall of 1996). The Senate further stated that although the act had been amended several times, none of those former amendments related to the contested part of the act.

The statement of the MPSV was more extensive. It has mainly accentuated the tradition of the institution of bend points in the Czech system of pension insurance (first established by Act No. 99/1948 Coll.), a fact that Act No. 155/1995 Coll. explicitly mitigated harshness in the system's settings, and a wide spectrum of degrees of equivalence that exist in the pension systems of other countries. In response to the plaintiff's interpretation of the function and nature of the institution of insurance, the Ministry distinguished between the social and private line of insurance, arguing that private insurance follows the principles stated in the complaint, while social insurance is designed differently. Bend points are, according to the MPSV, an element that affects the degrees of equivalence and solidarity of the system of pension insurance and reflects legislators' preferences on how strongly these principles should be enshrined in the system. They are, therefore, a matter of political decision. Bend points strengthen solidarity and reduce the risk of poverty in the older generation, which is one of the fundamental objectives of the pension system.

DECISION OF THE CONSTITUTIONAL COURT

On 16 April 2010, in its decision Ref. No. Pl. ÚS 8/07, **the Constitutional Court found the provision of Section 15 of Act No. 155/1995 Coll., on Pension Insurance, unconstitutional** and abolished the so-called reduction limit for calculating the percentage assessment of a pension.

The Constitutional Court supported its decision, among other things, by the then only recently published expert opinions on the degrees of equivalence and redistribution in the Czech pension system. These reports had been formulated over a period of political discussions on the future direction of the pension system. The decision quoted the Final Report of the Expert Advisory Forum on strong income redistribution, suppression of insurance elements, and a relatively high contribution rate within the pension system of the Czech Republic (MPSV 2010). Further, it relied on the Actuarial Report on Social Insurance published regularly by the MPSV, which described a possible pension system reform to diversify the system and strengthen the principle of equivalence (MPSV 2008). In its conclusion, the Constitutional Court stated that "...the entire complicated structure of the pension system is sufficiently non-transparent that it is de facto completely incomprehensible to its users; thus, for the majority of insured persons the calculated level of pension benefits becomes unverifiable" (Constitutional Court of the Czech Republic 2010).

The Constitutional Court (2010) stated that "it is not its role to evaluate the correctness (suitability) of the calculation of pension insurance benefits." The Court should neither "evaluate the chosen pension system model from political or economic viewpoints." Its judgement only assesses whether the construction of the pension system complies with the constitutional principles of the Czech Republic.

The decision by the Constitutional Court (2010) was dissented by two constitutional judges: Jan Musil and Jiří Nykodým. Jan Musil argued that "the Constitutional Court stepped into the territory of social policy, decisions on which are reserved only to the legislature." Jiří Nykodým refused to perceive the degree of solidarity and thus also the degree of equivalence in social security systems as a constitutional issue. In his opinion, it is in particular, an economic a political question. It does not, in his opinion, relate to "a case of flagrant injustice," and only under such circumstances would it become a constitutional law question (Constitutional Court of the Czech Republic 2010).

DECISION-MAKING PHASE

RESPONSE TO THE DECISION OF THE CONSTITUTIONAL COURT

Given the contemporary political situation (early elections), the reactions of party leaders were suggestive of campaign rhetoric. Right-wing political parties interpreted the judgement as an affirmation of the need for pension reforms to strengthen the system's degree of equivalence. The chairman of the governing Civic Democratic Party, Petr Nečas, stated that the Court's decision was a confirmation of the fact that the current pension system was unsustainable. He challenged the bend points as egalitarian and suggested capping pension insurance premiums. He stressed the need to rapidly adopt pension reforms.

Left-wing political parties opposed the decision critically and drew attention to the danger of devaluing the principle of solidarity in social security systems. The chairman of the then strongest opposition party (Czech Social Democratic Party), Jiří Paroubek, labeled the Court's decision as activism, arguing it was not appropriate to its jurisdiction. Representatives of the Communist Party of Bohemia and Moravia perceived the judgment as directly challenging the preservation of the system's solidarity.

One of the more restrained statements that came to the fore was that of Finance Minister Eduard Janota, who expressed concern about a potential additional burden on the state budget.

The Czech-Moravian Confederation of Trade Unions opposed the judgment while promoting the value of solidarity. It was concerned about the "promotion" of reform concepts that reinforce the degree of equivalence at the expense of solidarity, moreover, during the campaign before the elections to the Chamber of Deputies.

The preparation of a specific solution proposal took place after the elections. The new government was formed by a right-center coalition of the Civic Democratic Party, the TOP 09 and the Public Affairs. What follows are propositions on the shape of pension reform from the coalition partners' electoral programs.

Civic Democratic Party: "We promote various forms of supplementary pension insurance and retirement savings, including greater involvement of employers and competition between pension plans. We propose a voluntary option to transfer a part of the premiums (4% + a co-payment of 2%) to (private) pension funds."
(ODS 2010)

TOP 09: "Within the second phase, the government will transform the pension system into a so-called multi-component system: PAYG (pay-as-you-go) – funded by compulsory pension insurance contributions of 28%, or capitalization – citizens can voluntarily opt for entering. In this case their contributions to the PAYG component will be reduced to 24%, but they will be obliged to pay at least 6% to their capitalization accounts. If one's parents are pension beneficiaries then 2 percent of his/her account will be assigned to them (...) The decline of revenue in the PAYG system will be compensated from assets of the CEZ Group and if necessary from indirect taxes."
(TOP 09 2010)

Public Affairs: "Given the current shape of the pension system, we propose a three-component pension system funded from the following sources: the existing PAYG funding from social security contributions, optional saving of 4% from social security contributions in a single state pension fund, and private commercial supplementary insurance."
(Věci veřejné 2010)

In its policy statement, the government responded directly to the situation caused by the decision of the Constitutional Court. It undertook to comply with the decision by proposing modifications to the construction of newly granted pensions and capping the assessment base for insurance premiums. The policy statement also included a broader outline of pension reform to alleviate long-term financial unsustainability of the system.

PROPOSAL BY THE MPSV

In response to the decision of the Constitutional Court, the Ministry of Labor and Social Affairs put together three policy options – the so-called zero, formal, and substantive solutions (Maška, Rada 2011).

Change in the pension benefit formula – The recommendation of the MPSV[128] was to implement changes only to the expenditure side of the pension account. The Ministry proposed substantial revisions in the pension benefit formula designed for a neutral impact on the state budget. It also provided for a gradual "run-up" of the new formula during a transitional period from 2011 to 2015.

When discussing the adjustments proposed, critics focused mainly on additional parametric modifications. While the coalition parties pushed the amendment as a necessary step that was basically enforced by a decision of the Constitutional Court, opposition parties mainly criticized the impact of parametric adjustments on the amount of newly granted pensions for lower income categories and a lack of debate over the proposed shape of the pension reform.

The government submitted the draft amendment to the Chamber of Deputies on 2 March 2011. Critical responses to it stemmed mainly from two opposition parties – the Czech Social Democratic Party and the Communist Party of Bohemia and Moravia.

Czech Social Democratic Party: "The bill's response to the Constitutional Court decision is unjust, at the expense of middle-income earners. It will reduce newly awarded old-age pensions for 70% of policyholders (with monthly earnings ranging between 11 and 36 thousand CZK) in order to increase them for 10% of people with the highest earnings. This measure, along with the tightening of retirement conditions, has motivated a large number of applications for early retirement, which will cause an unintended rise of pension expenditure over the following years."
(ČSSD 2011)

Communist Party of Bohemia and Moravia: "The impacts will be tough and anti-social. Seventy percent of new pensioners will see their pensions reduced by up to three percent. Twenty percent of new pensioners with the highest incomes will see their pensions increased by up to seven percent."
(Dopady na lidi budou tvrdé 2011)

---

128 Details of the proposal are described in the section on the phase of implementation.

Within the **first reading** that took place at the 14th session of the Chamber of Deputies on March 15, 2011 the then Minister of Labor and Social Affairs Jaromír Drábek (TOP 09) presented the amendment in the context of the necessity for pension reform. There were additional parametric adjustments that went beyond a mere response to the decision of the Constitutional Court. In the debate, the proposal was supported by MP Jitka Chalánková (TOP 09) who considered a strengthening of the level of equivalence as the right step. Opposed to the proposal was MP Miroslav Opálka (Communist Party of Bohemia and Moravia) who described the proposed modifications as extremely harsh and antisocial. Prime Minister Petr Nečas (Civic Democratic Party) emphasized that the proposed changes were not so much an expression of one's political will as a response to the decision of the Constitutional Court. He described the amendment as an enforced decision.

The Committee on Social Policy of the Chamber of Deputies discussed the bill and on April 11, 2011 recommended it for approval without objections.

Within its **second reading,** the bill went through both general and detailed debate on May 4, 2011. Minister of Labor and Social Affairs Jaromír Drábek repeated the argumentation from the first reading and discussed current trends that were fully in line with the parametric modifications proposed.

Bohuslav Sobotka (Czech Social Democratic Party) rejected the bill, arguing that it was not only a response to the decision of the Constitutional Court, but included additional parametric adjustments to the pension system that the government wanted approved. He criticized more extensively a proposed extension of the retirement age. The proposed modifications would affect the expenditure side of the pension account without strengthening the revenue side. Prime Minister Petr Nečas (Civic Democratic Party) repeated his assertion that the amendments proposed responded to the decision of the Constitutional Court which required strengthening the principle of equivalence.

The **third reading** took place on May 11, 2011 and the bill was approved. In attendance were 136 MPs. 82 MPs of the government coalition or independent voted for the proposal, and 32 MPs, mostly from the Czech Social Democratic Party and the Communist Party of Bohemia and Moravia (plus one independent), voted against it.

DEBATE IN THE SENATE

The bill was tabled in the Senate on May 17, 2011. It was debated on June 8, 2011 and returned to the Chamber of Deputies with modifying proposals. The Senate proposed increasing the primary pension assessment from 9%

to 10% to mitigate a slump caused by strengthening equivalence, and capping premiums at the level of five times the average earning instead of six to four times.

DECISION OF THE CHAMBER OF DEPUTIES

The document of the Senate was delivered to the Chamber of Deputies and distributed on June 10, 2011. In a vote on the bill returned by the Senate on June 21, 2011, the Chamber of Deputies upheld the original bill. In attendance were 176 MPs, 105 MPs from the governmental coalition voted for the bill, against it were 71 MPs (Czech Social Democratic Party, Communist Party of Bohemia and Moravia), while no independent MPs were logged in.

PRESIDENT OF THE CZECH REPUBLIC

The amendment to Act No. 155/1995 Coll., on Pension Insurance, was delivered to the President for signature on June 23, 2011. The President expressed a dissenting opinion in which, among other things, he argued the constitutional judges had misunderstood the meaning and status of the pension system as a public good: "The state is neither a financial institution nor an insurance company, and pension insurance participants as well as recipients of state pensions are not its clients, as is very mistakenly believed by those Constitutional Court judges on whose initiative this amendment has been drafted. The principle of equivalence in this context has about as much sense as if each person paying significantly above-average taxes demanded, for example, that there should be more streetlight to shine on him/her or wanted from the state a higher level of police protection compared to others" (Klaus 2011). By July 7, 2011, the amendment to Act No. 155/1995 Coll., on Pension Insurance, had been neither signed into law by the president nor vetoed, and sent back to the Chamber of Deputies. The coming into force of the Act remained unaffected by this procedure since the Constitution does not specifically require the President's signature on the Act. Nevertheless, legal experts agreed that the procedure was on the verge of constitutionality.[129]

---

129 "The Constitution uses the exact wording of 'Laws which have been enacted shall be signed,' not 'has the right to sign' or 'may sign.' From this, commentaries infer a constitutional obligation to sign the act," says Jan Kysela from the Department of Legal Theory, Faculty of Law, Charles University. "Provided the President does not want to sign the act, he has the right to veto. If he does not want to veto the act, he has to sign it," he stated. For more details, see Macháček (2004).

PHASE OF IMPLEMENTATION

NEW WORDING OF SECTION 15 OF ACT NO. 155/1995 COLL., ON PENSION INSURANCE:

1. During the period from September 30, 2011 to December 31, 2014, the calculation base shall be determined from the personal assessment base (Section 16) by adding up:
   a) 100% of the amount up to the first reduction limit,
   b) of the amount above the first reduction limit and up to the second reduction limit, 29% during the period from September 30, 2011 to December 31, 2011, 28% in 2012, 27% in 2013 and 26% in 2014,
   c) of the amount above the second reduction limit and up to the third reduction limit, 13% during the period from September 30, 2011 to December 31, 2011, 16% in 2012, 19% in 2013 and 22% in 2014,
   d) of the amount above the third reduction limit, 10% during the period from September 30, 2011 to December 31, 2011, 8% in 2012, 6% in 2013 and 3% in 2014.
2. In the period after the end of 2014, the calculation base shall be determined from the personal assessment base (Section 16) by adding up:
   a) 100% of the amount up to the first reduction limit,
   b) 26% of the amount above the first reduction limit and up to the second reduction limit,
   c) none of the amount above the second reduction limit.
3. During the period from September 30, 2011 to December 30, 2014, the first reduction limit shall be 44% of the average wage, the second reduction limit shall be 116% of the average wage and the third reduction limit shall be 400% of the average wage. In the period after the end of 2014, the first reduction limit shall be 44% of the average wage and the second reduction limit shall be 400% of the average wage for the calendar year. The reduction limits shall be rounded up to the nearest CZK.

Even before the reform came into force, ČSSZ had registered an extraordinary increase in the number of applications for early retirement. 66,458 people applied during the first 8 months of 2011, which was three times more than in 2010. Early retirement helped eliminate the negative impacts for those 80% for which the Minor Pension Reform would entail a reduction in the newly granted pension. In contrast, over the years following the amendment, the number of pension applications among insured persons with a higher assessment base (for whom a postponement would mean more favorable calculation) did not show any significant fluctuations.

PHASE OF EVALUATION

Although the theory of the policy cycle places the phase of evaluating public policies only after the implementation phase, in the present case we encountered an earlier assessment effort referred to in the literature as *ex ante* evaluation.

Ex ante assessment of impacts of the proposed amendments to contested Section 15 was part of the RIA (Regulatory Impact Assessment) method adopted by the Ministry of Labor and Social Affairs.[130] The key criteria for selecting an option were – as determined by the actor constellation identified – an increase in the extent of equivalence, and fiscal neutrality with regard to the long-term financial sustainability of the pension system.

The MPSV conducted an *ex ante* evaluation of all three policy options (listed above in the paragraph on the decision making phase) on how to respond to the decision of the Constitutional Court and amend Section 15 of Act No. 155/1995 Coll., on Pension Insurance. Based on this evaluation, the MPSV recommended implementing a variant of option 3 – adjustments only on the expenditure side of the pension account.

- **Zero solution** (the provision in question would not be replaced). Pensions would be granted in their minimum amount. According to the assessment by the MPSV this option would result in substantial savings to the pension system but the level of pensions would not at all be tied to the amount of insurance contributions paid. Removing the principle of equivalence would not materialize the purpose of the decision of the Constitutional Court.
- **Formal solution** (to transform the existing insurance-based pension system into a social security system). According to the assessment by the MPSV, this would be both legislatively demanding and time-consuming. In addition there was a threat that this solution could provoke accusations of circumventing the decision of the Constitutional Court. However, the balance of the primary pension account would be unaffected.
- **Substantive solutions:**
  - **Modifications only to the expenditure side of the account.** According to the MPSV it was possible to draft proposals that did not create any additional pressure on the balance of the primary pension account.
  - **Modifications only to the revenue side of the account.** This solution was not considered appropriate because the Constitutional Court in its decision had directly annulled Section 15 of the Act on Pension Insurance and therefore probably expected its amendment. This solution would require a significantly lower level of the maximum assessment base, namely around 24 times the average wage per calendar year. That would directly worsen the balance without the possibility of counter-balancing. The balance of the primary pension account would deteriorate.

---

130 Cf. Chapter A9.

- **Combination of adjustments to the revenue and expenditure sides of the account.** According to the MPSV this measure would entail a risk of pressure on the pension account balance, at least during a transitional period due to a timing discrepancy between effects on the revenue and expenditure sides.

The goal of strengthening equivalence in the pension system of the Czech Republic implied, within the context of the adopted reform proposal, an increase in the replacement rate for individuals with the highest incomes, e.g., those from within the tenth income decile. For example, individuals with incomes above CZK 36,000 per month saw their replacement rate increased from 29% to 36%. The goal of maintaining solidarity without changing the level of the newly granted pensions was fulfilled only among low-income individuals in the first income decile (10% of the insured with incomes of up to about CZK 10,900 per month). 80% of the insured in between thus bore the costs of increasing the replacement rate for people with higher incomes by suffering reduced levels of pensions awarded using the new formula (a 2–6% decrease of their replacement rate). For example, the replacement rate for individuals with incomes between the first and second reduction levels declined by up to 3%.

CONCLUSION

The theory of actor-centered institutionalism made the explanation of the policy process analyzed more transparent. We proceeded from the institutional framework of the Constitution, which also defines the roles of key actors (the government, representative bodies, the President) within the legislative process. We also reviewed the roles and options of other political actors (political parties, social partners, experts), and specified their constellations and modes of interaction. The theory also helped us identify the politically symbolic actions of the President. Though he could not prevent the passing of a legislative act which he disapproved, he expressed his opinion at least through the act of "non-signature."

The theory of the policy cycle facilitated our understanding of the sequence of individual events, especially when looking at the legislative process itself. We were able to analyze public policy discourse in the phase of decision making where the theory of actor-centered institutionalism identified specific modes of interaction – in the given case, confrontational rather than consensual ones. On the other hand, the policy cycle model did not correspond with the fact that (at least within the case analyzed) the evaluation phase took place prior to the phases of decision making and implementation. Evaluation was already reflected within both initial stages of the policy process: in the course of specifying and recognizing the issue by the plaintiff and subsequently by the Constitutional Court, and in the course of decision making, which was based both on the explicit demand made by the Constitutional Court (to increase equivalence) and on the implicit political criterion of the government (fiscal discipline to achieve sustainability of the pension system). It is important to add that our case study did not include an *ex post* assessment, which possibly could have started a new policy cycle. Nevertheless, the theories applied serve for an instructive demonstration of identifying key stakeholders and critical policy events.

SOURCES

Bots, P. W. G. 2008. *Analyzing actor networks while assuming "frame rationality."* Paper presented at the conference on Networks in Political Science (NIPS). Kennedy School of Governance, Harvard University, Cambridge. Retrieved March 30, 2016 (http://www.hks.harvard.edu/netgov/files/NIPS/PWG_BOTS_Analyzing_actor_networks_14_June_2008.pdf.).

Burns, T. R., T. Baumgartner, P. Deville. 1985. *Man, Decisions, Society: The Theory of Actor-System Dynamics for Social Scientists.* New York: Gordon and Breach.

Constitutional Court of the Czech Republic. 2010. *Decision of the Constitutional Court – Pl. ÚS 8/07.* Prague: Constitutional Court of the Czech Republic. Retrieved March 30, 2016 http://www.usoud.cz/en/decisions/20100323-pl-us-807-right-to-adequate-material-security/).

ČMKOS. 2011. *Stanovisko ČMKOS* [Position of the Czech-Moravian Confederation of Trade Unions on Proposed Law on Pension Insurance, in Czech]. Prague: ČMKOS.

ČSSD. 2011. *Malá důchodová reforma je nespravedlivá, necitlivá a nedomyšlená, ČSSD s ní zásadně nesouhlasí* [Small Pension Reform is unfair, insensitive and ill-conceived, ČSSD strongly disagrees with it, in Czech]. Prague: ČSSD. Retrieved May 12, 2011 (https://www.cssd.cz/aktualne/aktuality/mala-duchodova-reforma-je-nespravedliva-necitliva-a-nedomyslena-cssd-s-ni-zasadne-nesouhlasi/).

"Dopady na lidi budou tvrdé." [Impacts on people will be tough, in Czech]. 2011. *Haló noviny*, Interview with the MP for KSČM Miroslav Opálka. May 6, 2011.

Holub, M. 2010a. "Rozhodnutí Ústavního soudu nemusí nutně znamenat dramatický zásah do důchodového systému" [Decision of the Constitutional Court need not signify a dramatic intervention into the pension system, in Czech]. *FÓRUM sociální politiky* 4 (4): 16–20.

Holub, M. 2010b. "Solidarita versus ekvivalence v českém důchodovém pojištění pohledem Ústavního soudu" [Solidarity versus equivalence in Czech pension insurance from the perspective of the Constitutional Court, in Czech]. *FÓRUM sociální politiky* 4 (3): 19–20.

Howlett, M. and M. Ramesh. 1995. *Studying Public Policy: Policy Cycles and Policy Subsystems.* Oxford: Oxford University Press.

Jaeger, C. C., O. Renn, E. A. Rosa and T. Webler. 2001. *Risk, Uncertainty, and Rational Action.* London: Earthscan Publications Ltd.

Klaus, V. 2011. "Stát není pojišťovna" [The state is not an insurance company, in Czech]. *MF DNES*, July 7. Retrieved July 7, 2011 (http://www.klaus.cz/clanky/2863).

Korpi, W. 2001. "Contentious Institutions: An Augmented Rational-Actor Analysis of the Origins and Path Dependency of Welfare State Institutions in the Western Countries." *Rationality and Society* 13 (2): 235–83.Macháček, D. 2004. "Prezident nepodepsal zákon, porušil Ústavu?" [The President did not sign the law, did he violate the Constitution?, in Czech]. *Hospodářské noviny*, May 4. Retrieved May 4, 2004 (http://archiv.ihned.cz/c1-14318020-prezident-nepodepsal-zakon-porusil-ustavu).

Maška, J., J. Rada. 2011. *Závěrečná zpráva Hodnocení dopadů regulace (RIA)* [Final Report on Regulatory Impact Assessment (RIA), in Czech]. Prague: MPSV ČR.

Mayntz, R. and F. W. Scharpf (eds.). 1995. *Gesellschaftliche Selbstregelung und politische Steuerung*. Frankfurt, Main: Campus.

MPSV. 2008. *Pojistněmatematická zpráva o sociálním pojištění* [Actuarial Report on Social Insurance, in Czech]. Prague: MPSV.

MPSV 2010. *The Expert Advisory Forum's Final Report*. Prague: MPSV. Retrieved August 6, 2016 (http://www.mpsv.cz/files/clanky/8897/Final_Report_PES.pdf).

ODS. 2010. *Podrobný volební program. Řešení, která pomáhají* [Detailed Election Program. Solutions that Help, in Czech]. Prague: ODS. Retrieved March 30, 2016 (http://www.ods.cz/docs/programy/volebni-program2010.pdf).

OECD. 2013. *Pensions at a Glance 2013: OECD and G20 Indicators*. Paris: OECD Publishing. Retrieved March 30, 2016, http://dx.doi.org/10.1787/pension_glance-2013-en.

Potůček, M., V. Rudolfová. 2015. Czech Pension Reform: How to Reconcile Equivalence with Fiscal Discipline. *Central European Journal of Public Policy*, 2015, 9 (1): 170–195.

Rahmatian, S. and C. Hiatt. 1989. "Toward an information-based theory of irrational systems behavior." *Systems Research* 6 (1): 7–16.

Scharpf, F. W. 1997. *Games Real Actors Play. Actor-Centered Institutionalism in Policy Research*. Boulder: Westview Press.

TOP 09. 2010. *Volební program. Volby 2010 do Poslanecké sněmovny* [Election program. Chamber of Deputies Election 2010, in Czech]. Prague: TOP 09. Retrieved March 30, 2016 (http://www.top09.cz/files/soubory/volebni-program-2010-do-poslanecke-snemovny_85.pdf).

Věci veřejné. Politická strana. 2010. *Politický program* [Political Program, in Czech]. Prague: Věci veřejné. Retrieved April 10, 2016. (http://www.olympic.cz/financovani/docs/VV.pdf).

LEGISLATION

Act No. 155/1995 Coll., on pension insurance.

Act No. 182/1993 Coll., on constitutional court.

Act No. 589/1992 Coll., on social security premiums and contributions to the state employment policy.

Act No. 99/1948 Coll., on national insurance.

Charter of Fundamental Rights and Freedoms. The Constitutional Act No. 2/1993 Coll. 1992. Retrieved June 11, 2016 (http://www.usoud.cz/fileadmin/user_upload/ustavni_soud_www/prilohy/Listina_English_version.pdf).

The Constitution of the Czech Republic. Constitutional Act No. 1/1993 Coll. 1992. Retrieved June 11, 2016 (http://www.psp.cz/en/docs/laws/constitution.html).

Act No. 403/2012 Coll., amending Act No. 427/2011, on supplementary pensions savings.

Act No. 427/2011Coll., on supplementary pensions savings.

/B4/

Rivalry of Advocacy Coalitions in the Czech Pension Reform[131]

Disputes about pension reform could be a good example of a public policy process in which forces with different opinions coalesce (and arm) for a clash of advocacy coalitions. According to the Advocacy Coalition Framework (hereinafter as ACF), differences in viewpoints of individual participants (ideologically driven) are the key attribute of such a clash. Behind them, however, one can sense a number of differentiated interests (though often under the veil of ideological beliefs). It is not surprising that over time, this ideologically polarized issue gave rise to coalitions of stakeholders from different spheres, who were brought together by a common vision for this particular reform

---

131 This is an updated version of a paper written by Potůček and Rudolfová (2016).

strategy. With a large degree of simplification, such camps can be defined along the line of a left-right political cleavage, or by the ways the values they accentuate are reflected in pension policy. The values which resonate on the right side of the political spectrum are ones associated with an emphasis on the regulatory role of the market and individual responsibility, strengthening the degree of equivalence in the pension system (the more one contributes now, the more one gets back later) and the role of private insurance in old-age security. On the left side of the political spectrum, the value of solidarity in pensions is supported by the role of public authorities and institutions, and the first pillar of the pension system is stressed. There are, of course, exceptions to this simplification.

This case study deals with the history of the establishment and shutdown of a voluntary, private, defined-contribution (DC), fully-funded (FF) pension savings subsystem co-funded from individual reallocations from the first (public) pillar within the Czech pension system (the so-called "second pillar").[132] In applying ACF, we work mainly with an analysis of policy documents, public statements of individual actors and voting on the relevant law in both chambers of the Czech Parliament in order to identify the process of crystallization of two distinct coalitions of actors from both sides of the political spectrum. An ideological shift occurred in both camps (advocacy coalitions with different beliefs) as members of each fell into extreme positions to affirm the correctness of their arguments and positions. In the case of an important long-term cyclical system such as the pension system, if this ideological and political struggle does not result in a political compromise and agreement, the likelihood increases that the adopted solution will not be maintained.

ADVOCACY COALITION FRAMEWORK (ACF) THEORY

ACF (based on Sabatier, Weible 2007) examines a subsystem of public policies, with coalitions, their sources and beliefs, alongside the outputs and outcomes of public policies. The subsystem is anchored in the broader political system with relatively stable parameters and external events (dynamic element).

ACF works with a social-psychological model of the individual, which is different from the model of the rational individual used by public choice theory. The key element of the concept is the existence of belief systems. ACF perceives core beliefs and values as the main driving forces of political behavior, i.e., the dealings of actors. Inspired by prospective theory (Quattrone, Tversky 1988), individual aversion to loss is another ACF assumption. We simply tend to remember more of our losses than gains.

---

132 Refer to the Terminology of Pillars in the Czech Pension System in the beginning of Part B of this book.

An advocacy coalition (AC) is defined as a group of actors who share basic beliefs about a public policy domain (policy core beliefs) and coordinate their actions. ACs form a dynamic environment in which the actors belonging to a coalition may vary in their beliefs and attitudes toward current public policy issues.

STUDY TIP: Refer to **Chapter A5** for more on the Advocacy Coalition Framework.

ESTABLISHMENT AND TERMINATION OF A FULLY FUNDED, DEFINED CONTRIBUTION "SECOND PILLAR": AN ACF PERSPECTIVE

In the following, we are going to analyze the behavior and development of two advocacy coalitions (hereinafter as AC1 and AC2). AC1 promoted the introduction of a private, defined-contribution, fully-funded pillar (shortly, the second pillar) to the Czech pension system. AC2 was opposed to the introduction of the second pillar.

FORMATION OF AN ADVOCACY COALITION SUPPORTING THE INTRODUCTION OF A SECOND PILLAR (AC1)

Formation of AC1 in the Czech pension system started slowly, with attempts to convince experts as well as the general public about the fiscal unsustainability of the public, defined benefit, pay-as-you-go (PAYG) public pension system (shortly, the first pillar) due to population aging. This topic had been present in the discussions since 1995, but the attention and political support it received peaked in the dawn of the new millennium.

Under a caretaker government before the 2010 snap election, an Expert Advisory Forum (PES) was established in January 2010. Its main objective was to analyze the current state of the pension issue in a broader context and recommend to future governments possible ways of reforming the pension system. The formation of the team was delegated to Mr. Vladimír Bezděk, who had originally worked at the Czech National Bank (ČNB) and led another commission which played an important role in designing an unsuccessful reform of the pension system in 2005.

Vladimír Bezděk was given *carte blanche* to select his associates. He approached this task in particular by inviting to the Forum such professionals whose opinions were relatively close to his own. A political component was not included in PES. Most experts appointed to the Forum worked in the commercial sector, some even with entities who were potential sellers of the product under consideration. The establishment of the second pillar was also recommended in the final report of PES.

The pension reform proposal of the Expert Advisory Forum (PES) included Variant I (majority) and Variant II (minority). Under Variant I the first pillar would decrease the contribution rate from 28 to 25% and would be adjusted according to the reform proposals. The second pillar would obtain three percentage points of the 28% contribution rate plus an individual contribution of 2% of gross wage of the insured individual. Participation would be mandatory for all persons under 40 years (in the year of the start of the reform).

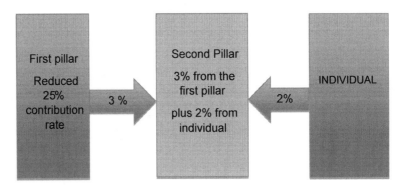

Figure B4.1 Majority option
Source: Authors.

Variant II involved the following arrangements. The contribution rate (28 percent) of the first pillar would not change. "The 2nd pillar will be managed by the reformed pension funds; the direct state support will be 3 percentage points of the contribution rate, provided the participant saves at least the same amount. The same ceiling on premiums applies to this state support as in the PAYG pillar, i.e., up to the amount of three times the average wage. The entry into the 2nd pillar will be voluntary, but after entering, participation and payment of the premiums will be compulsory" (MPSV 2010: 20).

The snap election to the Chamber of Deputies of the Czech Parliament held in 2010 resulted in the formation of a new right-wing coalition government composed of the Civic Democratic Party (ODS), TOP 09, and the Public Affairs (VV). This coalition brought together parties whose election programs consistently suggested a fundamental pension reform, albeit with differences in individual concepts. Led by ODS Chairman Petr Nečas, the government restored the activities of the National Economic Council (hereinafter as NERV). The experts were invited to NERV to contribute to the preparation of key government reforms, not excluding pensions.

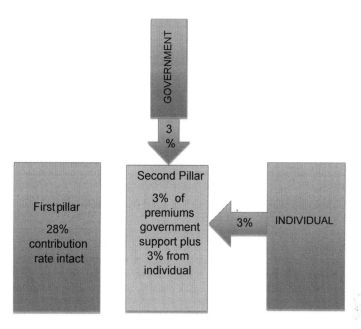

Figure B4.2 Minority option
Source: Authors.

The activities of NERV followed Variant I of the Expert Advisory Forum. The proposed solution was based on arguments about financial unsustainability of the Czech pension system and promoted strengthening the degree of equivalence supported by, among other things, the introduction of the second (private, fully-funded, defined-contribution) pillar to the Czech pension system.

NERV'S DECEMBER 2010 PROPOSAL INCLUDED:

3% opt-out from the 28% contribution rate levied for PAYG public pension insurance.
Premium collection and management would be done by the public Social Security Administration.
Investment management would be entrusted to reputable pension funds, investment companies, banks – according to the participant's choice.
The money saved would be channelled into a mandatory annuity.
Opt-out would be mandatory for persons under 40 years of age at the start of the reform.
A voluntary opt-out would be utilized only by a part of the population, making the reforms meaningless. (NERV 2011)

Other allies in AC1 were potential sellers of the new products, including pension savings funds which would be established as a result of the pension reform. The voluntary Association of Pension Funds (later renamed as Association of Czech Pension Companies), which brings together firms operating in the pension market and capital savings (operators of retirement savings, supplementary pension savings and supplementary pension insurance), participated in the debates as active supporter of the introduction of the second pillar and additional forms of pension savings, releasing numerous press statements and comments, including an online information campaign under the motto, "You are getting old. Think."

The umbrella organization united the fragmented arguments of individual entities and thus strengthened its position both within AC1 and on the outside, vis-à-vis representatives of AC2. The individual entities, each on its own, continued to support the government's defined strategy to introduce the second pillar. Financial institutions participated in presentations and workshops articulating the need for the introduction of a second pillar.

Pension companies also participated in the funding and implementation of academic studies. ČSOB PF Stabilita, for example, engaged an academic think-tank, IDEA-CERGE, which supported the argument about financial unsustainability of the PAYG pillar (ČSOB 2012).

The joint effort of AC1 resulted in the government pension reform proposal, which allowed for the introduction of the second pillar. However, the second pillar was constructed on a voluntary basis due to the inevitable compromises that were required to sustain the fragile coalition government.

THE GOVERNMENT PROPOSAL INCLUDED THE FOLLOWING PROVISIONS:

Opt-out of 3% from the 28% rate levied on insurance premiums plus a mandatory additional 2% (overall a citizen would thus be burdened with 30%).
Collection would be carried out by a single collection point (SCP).
Administration would be carried out by transformed pension funds and newly established pension companies.
Drawing funds in the form of a life annuity, life annuity with survivor pension for three years, or a 20 years' allowance.
Opt-out would be voluntary.

The voluntary nature of the second pillar as proposed by the government eventually caused profound disagreements between the government and NERV members on what could be accepted as a compromise solution without jeopardizing the potential success of pension reforms. Some NERV members distanced themselves from the government proposal (Kohout 2011, Hejkrlík 2011). The government significantly modified NERV's pension reform recommendations, prompting NERV to present the deviation from its original ideas.

One of the members of NERV, Jiří Rusnok, commented on the government's compromise proposal as follows: "The government reached, after difficult negotiations, this compromise that was merely politically acceptable for it but certainly not optimal. I am afraid that under the given conditions many people will not voluntarily choose to bring in money from the PAYG system as well as the additional payment. I do not know how they would be motivated by this..." (Parol 2011).

Dissenting opinions of individual NERV members also led the entire advisory board to express their vision of the reform of the pension system and to highlight the differences of their presented proposal from the government proposal: "Recommendations of the National Economic Council were often distorted and even misinterpreted. (...) NERV recommended a number of so-called parametric modifications to the first pillar (...) NERV also recommended the introduction of a small but mandatory second pillar where citizens under 40-years old would be obliged to save for a part of their pension. (...) The National Economic Council's position on pension reform is much more comprehensive; however, the above aspects are frequently misinterpreted. Therefore, the members of NERV listed wanted to take this opportunity to set the record straight" (Bezděk et al. 2011).

Although the final decision in the coalition of actors led to disagreements, the entire process of preparation and formulation of the reform concept linked the same opinions of actors from different areas into a relatively comprehensive whole.

The activity of this advocacy coalition culminated in the approval of Act No. 426/2011 Coll., which introduced the second pillar into the Czech pension system.

FORMATION OF AN ADVOCACY COALITION REFUSING THE SECOND PILLAR (AC2)

An advocacy coalition on the left side of the political spectrum (AC2) cemented the opposite opinion. Its members did not believe that a second pillar had to be introduced to address the issue of pension security. In their view, strengthening equivalence in the system connected to the second pillar meant limiting the solidarity provided by the public system, as a core value. At the same time they were concerned about weakening the revenue side of the public PAYG first pillar without adequate reductions on the expenditure side in the same time period.

A key actor in the coalition was the Czech Social Democratic Party (ČSSD). This party announced its comprehensive approach to pension reform at the end of 2011. "Retirement provision is the most important element of social protection. A key objective of pension reform is to ensure that everyone, present and future pensioners alike, has enough money for a peaceful and dignified living, to maintain an adequate standard of living and the ability to participate in the public, social, economic and cultural life of society. (...) The reform must be viewed more broadly, especially in relation to the labor market and demographic development, which are affected by the pension system retroactively." The policy document also explicitly rejected the creation of an additional fully-funded pillar within the pension system (ČSSD 2011).

Formed in January 2011, CESTA (Center for Social Market Economy and Open Democracy) was another important actor. In December 2011, this think-tank presented two alternative pension reform scenarios – a version with an NDC scheme similar to the Swedish one, and a version taking parenting into account in the PAYG system. Although the entire AC2 consistently refused to introduce a second pillar in the Czech pension system, disagreements in this coalition could be found on detailed ideas about the concepts and alternatives of the reform, which are illustrated in the presentation of different reform concepts (Vostatek, Zborník, Fiala 2011, Rusý, Zborník, Fiala 2011).

A traditional ally of the Social Democracy, labor unions, were represented mainly by the Czech-Moravian Confederation of Trade Unions (ČMKOS). It was therefore not surprising that these partners had traditionally shared beliefs with regard to pension policy, too. The unions are a relatively strong actor in pension policy in the Czech Republic. In the pension reform discussions, they protested against the introduction of the second pillar and criticized the government for its reluctance to discuss alternative proposals. In their statements, they critiqued the government proposals in detail and submitted their own concepts. They rejected "...pension reform's simplistic and one-sided focus on the financial operation of creating a more costly infrastructure of the second pillar of private savings schemes" (ČMKOS 2011).

The other major actor of the center-left spectrum, the Communist Party (KSČM), consistently insisted on only parametric adjustments to the existing PAYG public pillar and opposed the second pillar in the Czech pension system. The Communist Party's opposition to the introduction of the second pillar (or support for its abolition) was thus evident, though neither the Social Democrats nor ČMKOS ever obtained an explicit certificate of KSČM's opinions. Alternative pension reform proposals were indeed one of the many weapons used in the political battle for voters on the left side of the political spectrum.

THE LEGISLATIVE PROCEDURE

Adoption of Act No. 426/2011 Coll. regarding pension savings was preceded by debates in the Chamber of Deputies and then in the Senate. The resulting vote reflected a line of dispute between advocacy coalitions. The introduction of a second pillar was supported exclusively by parties on the right side of the political spectrum and by members of AC1, whereas members of AC2 (ČSSD, KSČM) were adamantly opposed. The discussion was conducted in the same argumentative spirit that had accompanied previous ideological battles between the ACs. On the one hand, the financial instability of the system was emphasized, as well as the need to strengthen the degree of equivalence. On the other hand, there was a resounding defense of solidarity and concern about weakening the first pillar of the pension system. The "devil shift" was also reflected in the sharp rhetoric used during the approval process.

The government submitted the bill on June 30, 2011. The first reading in the Chamber of Deputies of the Czech Parliament took place on July 13, 2011. The second reading, with both general and detailed debate, took place on August 30, 2011. The third reading took place on September 9, 2011. The bill was approved by 86 out of the 147 deputies present (ODS, TOP 09, VV, 1 independent member). Against the proposal were 61 deputies (ČSSD, KSČM, 1 independent member). On September 19, 2011, the bill was forwarded to the Senate.[133] The Senate voted it down. Of the 61 senators attending the vote, 43 rejected the bill (ČSSD, KDU-ČSL, 2 independent senators) and 18 supported it (ODS, TOP 09 plus the Mayors Party).

The bill returned by the Senate was voted on at the Chamber of Deputies on the 3rd and 6th of November 2011. The lower chamber reaffirmed the original bill. 109 out of the 179 deputies present voted for it (ODS, TOP 09, VV, 1 independent member) and 70 deputies were against it (ČSSD, KSČM, 2 independent members).

The Act was delivered to the President for signature on November 9, 2011. The President neither signed nor vetoed it, and therefore it became law on November 24, 2011 and came into force on January 1, 2013.

The vote on the law in the parliament only confirmed the composition of the two ACs that had been formed in the previous coordinative and communicative discourse.

In terms of actors' resources, we can consider AC1 as dominant. Among its members were actors who held offices in the executive branch of government or had access to other actors who were able to influence political decisions or possessed information resources (parties of the government coalition, Ministry of Finance, Ministry of Labor and Social Affairs, government advisory bodies, pension funds, the IDEA-CERGE research institute), which was formidable compared to the other AC. Considering the resources of its actors, AC2 must be considered minor.

---

133 The Czech Parliament consists of two chambers: the lower one, Chamber of Deputies, and the upper one, the Senate.

AFTER THE GENERAL ELECTION – DISINTEGRATION AND TRANSFORMATION OF THE ADVOCACY COALITIONS

New snap elections to the Chamber of Deputies took place at the end of 2013. A proposal to abolish the newly instituted element of the pension system came to the forefront of the election debate, supported by all members of AC2. The election programs of ČSSD and KSČM explicitly expressed that they would seek its abolishment in the event of an electoral victory. Their argumentative strategies were dominated by the defense of solidarity as a key element in the compulsory public social insurance, which was weakened by this newly introduced element of the system, and by the effort to maintain the sustainability of the first pillar of the pension system.

The center-left Social Democrats (ČSSD) won the parliamentary elections in 2013 and formed the government coalition which opened up opportunities to promote the objectives and opinions of the partners united in opposition to the introduction of the second pillar of the pension system. In the coalition agreement (ČSSD, the recently established political movement ANO, and KDU-ČSL) and subsequently in the government's policy statement (2014), there were explicit mentions of the intention to create an expert commission to consider further orientation of the pension reform and to advise on how to abolish the second pillar (Government of the Czech Republic 2014). The Christian Democrats (KDU-ČSL) became a new ally. They joined the government's criticism of the second pillar of the pension system, which they deemed as incapable of reform, and agreed with its abolition. The ANO political movement was one surprising ally. In its election program it did not dispute the existence of the second pillar; to the contrary, its aim was to strengthen its robustness. In the end, however, ANO agreed with the government's policy statement in which the coalition partners committed to abolishing the second pillar.

A situation arose after the election that the ACs were hit by external (indirect) change. Groupings with significantly different political orientations took power in the state. Some political parties "disappeared" from the arena of key actors (e.g., VV – Public Affairs), while others returned (KDU-ČSL). The old ACs that had been formed primarily on the basis of former government coalition vs. former opposition crumbled. AC2 gained, as its actor, formal authority and the right to make policy decisions. This change flipped the roles of both ACs and thus paved the way for the fulfillment of one of AC2's important goals.

On the basis of the coalition agreement and the government policy statement, the Expert Committee on Pension Reform (the acronym "OK") was established in order to seek broad political consensus about the continuation of pension reform. The key criteria of the draft pension reform were defined as follows: ability of the system to ensure adequate and decent pensions, strengthening the degree of equivalence, settlement transfers between family and society, and long-term sustainability of the pension system (Mandate 2014). OK's initial meetings, which were concerned with the question of how to end the second pillar, saw a clash of the former two ACs regarding other activities of the Committee. When attention was focused on the broader concept of pension reform, an interesting shift occurred. Former members of ACs began looking for space to promote their interests in the new situation, forming new alliances. The attention of some members of the former government coalition moved to robust support for the third pillar (voluntary pension insurance/savings with state contribution, established as early as in 1995).

On 23 October 2015, the Czech parliament passed Act No. 376/2015 Coll. which abolished the second pension pillar and Act No. 377/2015 Coll. which strengthened the third pillar starting 2016.

DISCUSSION

It seems to be obvious that representation in the executive branch of government was crucial in the battle of ACs to orientate pension reform. Furthermore, possession of government offices in AC1 increased the likelihood of effecting the changes. Government's participation in AC1 increased the likelihood of success – the concept presented by AC1 was pushed through, while the AC without government representation was less successful. Within the framework of two rival ACs in the case of pension reform in the Czech Republic, the government and political parties were the key members of the AC whose concept was pushed through.

In turn, the absence of government offices in an advocacy coalition can (given the inability to push through one's own concepts) limit the activities of this AC, namely its attempt to block the implementation of the other AC's proposals. Nevertheless, AC2 was focused not only on a "negative" campaign or attempts to block the introduction of the second pillar, but also on formulating alternative proposals for solutions. AC2 was not successful until the snap parliamentary elections redistributed power.

Our analysis also focused on the uniformity of opinions within each coalition. Both ACs identified showed unity and consensus among their members with regard to the primary focus. In this case, the focus was the introduction (or abolishment) of the second pillar of the pension system. Upon a more detailed examination, however, we can identify differences of opinion. In AC1, such differences were expressed regarding the very nature or construction of the second pillar. NERV, concurring with financial institutions, promoted compulsory participation as an essential parameter for the pillar to work effectively. By contrast, the government, certainly under internal political pressure, eventually pushed for the concept of voluntary participation. AC2 was united in its negative stance on the second pillar, whereas no consensus was achieved on the question of a "correct alternative concept of pension reform." Due to the variability of opinion among members of this coalition, a unified pension reform counterproposal was not advanced. The various proposals included: complex reform concepts with the goal of keeping the system sustainable while maintaining a high degree of solidarity; introduction of a Notional Defined Contributions (NDC) scheme via adjustments, taking parenting and other things into account; or a "mere" parametric modification of the first pillar.

We also paid attention to the motivations of actors to join a coalition. We have already demonstrated that some actors were motivated to coalesce with members of the executive, mainly because of the higher probability of bringing about change. Due to its higher potential to succeed, this type of AC is more attractive to actors. If the aim of the actors is to promote particular interest, then ideological background may not necessarily be the only factor that determines membership in a coalition. AC1 lost its executive and legislative powers. Discussions about the Expert Committee on Pension Reform, established by the new government of the Czech Republic after the snap parliamentary elections in 2014, suggest a shift of "interests" of some actors. Financial institutions pragmatically abandoned support for the second pillar (after the decision on its dissolution), and strategically focused on strengthening the complementary third pillar. Based on this observation, we can confirm that ideological closeness may not be the only factor that determines membership of the actors in ACs. In particular, it is necessary to take into account differences of ideology and interest between the actors. Actors may have different reasons to get involved in the activities of a coalition. In some actors (such as political parties), a key role is played by ideological affinity with other actors. For others (such as private or public institutions), the ability/inability or to promote (individually or collectively) their vested interests plays an important role.

Advocacy coalitions' rivalry can also be a source of an additional flow of information relevant to political decision making. It is the clash of opposing views which strengthens an ACs' argumentative strategies. The positive information effect of a coordinated argumentative strategy can even be traced in the variants of reform concepts presented by actors within the same AC. Joint activities (seminars, presentations, studies) were addressed to the public as well as to coalition partners by financial, research, and even educational institutions that were associated with the different reform options. A parallel increase in interpretive efforts in AC2 was represented by the sharing and use of information between the traditional social partners: the unions (ČMKOS), political parties of the political left, and NGOs (CESTA). The value of information is reflected in the treatment of the subject by political parties and, ultimately, in the final presentation of the topic by government executives. One of the most significant informational effects of the clash of ACs is the presence of the issue on the media agenda (and in turn, increased interest by the public). This benefit may be weakened by special interest misinterpretations, resulting biases, and sometimes by unprofessional news reporting on factually complex themes like the pension system and its reform.

CONCLUSION

The Advocacy Coalition Framework proved functional in the explanation of situations where there were sharp political conflicts. An ideological shift occurred within both camps (ACs with different beliefs) as each fell into extreme positions to affirm the correctness of their arguments and positions. Shared beliefs, opinions and views became more entrenched, the cleavage between the coalitions deepened, and the convictions of political opponents solidified.

From an analytical point of view, the application of ACF was tied to specific forms of political institutions, actual distribution of political power, and differentiated interests. For an institutional environment set up in a way that does not necessarily require agreement across the political spectrum and within a wider range of actors, an ACF-informed analysis identified an unwillingness and inability to seek compromise between competing coalitions. We witnessed the adoption of sometimes extreme solutions, which were pushed through by actors using their current position in the political arena, using their radicalism as potential for at least some success, especially in an underdeveloped political culture of negotiation skills and preparedness to compromise.

In situations where the actors are forced to roundtable negotiations, whether by the institutional environment (political culture of negotiation and compromise, tradition of tripartite agreements, etc.) and/or external influences (e.g., the results of elections), ACF can be applied sparingly. In such conditions, it is interesting to see the regrouping of ACs under changing institutional conditions and the effects of these rearrangements, as well as the influence of marginal actors on the argumentative strategies and decision-making potential of the main actors. We are still faced with the limits of the Advocacy Coalition Framework itself, since in such an environment, actors' beliefs and views recede into the background and the actors are more inclined towards promoting their specific differentiated interests.

SOURCES

Bezděk, V., D. Münich, J. Procházka, J. Rusnok, P. Zahradník, M. Zámečník. 2011. "Experti z NERVu: Důchodová reforma očima NERVu" [NERV Experts: The Pension Reform from NERV's Perspective, in Czech]. *Hospodářské noviny*, March 14, 2011. Retrieved June 2, 2016 (http://archiv.ihned.cz/c1-51131930-experti-z-nervu -duchodova-reforma-ocima-nervu).

ČMKOS. 2011. *Stanovisko ČMKOS*. [Position of the Czech-Moravian Confederation of Trade Unions on Proposed Law on Pension Insurance, in Czech]. Prague: ČMKOS.

ČSOB. 2012. *Státní důchody čeká strmý propad, vstup do II. pilíře se vyplatí téměř polovině populace* [State pensions will fall down sharply, nearly one-half of the population will profit from entering the second pillar, in Czech]. Prague: ČSOB.

ČSSD. 2011. *Programový dokument – Důchodová reforma ČSSD 2011* [Policy Document – Pension reform of the ČSSD 2011, in Czech]. Prague: ČSSD. Retrieved March 30, 2016 (http://www.cssd.cz/data/files/duchody-0004.pdf).

Government of the Czech Republic. 2014. *Policy Statement of the Government of the Czech Republic,* February 14, 2014. Retrieved April 4, 2016 (http://www.vlada.cz /en/media-centrum/dulezite-dokumenty/policy-statement-of-the-government -of-the-czech-republic-116171/).

Hejkrlík, P. 2011. "Člen NERV Zámečník se distancuje od penzijní reformy" [NERV Member Zámečník Dissociates himself from Pension Reform, in Czech]. *Týden.cz*, March 3, 2011. Retrieved March 3, 2011 (http://www.tyden.cz/rubriky/byznys/cesko/clen-nerv -zamecnik-se-distancuje-od-penzijni-reformy_195447.html?showTab=kurzovni-listek #.VMk3ncb8EZk).

Kohout, P. 2011. "Důchodová reforma se důsledně vyhýbá návrhům NERVu a Bezděkovy komise" [Pension reform consistently avoids NERV's and Bezděk Commission's proposals, in Czech]. *Naše peníze.cz*, July 1, 2011. Retrieved July 1, 2011 (http://www.nasepenize .cz/pavel-kohout-duchodova-reforma-se-dusledne-vyhyba-navrhum-nervu-a-bezde-kovy-komise-9300).

Mandate of the Expert Committee on Pension Reform. 2015. Prague: MPSV. Retrieved June 6, 2016 (http://www.duchodova-komise.cz/wp-content/uploads/2015/02/Man-date-of-the-Expert-Committee.pdf).

MPSV. 2010. *The Expert Advisory Forum's Final Report.* Prague: MPSV. Retrieved August 6, 2016 (http://www.mpsv.cz/files/clanky/8897/Final_Report_PES.pdf)

NERV. 2011. *Důchodová reforma* [Pension Reform, in Czech]. Prague: National Economic Council of the Government. Retrieved March 30, 2016 (http://www.vlada.cz/assets /media-centrum/aktualne/NERV_Duchodova-reforma.pdf).

Parol 2011. "Vládní návrh penzijní reformy je taková bramboračka." Rozhovor s Jiřím Rusnokem [The government pension reform proposal is a kind of *Eintopf.* Interview with Jiří Rusnok, in Czech]. *Parlament, vláda, samospráva.* Prague: Parol. Retrieved June 26, 2012 (http://www.parlament-vlada.eu/index.php/rozhovor-finance /53-vladni-navrh-penzijni-reformy-je-takova-bramboraka).

Potůček, M., V. Rudolfová. 2016. "Rivalry of Advocacy Coalitions in the Czech Pension Reform." *The NISPAcee Journal of Public Administration and Policy* IX, No. 1, pp. 117–134.

Quattrone, G. A., A. Tversky. 1988. "Contrasting Rational and Psychological Analyses of Political Choice." *American Political Science Review* 82 (3): 719–736, http://dx.doi.org/10.2307/1962487.

Rusý, P., P. Zborník, T. Fiala. 2011. "Návrh penzijní reformy (verze se zohledněním výchovy dětí v průběžném systému)" [Pension reform proposal (version taking parenting into account in the PAYG system), in Czech]. Prague: CESTA. Retrieved March 30, 2016 (http://www.centrum-cesta.cz/files/prectete-si/publikace/navrhy-penzijni-reformy-pro-ceskou-republiku/navrh-penzijni-reformy-2-verze-se-zohlednenim-deti-v-prubeznem-systemu.pdf).

Sabatier, P., C. Weible. 2007. "The advocacy coalition framework: Innovations and clarifications." Pp. 189–222 in *Theories of the Policy Process*, edited by P. Sabatier. 2nd ed. Boulder: Westview Press.

Vostatek, J., P. Zborník, T. Fiala. 2011. "Návrh penzijní reformy (verze s NDC)" [Pension reform proposal (NDC version), in Czech]. Prague: CESTA. Retrieved March 30, 2016 (http://www.centrum-cesta.cz/files/prectete-si/publikace/navrhy-penzijni-reformy-pro-ceskou-republiku/navrh-penzijni-reformy-1-verze-s-NDC.pdf).

LEGISLATION

Act No. 426/2011 Coll., on pension savings.

Act No. 376/2015 Coll., on the termination of pension savings systems.

Act No. 377/2015 Coll., amending certain Acts in relation to the adoption of the Act on termination of the pension savings system.

/B5/
Pensions Basics

There is a wide range of parameters that characterize pension systems or their parts (pillars) thereof. They include the **type of financing, the way benefits are calculated, nature of participation in the system, and indexation of benefits**.

FINANCING PENSIONS

The basic distinction is made between:
    (a) pay-as-you-go schemes (PAYG) and
    (b) fully funded schemes (FF).

In a **PAYG scheme**, pension benefits are financed from the incomes of individuals who are currently economically active; there are no accumulated assets. So-called partially-funded pension schemes are also included in the **PAYG** category.

Table B5.1 Pay-as-you-go funding (PAYG)

Strengths	Weaknesses
major role in eliminating poverty	dependence on demographic parameters (birth rate, migration)
wide coverage of the general population	dependence on economic factors (growth)
potential for both intra- and intergenerational solidarity	governments may be unable to fully meet their commitments
benefits can be paid without prior long-term accumulation of assets	
resistance to fluctuations of economic cycle	
high level of transparency	
low impacts on labor force mobility	

Source: Authors.

(b) In **fully funded schemes**, benefits are paid out of resources previously accumulated and invested into financial assets.

Table B5.2 Fully funded schemes (FF)

Strengths	Weaknesses
independence of demographic development	no guarantee of intra- or intergenerational solidarity
accumulation of assets may have positive effects on the economy – savings and growth (questionable)	risk of capital market losses
provided high rates of return on investment, there is room for alleviating the tax burden on employees and/or employers (in case of high rates of return, tax/contribution burden on employees and/or employers can be reduced). This argument tends to be controversial. Although positive effects of FF schemes on capital market development are generally acknowledged, some authors argue that the relationship between capital market growth, aggregate savings and economic growth is not clearly supported by evidence (Hughes & Singh 1987, Warshawsky 1987, Eatwell 2003)	high administrative costs

	high importance of the quality of institutional environment (risk of nationalization, embezzlement, etc.)
	benefits are not indexed according to the wage growth and inflation
	risk of poverty (especially in specific population groups)

Source: Authors.

CALCULATION OF BENEFITS

According to the way the amount of benefits is determined, one distinguishes between **defined-benefit** and **defined-contribution** schemes.

Defined-benefit schemes provide specific amounts of money upon reaching retirement age. The amount of benefits may be fixed explicitly (e.g., €300 per month), but typically depends on a more complex formula with variables such as level of income or length of insurance period. Defined-benefit systems are characterized by higher levels of intragenerational redistribution.

Table B5.3 Defined-benefit schemes (DB)

Strengths	Weaknesses
can be launched anytime, benefits can be paid immediately	pension benefits not transferable
large schemes can achieve economies of scale (administrative, operational expenditure)	system's stability depends on the condition of the economy (DB schemes profit from high levels of employment, births and labor market participation)
are able to guarantee some level of solidarity	lower potential of political legitimacy when calculation formulae are difficult to understand
can also finance benefits for cases of "disadvantaged" members of society (sickness, accident, etc.)	amount of benefit uncertain in case of adverse economic or demographic development, political risk
are able to guarantee price and/or wage indexation	adverse impact on labor market participation
one cannot "outlive" one's "savings" (entitlements in FF schemes can be outlived or exhausted, unless defined as lifelong annuities)	

Source: Authors.

Defined-contribution schemes do not guarantee the amount of benefits obtained by participants following retirement. They increase the level of equivalence, thus necessarily limiting the potential for solidarity.

Table B5.4 Defined-contribution schemes (DC)

Strengths	Weaknesses
pension benefits transferable	risk of poverty for specific population groups
able to respond to increasing life expectancy	solidarity difficult to guarantee
the simple principle of "each on their own" can be more politically feasible	
motivates to stay in the labor market	

Source: Authors.

Simply speaking, in a defined-benefit scheme one knows the amount of benefits one gets but has little idea of how much one will have to contribute. In a defined-contribution scheme, the amount of money paid in can be influenced but it remains unclear how much the benefits will be one day.

A special category is comprised by **notional defined-contribution schemes (NDC)**, also referred to as notional accounts. In such pay-as-you-go or partially funded schemes,[134] participants' contributions are (notionally, virtually) accumulated in notional accounts. The amount of benefits received better reflects the amount of money contributed. However, no funds are actually accumulated. The goal of such schemes is to tap the advantages of **PAYG** funding while increasing the level of equivalence (limiting the redistribution effects that are typical of **DB** schemes).

NATURE OF PARTICIPATION

Participation in a certain part of the pension system (pillar or scheme) may be **mandatory** or **voluntary**. It can be deemed essential to oblige every individual to participate in at least one scheme. This is due to the anthropological fact that few people are able and willing to make strategic considerations about their life and secure their needs for tens of years ahead. Therefore, the central goal is to make sure that the future pension needs of the broadest possible population are taken care of.

Specific risks are associated with the different ways of participation in pension schemes.

---

134 Partially funded schemes rely on some level of accumulated assets, and as such tend to be classified in the **PAYG** category.

In the case of **voluntary retirement schemes,** there is a risk that a part of the population will fail to accumulate any savings and, by the time they reach retirement age, they will either demand an alternative provision (funded from tax revenue, for instance) or find themselves at risk of poverty. In the expert community, such a *laissez faire* approach to pension schemes tends to be regarded as a curiosity. It is associated both with a high level of risk for the so-called more responsible part of the population, and with risk of poverty for the "less responsible" part. Ultimately, failure to cover any segment of the population by pension benefits exposes the society as a whole to a risk of social disorder or even riots, with potentially destabilizing outcomes.

Mandatory participation in a pension scheme, too, has its strengths and weaknesses. If participation is prescribed by the government, then the state should, as a rule, also guarantee proper operation of the mandatory schemes. This is a critical issue especially for private savings funds. In addition to the risk of low return on investment or high administrative expenditure, a number of other problematic moments that may importantly determine the amount of savings accumulated have emerged in more-or-less recent history – such as embezzlement, monetary reform, war, or the change of a political regime.

Voluntary and mandatory pillars tend to exist side-by-side in practice. The choice between these two options has implications for the extent of coverage in society: mandatory schemes include as many people as possible, while voluntary schemes imply that the extent of coverage is not a priority.

INDEXATION OF BENEFITS

There are different perceptions of the terms "valorization" and "indexation" of pension benefits, albeit these are sometimes regarded as synonymous.

Valorization may be perceived as pre-retirement indexation, i.e., adjustment to change in the level of earnings and prices between the time periods when pension entitlements are accrued and benefits are paid. In order to bridge this gap, earnings are typically converted using a set coefficient. To put it simply, if the amount of benefits in the year 2017 were to depend on the nominal level of earnings over the past, say, 30 years of one's career, then the mean wage from the year 1987 onward would give rise to a curiously low pension entitlement and the pension system would fail even its most basic function – protection from the risk of poverty. For that reason, past earnings must be converted to current levels of prices and wages.

Indexation of pension benefits in payment is the standard option. Here, benefits are basically adjusted according to changes in living expenses as measured by the rates of growth of prices and wages.

Table B5.5 Price and wage indexation

Price indexation	Wage indexation
Pensions vary with the **level of prices** and their **purchasing power is preserved**. The risk of change in the standard of living is borne by the economically active generation. When economic performance declines, it is necessary to increase the level of benefits paid in order to preserve their real value. Isolated price indexation means that seniors do not benefit from any wage growth that occurs after their retirement.	Pensions adjust to **growth of wages.** Thus, economically inactive individuals benefit from increasing productivity of labor and economic performance. This can be a 100% or partial adjustment. If productivity remains constant then wage indexation is equivalent to price indexation.

Source: Authors.

Some countries prefer price indexation (e.g., Belgium or France) with the aim to slow down the growth of pension expenditure. **Price indexation alone leads to a lower replacement ratio (pensions to wages). In other words, pensioners no longer benefit from any growth of welfare in society.**

In **progressive indexation** (e.g., in Italy), lower pensions are increased relatively more than higher pensions.

Albeit price indexation is currently more popular among policymakers, path dependence in pension systems typically results in a mix of both indexation methods applied in different proportions. Wage indexation alone is not commonplace.

TYPES OF PENSION REFORMS

Contemporary literature predominantly distinguishes between two types of reform measures – **incremental reforms (parametric adjustments) and paradigmatic reforms (structural, institutional changes).**

PARAMETRIC REFORMS

In parametric reforms, policymakers adjust existing parameters of public pay-as-you-go systems without changing them fundamentally. Adjustments can be made on the side of contributions and/or benefits.

Table B5.6 Parametric adjustments in public PAYG systems

On the side of benefits	On the side of contributions
increase retirement age restrict indexation of benefits increase the contributory insurance period restrict indexation of earnings in the pension formula introduce or increase taxation of benefits cut down the crediting of non-contributory insurance periods penalize early retirement change the level of equivalence within the system	increase contributions (**expand the** **assessment base** or **increase the** **percentage of it paid**) decrease contributions (lower the rate, set maximum amounts of assessment) redefine the group of mandatory participants

Source: Authors.

Parametric reforms tend to combine adjustments on both sides. Statistical modeling is the only way to determine the exact effects of the different changes. Therefore, the intensity and nature of changes cannot be readily defined and presented in political debate (some policymakers may deliberately conceal the real effects of parametric changes such as shrinking benefits).

PARADIGMATIC REFORMS

Such reforms are associated with changes to the system as a whole. They imply substantial changes in one or several of the following criteria: **change of provider, change in type of funding, and/or structural change in calculation of benefits**. However, concrete reform measures may vary.

The most typical example of fundamental reform is when a new, private, fully funded pillar is introduced and replaces a part of the public **PAYG** pillar (this operation is referred to as opt-out). Such reforms are mostly associated with changes in funding and in the calculation of benefits – from **DB** to **DC**.

Another way to fundamentally reform a public pay-as-you-go pillar is when **calculation of benefits shifts from DB to DC**, or to **NDC** when **PAYG** funding is to be preserved.

Change in provider, namely from public to private one, also represents a fundamental change. In the same category, one can further distinguish the sub-criterion of type of responsibility (Lesay 2007) – collective or individual – which translates into the way benefits are calculated. **DB** schemes rely on collective responsibility, while individuals are solely responsible in **DC** schemes. Privately managed schemes are not necessarily associated with the individual type of responsibility. On one hand, there are public systems with individual responsibility (and defined contributions), such as **NDC** systems in

Sweden or Poland. On the other hand, some "private" employer schemes are based on collective responsibility and defined benefits – e.g., in Germany, the USA or the UK (Lesay 2007).

The pension system should always be regarded as a part (albeit a large one) of a broader whole (the social system, the economy, the society). Given its complexity, it overlaps with a number of other policy areas. At the most general level, one can think of such pension system reforms that go hand-in-hand with reforms of the tax system or of the system of so-called non-insurance welfare benefits. For example, Vostatek (2014) proposes a comprehensive reform that would include not only the above elements but also the management and funding of health care in the Czech Republic.

SOURCES

Eatwell, J. 2003. *The Anatomy of the Pensions Crisis and Three Fallacies On Pensions.* Retrieved July 8, 2016 (http://mbz.net.pl/eftepe/Eatwell.pdf).

Hughes, A., A. Singh. 1987. *Takeovers and the stock-market. Contributions to Political Economy* 6: 73–85.

Lesay, I. 2007. *Czech Pension Reform: Will it Go Fundamental?* 2007. Brno: Economy and Society Trust. Discussion Paper No. 2. Retrieved July 11, 2016. (http://www.akademickyrepozitar.sk/sk/repozitar/czech-pension-reform-will-it-go-fundamental.pdf).

Vostatek, J. 2014. "Zdanění příjmů a pojistné" [Income Taxation and the Insurance Premium, in Czech]. *Bulletin Komory daňových poradců ČR* 4: 36–41.

Warshawsky, M. 1987. "Private Annuity Markets in the United States: 1919-1984." *Research Papers in Banking and Financial Economics* 96. Board of Governors of the Federal Reserve System.

RECOMMENDED SOURCES

Arza C., P. Johnson. 2005. "The development of public pensions from 1889 to the 1990s." in *Oxford Handbook of Pensions and Retirement Income*, edited by G. Clark, A. Munnell, M. Orszag. Oxford: Oxford University Press.

Baroni, E. 2007. *Pension Systems and Pension Reform in an Aging Society: An Introduction to the Debate.* Working Paper 2007: 6. Stockholm: Institute for Future Studies.

Barr, N., P. Diamond. 2008. *Reforming pensions: principles and policy directions.* Oxford: Oxford University Press.

Barr, N., P. Diamond. 2009. "Reforming pensions: principles, analytical errors and policy directions." *International Social Security Review* 62 (2): 5–29.

Bezděk, V., A. Krejdl, P. Pergler, J. Škorpík, Z. Šmídová, Z. Štork. 2005. Závěrečná zpráva [Final report, in Czech]. Prague: Výkonný tým. Retrieved June 2, 2016 (http://www.mpsv.cz/files/clanky/2235/zaverecna_zprava.pdf).

Blake, D. 2006. *Pension Economics*. West Sussex: John Wiley & Sons.

European Commission. 2015. *The 2015 Aging Report. Economic and Budgetary Projections for the 28 EU Member States (2013-2060)*. Brussels: European Commission, Directorate-General for Economic and Financial Affairs. Retrieved July 18, 2016 (http://europa.eu/epc/pdf/ageingreport_2015_en.pdf).

Green Paper. 2010. *Towards adequate, sustainable and safe European pension systems*. SEC (2010) 830. Brussels: European Commission,

Hinrichs, K. 2000. Elephants on the Move: Patterns of Public Pension Reform in OECD. *European Review* 8: 353–378.

OECD. 2013. *Pensions at a Glance 2013: OECD and G20 Indicators*. Paris: OECD Publishing. Retrieved March 30, 2016 (http://dx.doi.org/10.1787/pension_glance-2013-en).

OECD. 2015. *Pensions at a Glance 2015: OECD and G20 Indicators*. Paris: OECD Publishing. Retrieved July 18, 2016
http://static.politico.com/d9/2d/a9fe45a241eba663b8e935d4e41d/oecd-pensions-at-a-glance-2015.pdf).

Orszag, P. R., J. E. Stiglitz. 2001. "Rethinking Pension Reform: Ten Myths about Social Security Systems." Pp. 17–56 in *New Ideas about Old Age Security: Toward Sustainable Pension Systems in the Twenty-First Century*, edited by R. Holzmann, J. E. Stiglitz. Washington, D.C.: World Bank.

Pierson, P. 1994. *Dismantling the Welfare State? Reagan, Thatcher, and the Politics of Retrenchment*. Cambridge, New York: Cambridge University Press.

Potůček, M. 1995. *Sociální politika*. [Social Policy, in Czech]. Prague: SLON.

Schludi, M. 2005. *The Reform of Bismarckian Pension Systems: A Comparison of Pension Politics in Austria, France, Germany, Italy and Sweden*. Amsterdam: Amsterdam University Press.

Weaver, K. 2003. *The Politics of Public Pension Reform*. Retrieved July 8, 2016 (http://ssrn.com/abstract=1136874).

Wheeler, P. M., J. R. Kearney. 1996. "Income Protection for the Aged in the 21st Century: A Framework to Help Inform the Debate." *Social Security Bulletin* 59 (2): 3–19.

World Bank. 1994. *Averting the Old Age Crisis: Policies to Protect the Old and Promote Growth*. Oxford: Oxford University Press.

Literature – Part B

Arza C., P. Johnson. 2005. "The development of public pensions from 1889 to the 1990s." In *Oxford Handbook of Pensions and Retirement Income*, edited by G. Clark, A. Munnell, M. Orszag. Oxford: Oxford University Press.

Ash, T. G. 1990. *The Magic Lantern: The Revolution of '89 Witnessed in Warsaw, Budapest, Berlin and Prague.* New York: Random House.

"Dopady na lidi budou tvrdé." [Impacts on people will be tough, in Czech]. 2011. *Haló noviny,* Interview with the MP for KSČM Miroslav Opálka. May 6, 2011.

Baroni, E. 2007. *Pension Systems and Pension Reform in an Aging Society: An Introduction to the Debate.* Working Paper 2007:6. Stockholm: Institute for Future Studies.

Barr, N., P. Diamond. 2008. *Reforming pensions: principles and policy directions.* Oxford: Oxford University Press.

Barr, N., P. Diamond. 2009. "Reforming pensions: principles, analytical errors and policy directions." *International Social Security Review* 62 (2): 5–29.

Benford, R. D., D. A. Snow. 2000. "Framing Processes and Social Movements: An Overview and Assessment." *Annual Review of Sociology* 26: 611–639.

Beveridge, W. 1942. *Social insurance and allied services.* Report by Sir William Beveridge. London: HMSO.

Bezděk, V., A. Krejdl, P. Pergler, J. Škorpík, Z. Šmídová, Z. Štork. 2005. Závěrečná zpráva [Final report, in Czech]. Praha: Výkonný tým. Retrieved June 2, 2016 (http://www.mpsv.cz/files/clanky/2235/zaverecna_zprava.pdf).

Bezděk, V., D. Münich, J. Procházka, J. Rusnok, P. Zahradník, M. Zámečník. 2011. "Experti z NERVu: Důchodová reforma očima NERVu" [NERV Experts: The Pension Reform from NERV's Perspective, in Czech]. *Hospodářské noviny,* March 14, 2011. Retrieved June 2, 2016 (http://archiv.ihned.cz/c1-51131930-experti-z-nervu-duchodova-reforma-ocima-nervu).

Blake, D. 2006. *Pension Economics.* West Sussex: John Wiley & Sons.

Bots, P. W. G. 2008. *Analyzing actornetworks while assuming "frame rationality." Paper presented at the conference on Networks in Political Science (NIPS).* Kennedy School of Governance, Harvard University, Cambridge. Retrieved March 30, 2016 (http://www.hks.harvard.edu/netgov/files/NIPS/PWG_BOTS_Analyzing_actor_networks_14_June_2008.pdf.).

Burns, T. R., T. Baumgartner, P. Deville. 1985. *Man, Decisions, Society: The Theory of Actor-System Dynamics for Social Scientists.* New York: Gordon and Breach.

Clark, G., A. Munnell, M. Orszag (eds.) 2006. *Oxford Handbook of Pensions and Retirement Income.* Oxford: Oxford University Press.

Constitutional Court of the Czech Republic. 2010. *Decision of the Constitutional Court – Pl. ÚS 8/07.* Prague: Constitutional Court of the Czech Republic. Retrieved March 30, 2016 http://www.usoud.cz/en/decisions/20100323-pl-us-807-right-to-adequate-material-security/).

ČMKOS. 2011. *Stanovisko ČMKOS.* [Position of the Czech-Moravian Confederation of Trade Unions on Proposed Law on Pension Insurance, in Czech]. Prague: ČMKOS.

ČSOB. 2012. *Státní důchody čeká strmý propad, vstup do II. pilíře se vyplatí téměř polovině populace* [State pensions will fall down sharply, nearly one-half of the population will profit from entering the second pillar, in Czech]. Prague: ČSOB.

ČSSD. 2011. *Malá důchodová reforma je nespravedlivá, necitlivá a nedomyšlená, ČSSD s ní zásadně nesouhlasí.* [Small Pension Reform is unfair, insensitive and ill-conceived, ČSSD strongly disagrees with it, in Czech]. Prague: ČSSD. Retrieved May 12, 2011 (https://www.cssd.cz/aktualne/aktuality/mala-duchodova-reforma-je-nespravedliva-necitliva-a-nedomyslena-cssd-s-ni-zasadne-nesouhlasi/).

ČSSD. 2011. *Programový dokument – Důchodová reforma ČSSD 2011* [Policy Document – Pension reform of the ČSSD 2011, in Czech]. Prague: ČSSD. Retrieved March 30, 2016 (http://www.cssd.cz/data/files/duchody-0004.pdf).

Eatwell, J. 2003. *The Anatomy of the Pensions Crisis and Three Fallacies On Pensions.* Retrieved July 8, 2016 (http://mbz.net.pl/eftepe/Eatwell.pdf).

Entman, R. M. 1993. "Framing: Toward clarification of a fractured paradigm." *Journal of Communication* 43 (4): 51–58.

European Commission. 2015. *The 2015 Aging Report. Economic and Budgetary Projections for the 28 EU Member States (2013–2060).* Brussels: European Commission, Directorate-General for Economic and Financial Affairs. Retrieved July 18, 2016 (http://europa.eu/epc/pdf/ageing_report_2015_en.pdf).

Expert Committee on Pension Reform. 2015. *Final report on activities in 2014.* Prague: The Expert Committee on Pension Reform. Retrieved March 23, 2016 (http://www.duchodova-komise.cz/wp-content/uploads/2015/02/Final-report-CoE-2014.pdf).

Expert Committee on Pension Reform. 2016. *Final report on activities in 2015.* Prague: The Expert Committee on Pension Reform. Retrieved March 23, 2016 (http://www.duchodova-komise.cz/wp-content/uploads/2016/02/Final-report-ECPR-2015.pdf)

Expert Committee on Pension Reform. 2017. *Final report on activities in 2016.* Praha: The Expert Committee on Pension Reform. Retrieved September 18, 2017

(http://www.duchodova-komise.cz/wp-content/uploads/2017/02/Zpráva-o-činnosti -OK-za-rok-2016.pdf)

Goffman, E. 1974 (reprint 1986). *Frame Analysis*. New York: Harper and Row. Retrieved June 2, 2016 (https://nellalou.files.wordpress.com/2014/07/83646510-erving-goffman-frame-analysis-an-essay-on-the-organization-of-experience-1974.pdf).

Government of the Czech Republic. 2014. *Policy Statement of the Government of the Czech Republic*, February 14, 2014. Retrieved April 4, 2016 (http://www.vlada.cz/en/media-centrum/dulezite-dokumenty/policy-statement-of-the-government-of -the-czech-republic-116171/).

Green Paper. 2010. *Towards adequate, sustainable and safe European pension systems*. SEC (2010) 830. Brussels: European Commission.

Hejkrlík, P. 2011. "Člen NERV Zámečník se distancuje od penzijní reformy" [NERV Member Zámečník Dissociates himself from Pension Reform, in Czech]. *Týden.cz*, March 3, 2011. Retrieved March 3, 2011 (http://www.tyden.cz/rubriky/byznys/cesko/clen-nerv -zamecnik-se-distancuje-od-penzijni-reformy_195447.html?showTab=kurzovni-listek #.VMk3ncb8EZk).

Hinrichs, K. 2000. Elephants on the Move: Patterns of Public Pension Reform in OECD. *European Review* 8: 353–378.

Holub, M. 2010a. "Rozhodnutí Ústavního soudu nemusí nutně znamenat dramatický zásah do důchodového systému." [Decision of the Constitutional Court need not signify a dramatic intervention into the pension system, in Czech]. *FÓRUM sociální politiky* 4 (4): 16–20.

Holub, M. 2010b. "Solidarita versus ekvivalence v českém důchodovém pojištění pohledem Ústavního soudu." [Solidarity versus equivalence in Czech pension insurance from the perspective of the Constitutional Court, in Czech]. *FÓRUM sociální politiky* 4 (3): 19–20.

Holzmann, R., R. Hinz. 2005. *Old-Age Income Support in the 21st Century*. Washington, D.C.: World Bank.

Howlett, M. and M. Ramesh. 1995. *Studying Public Policy: Policy Cycles and Policy Subsystems*. Oxford: Oxford University Press.

Hughes, A., A. Singh. 1987. Takeovers and the stock-market. Contributions to Political *Economy* 6: 73–85.

Iglesias, A. 2003. *Strengthening of the Private Voluntary Pension Scheme in the Czech Republic*. Unpublished manuscript.

Jaeger, C. C., O. Renn, E. A. Rosa and T. Webler. 2001. *Risk, Uncertainty, and Rational Action*. London: Earthscan Publications Ltd.

Klaus, V. 2011. "Stát není pojišťovna." [The state is not an insurance company, in Czech]. *MF DNES*, July 7. Retrieved July 7, 2011 (http://www.klaus.cz/clanky/2863).

Kohout, P. 2011. "Důchodová reforma se důsledně vyhýbá návrhům NERVu a Bezděkovy komise." [Pension reform consistently avoids NERV's and Bezděk Commission's proposals, in Czech]. *Naše peníze.cz*, July 1, 2011. Retrieved July 1, 2011 (http://www .nasepenize.cz/pavel-kohout-duchodova-reforma-se-dusledne-vyhyba-navrhum-nervu -a-bezdekovy-komise-9300).

Korpi, W. 2001. "Contentious Institutions: An Augmented Rational-Actor Analysis of the Origins and Path Dependency of Welfare State Institutions in the Western Countries." Rationality and Society 13 (2): 235–83.

Lasagabaster E., R. Rocha. P. Wiesse. 2002. *Czech Pension system: Challenges and Reform Options*. Washington, D.C.: World Bank.

Lesay, I. 2007. *Czech Pension Reform: Will it Go Fundamental?* 2007. Brno: Economy and Society Trust. Discussion Paper No. 2. Retrieved July 11, 2016. (http://www.akademickyrepozitar.sk/sk/repozitar/czech-pension-reform-will-it-go-fundamental.pdf).

Leweke, R. W. 1999. *News Frames and Policy: Frame-building in Mainstream News and Political Commentary Media, 1992–1997*. Unpublished dissertation. University of North Carolina at Chapel Hill.

Macháček, D. 2004. "Prezident nepodepsal zákon, porušil Ústavu?" [The President did not sign the law, did he violate the Constitution?, in Czech]. *Hospodářské noviny*, May 4. Retrieved May 4, 2004 (http://archiv.ihned.cz/c1-14318020-prezident-nepodepsal-zakon-porusil-ustavu).

Mandate of the Expert Committee on Pension Reform. 2015. Prague: MPSV. Retrieved June 6, 2016 (http://www.duchodova-komise.cz/wp-content/uploads/2015/02/Mandate-of-the-Expert-Committee.pdf).

Maška, J., J. Rada. 2011. *Závěrečná zpráva Hodnocení dopadů regulace (RIA)* [Final Report on Regulatory Impact Assessment (RIA), in Czech]. Prague: MPSV ČR.

Mayntz, R. and F. W. Scharpf (eds.). 1995. *Gesellschaftliche Selbstregelung und politische Steuerung*. Frankfurt, Main: Campus.

Mimra, S. 1936. *Systém nemocenského, invalidního a starobního pojištění dělníků* [System of workers' sickness, disability and old age insurance, in Czech]. Prague: Čs. ústředí nemocenských pojišťoven.

Morávek, J. 2011. "Analýza rámců" [Frame Analysis, in Czech]. Pp. 105–135 in M. Nekola, H. Geissler, M. Mouralová (eds.). *Současné metodologické otázky veřejné politiky* [Contemporary Methodological Issues of Public Policy, in Czech]. Prague: Karolinum.

MPSV. 2005. *Final Report: Executive Team*. Prague: MPSV. Retrieved August 6, 2016 (www.mpsv.cz/files/clanky/3445/Final_report.pdf)

MPSV. 2008. *Pojistněmatematická zpráva o sociálním pojištění* [Actuarial Report on Social Insurance, in Czech]. Prague: MPSV.

MPSV. 2010. *The Expert Advisory Forum's Final Report*. Prague: MPSV. Retrieved August 6, 2016 (http://www.mpsv.cz/files/clanky/8897/Final_Report_PES.pdf).

NERV. 2011. *Důchodová reforma* [Pension Reform, in Czech]. Prague: National Economic Council of the Government. Retrieved March 30, 2016 (http://www.vlada.cz/assets/media-centrum/aktualne/NERV_Duchodova-reforma.pdf).

ODS. 2010. *Podrobný volební program. Řešení, která pomáhají.* [Detailed Election Program. Solutions that Help, in Czech]. Prague: ODS. Retrieved March 30, 2016 (http://www.ods.cz/docs/programy/volebni-program2010.pdf).

OECD. 2013. *Pensions at a Glance 2013: OECD and G20 Indicators*. Paris: OECD Publishing. Retrieved March 30, 2016, http://dx.doi.org/10.1787/pension_glance-2013-en.

OECD. 2015. *Pensions at a Glance 2015: OECD and G20 Indicators*. Paris: OECD Publishing. Retrieved July 18, 2016 http://static.politico.com/d9/2d/a9fe45a241eba663b8e935d4e41d/oecd-pensions-at -a-glance-2015.pdf).

Orszag, P. R., J. E. Stiglitz. 2001. "Rethinking Pension Reform: Ten Myths about Social Security Systems." Pp. 17–56 in *New Ideas about Old Age Security: Toward Sustainable Pension Systems in the Twenty-First Century*, edited by R. Holzmann, J. E. Stiglitz. Washington, D.C.: World Bank.

Paine, T. 2004. *Common Sense [with] Agrarian Justice*. London: Penguin.

Parol. 2011. "Vládní návrh penzijní reformy je taková bramboračka." Rozhovor s Jiřím Rusnokem [The government pension reform proposal is a kind of Eintopf. Interview with Jiří Rusnok, in Czech]. *Parlament, vláda, samospráva*. Prague: Parol. Retrieved June 26, 2012 (http://www.parlament-vlada.eu/index.php /rozhovor-finance/53-vladni-navrh-penzijni-reformy-je-takova-bramboraka).

Pierson, P. 1994. *Dismantling the Welfare State? Reagan, Thatcher, and the Politics of Retrenchment*. Cambridge, New York: Cambridge University Press.

Potůček, M. 1995. *Sociální politika*. [Social Policy, in Czech]. Prague: SLON.

Potůček, M., V. Rudolfová. 2015. "Czech Pension Reform: How to Reconcile Equivalence with Fiscal Discipline." *Central European Journal of Public Policy* 9 (1): 170–195.

Potůček, M., V. Rudolfová. 2016. "Rivalry of Advocacy Coalitions in the Czech Pension Reform." *The NISPAcee Journal of Public Administration and Policy* IX, No. 1, pp. 117–134.

Potůček, M., V. Rudolfová. 2017. "The Role of Politicians and Experts in the Preparation of the Czech Pension Reform." In: Sánches-Cabeduzo, S. S., López Peláez, A. (eds.) *The Ailing Welfare State*. Navarra: Thomson Reuters Aranzadi, pp. 165–190.

Quattrone, G. A., A. Tversky. 1988. "Contrasting Rational and Psychological Analyses of Political Choice." *American Political Science Review* 82 (3): 719–736, http://dx.doi .org/10.2307/1962487.

Rahmatian, S. and C. Hiatt. 1989. "Toward an information-based theory of irrational systems behavior." *Systems Research* 6 (1): 7–16.

Rákosník, J., I. Tomeš et al. 2012. *Sociální stát v Československu*. [Welfare State in Czechoslovakia, in Czech]. Prague: Auditorium.

Rein, M., D. Schön. 1993. "Reframing policy discourse." Pp. 145–166 in *Argumentative Turn in Policy Analysis and Planning*, edited by Fischer, F. London: Routledge.

Rein, M., D. Schön. 1996. "Frame-critical policy analysis and frame reflective policy practice." *Knowledge and Policy* 9 (1): 88–90.

Rusý, P., P. Zborník, T. Fiala. 2011. "Návrh penzijní reformy (verze se zohledněním výchovy dětí v průběžném systému)" [Pension reform proposal (version taking parenting into account in the PAYG system), in Czech]. Prague: CESTA. Retrieved March 30, 2016 (http://www.centrum-cesta.cz/files/prectete-si/publikace/navrhy-penzijni -reformy-pro-ceskou-republiku/navrh-penzijni-reformy-2-verze-se-zohlednenim-deti -v-prubeznem-systemu.pdf).

Sabatier, P., C. Weible. 2007. "The advocacy coalition framework: Innovations and clarifications." Pp. 189–222 in *Theories of the Policy Process*, edited by P. Sabatier. 2nd ed. Boulder: Westview Press.

Scharpf, F. W. 1997. *Games Real Actors Play. Actor-Centered Institutionalism in Policy Research*. Boulder: Westview Press.

Schmidt, V. A. 2008. "Discursive Institutionalism: The Explanatory Power of Ideas and Discourse." *Annual Review of Political Science* 11: 303–326.

Schön, D., M. Rein. 1994. *Frame Reflection: Toward the Resolution of Intractable Policy Controversies*. New York: Basic Books. Retrieved June 2, 2016 (http://www.colorado.edu/conflict/peace/example/Frame_refl_sum.htm).

Schludi, M. 2005. *The Reform of Bismarckian Pension Systems: A Comparison of Pension Politics in Austria, France, Germany, Italy and Sweden*. Amsterdam: Amsterdam University Press.

Shepherd, R. H. E. 2000. *Czechoslovakia. The Velvet Revolution and Beyond*. New York: Palgrave.

Stone, D. A. 1997. *Policy paradox. The art of political decision making*. New York: Norton, W. W. & Company, Inc.

Tomeš, I. 1996. *Sociální politika. Teorie a mezinárodní zkušenost* [Social Policy. Theory and International Experience, in Czech]. Prague: SOCIOKLUB.

TOP 09. 2010. *Volební program. Volby 2010 do Poslanecké sněmovny* [Election program. Chamber of Deputies Election 2010, in Czech]. Prague: TOP 09. Retrieved March 30, 2016 (http://www.top09.cz/files/soubory/volebni-program-2010-do-poslanecke-snemovny_85.pdf).

Ústavní soud ČR. 2010. *Nález Ústavního soudu Pl. ÚS 8/07* [Ruling of the Constitutional Court, in Czech]. Retrieved June 14, 2016 (http://www.usoud.cz/en/decisions/20100323-pl-us-807-right-to-adequate-material-security-1).

Věci veřejné. Politická strana. 2010. *Politický program* [Political Program, in Czech]. Prague: Věci veřejné. Retrieved April 10, 2016. (http://www.olympic.cz/financovani/docs/VV.pdf).

Vostatek, J. 2014. "Zdanění příjmů a pojistné" [Income Taxation and the Insurance Premium, in Czech]. *Bulletin Komory daňových poradců ČR* 4: 36–41.

Vostatek, J., P. Zborník, T. Fiala. 2011. "Návrh penzijní reformy (verze s NDC)" [Pension reform proposal (NDC version), in Czech]. Prague: CESTA. Retrieved March 30, 2016 (http://www.centrum-cesta.cz/files/prectete-si/publikace/navrhy-penzijni-reformy-pro-ceskou-republiku/navrh-penzijni-reformy-1-verze-s-NDC.pdf).

Warshawsky, M. 1987. "Private Annuity Markets in the United States: 1919–1984." *Research Papers in Banking and Financial Economics* 96. Board of Governors of the Federal Reserve System.

Weaver, K. 2003. *The Politics of Public Pension Reform*. Retrieved July 8, 2016 (http://ssrn.com/abstract=1136874).

Wheeler, P. M., J. R. Kearney. 1996. "Income Protection for the Aged in the 21st Century: A Framework to Help Inform the Debate." *Social Security Bulletin* 59 (2): 3–19.

Wodsak V., M. Koch. 2010. "From three to five: The World Bank's pension policy norm." Pp. 48–69 in *Owning Development*, edited by S. Park, A. Vetterlein. Cambridge: Cambridge University Press.

World Bank. 1994. *Averting the old age crisis : policies to protect the old and pro-mote growth.* Washington, D.C.: Oxford University Press. Retrieved June 2, 2016 (http://documents.worldbank.org/curated/en/973571468174557899/Averting -the-old-age-crisis-policies-to-protect-the-old-and-promote-growth).

World Bank. 2006. *Hodnocení spolupráce České republiky a Světové banky 1998–2005* [Evaluation of Collaboration, the Czech Republic and the World Bank 1998–2005, in Czech]. Retrieved July 8, 2016 (http://siteresources.worldbank.org/INTCZECH /Resources/evaluation-Czech-partnership-cz.pdf).

List of Tables – Part B

List of Figures – Part B

Subject Index
(relating to part A)

accountability 65

actors **71–72**

administration 63, 91, **92**, 96, 137–138, 141–142

  government administration 51, 62, 76, 137, 207, 213

    public 7, 20, 42, 50–52, 55, 59, 72, 74–76, **84**, 87–90, 92, 100, 113, **142**, 143

    regional 96

agenda 25, 32, 35, 51, 73–74, 78–79, 87–88, 108–110, 113, 125

arenas 26, 78–79, 113

budget 18, 23, 53, 89–90, 114, 125, 137, 139, 143

  government budget **89–90**, 91, 96, 99

  public 53, 89, 90

bureaucracy 19, 20, 26, 76, **134**, 137, **141**, 142, **146**

centralization, decentralization 35, **88**, 120

citizenship 37, 53

coalition 58, 79, 127, **134**, 135, 139

  advocacy coalition 26, **94**, 95, **103**, **134**, 135

cohesion, social 35, 40, 65

communication 26, 32, 34, 59, 61, 65, 78–80, **84**, 92, **93**, 96, 98, 136

communities 16–18, 23, 30, 63, 93, 113, 155

  epistemic **61**, 72

  policy communities 94–95, 113

competence 42, 76, **136**, 140–142, 156

competition 17, 30, 33, 57–58, 77–78, 125, 142

concentration, deconcentration **88**, 89, 98

conception 95, 97

conflict 15–19, 22, 29, 41–42, 48, 58, 74, 77–78, 95, 110, 112–113, 120, 122, **126**, 127, 134, 137, 140, 156

constitution 8, 23, 32, 72, 74, **75**, **88**, 140

construction, social 26, 108

coordination 65, 77, **88**, 134, **136**

corporation 16, 36, 64

corruption 41–42, **62**, 128, 151

criteria 30, 32, 39, **55**, **57**, 59, 61, 91, 122, 130, 148, **149–150**, **153**, 165

culture 15, 20, 30, 32, 54, 63, 74, 91, 98, 124, 142, 167, 169

  political 54

decision-making 7–8, 26, 34, 62, 84, 90, 94, 96, 98, 100, 107, **120**, 121, **122–124**, 125, **126**, 127–128, **129**, 130, 133, 141, 144, 152

Personal Index (relating to part A)